# Masochism

# Masochism

ထ

## Coldness and Cruelty

Gilles Deleuze

## Venus in Furs

Leopold von Sacher-Masoch

ထ

ZONE BOOKS · NEW YORK

1991

© 1989 Urzone, Inc.
ZONE BOOKS
611 Broadway, Suite 608
New York, NY 10012

*First Paperback Edition*
*Sixth Printing, 1999*

Reprinted by permission of George Braziller, Publishers.
© 1971 Faber and Faber, Ltd., under the title *Sacher-
Masoch*. Originally published in France under the title
"Le Froid et le Cruel" in *Présentation de Sacher-Masoch*
© 1967 Editions de Minuit.

Printed in the United States of America

Distributed by The MIT Press,
Cambridge, Massachusetts, and London, England

Library of Congress Cataloging in Publication Data

Masochism / translated by Jean McNeil
    p. cm.
    Reprint. Originally published: New York: G. Braziller,
1971. Includes bibliographical references.
    Contents: Coldness and cruelty / by Gilles Deleuze —
Venus in furs / by Leopold von Sacher-Masoch.
    ISBN 0-942299-55-8 (pbk.)
    1. Sacher-Masoch, Leopold, Ritter von, 1835–1895 —
Criticism and interpretation. 2. Sade, marquis de,
1740–1814 — Criticism and interpretation. 3. Masochism
in literature. 4. Sadism in literature. I. Deleuze, Gilles.
Présentation de Sacher-Masoch, le froid et le cruel.
English. 1989. II. Sacher-Masoch, Leopold, Ritter von,
1835–1895. Venus im Pelz. English, 1989.
[PT2461.83Z86        1989]
833'.8–dc19                                88-20823
                                            CIP

# Contents

# Coldness and Cruelty

GILLES DELEUZE

# Foreword

Most of the information on the life of Sacher-Masoch comes to us from his secretary, Schlichtegroll (*Sacher-Masoch und der Masochismus*) and from his first wife, who took the name of the heroine of *Venus in Furs*, Wanda (Wanda von Sacher-Masoch, *Confessions of My Life*). Wanda's book is excellent, but it was severely judged by subsequent biographers, who often merely present us with subjective impressions of the work. In their opinion, the image she offers of herself is too innocent, and they assumed her to be a sadist, since Masoch was a masochist. But this may well be a misstatement of the problem.

Leopold von Sacher-Masoch was born in 1835 in Lemberg, Galicia. He was of Slav, Spanish and Bohemian descent. His ancestors held official positions in the Austro-Hungarian Empire. His father was Chief of Police of Lemberg, and as a child he witnessed prison scenes and riots which were to have a profound effect on him. His work is deeply influenced by the problems of nationalities, minority groups and revolutionary movements in the Empire, hence his Galician, Jewish, Hungarian, Prussian tales, etc. He often describes the organization of agricultural communes and the struggle of the peasants against the Austrian administration and especially against the landowners. He became involved in the Panslavic movement. The men he admired, besides Goethe, were Pushkin and Lermantov, and he was known himself as the Turgeniev of Little Russia.

He was appointed Professor of History at Graz and began his literary career by writing historical novels. He met with rapid success: one of his first *genre* novels, *The Divorced Woman* (1870) aroused interest even in America; in France, Hachette, Calmann-Lévy and Flammarion published translations of his novels and stories. One of his translators was able to present him as a strict moralist who drew his inspiration from history and folklore, without making the slightest allusion to the erotic character of his works. His fantasies were probably made more acceptable by the fact that they could be attributed to the spirit of the Slav people. We must also take into account the more general explanation that the standards of "censorship" and tolerance of the nineteenth century were very different from our own; diffuse sexuality being more acceptable than specific physical and mental details.

In the language of Masoch's folklore, history, politics, mysticism, eroticism, nationalism and perversion are closely intermingled, forming a nebula around the scenes of flagellation; he was consequently disturbed when Krafft-Ebing used his name to designate a perversion. Masoch was a famous and honored writer; in 1886 he made a triumphant journey to Paris where he was decorated and entertained by the *Figaro* and the *Revue des Deux Mondes*.

Masoch's tastes in matters of love are well known: he enjoyed pretending to be a bear or a bandit or having himself pursued, tied up and subjected to punishments, humiliations and even acute physical pain by an opulent fur-clad woman with a whip; he was given to dressing up as a servant, making use of all kinds of fetishes and disguises, placing advertisements in newspapers, signing contracts with the women in his life and if need be prostituting them.

An affair with Anna von Kottowitz inspired *The Divorced Woman*, another affair, with Fanny von Pistor, *Venus in Furs*. Then a young lady by the name of Aurore Rümelin approached him by means of a somewhat ambiguous correspondence, took the pseudonym of Wanda, and married Masoch in 1873. As a companion she was at once docile, demanding and overwhelmed. Masoch was fated to be disappointed as though the masquerades he planned were bound to give rise to misunderstandings. He was always attempting to introduce a third party into his ménage, the character he calls "the Greek." During his period with Anna von Kottowitz, a sham Polish count entered their life, revealing himself later to be a chemist's assistant wanted for theft and dangerously ill. Then there is the strange adventure involving Aurore/Wanda, the hero of which appears to be Ludwig II of Bavaria; the story is included among the appendices to this book. Here again the ambivalence of the characters, the disguises, the parrying of the parties involved turn the whole episode into an extraordinary ballet ending in disappointment. Finally there is the adventure with Armand of the *Figaro*, of which Wanda gives an excellent account, leaving the reader to make his own amendments. This episode was the reason for Masoch's journey to Paris in 1886, and it also marks the end of his union with Wanda; in 1887 he married his children's governess. In a novel by Myriam Harry, *Sonia in Berlin*, we find an interesting portrait of Masoch in retirement. He died in 1895, saddened by the neglect into which his work had fallen.

And yet his writings are important and unusual. He conceived of them as a cycle or rather as a series of cycles. The principal one is entitled *The Heritage of Cain* and was to have treated six themes: love, property, money, the State, war and death; only the first two parts were finished, but the other four themes can already be discerned in them. The folktales and the ethnic tales

form secondary cycles; they include in particular two somber novels dealing with mystical sects in Galicia which rank among the
best of Masoch's works and reach heights of anguish and tension
rarely equaled elsewhere (*The Fisher of Souls* and *The Mother of
God*). What is the meaning of the term "heritage of Cain"? It is
intended first to express the burden of crime and suffering inherited by humanity; however, this apparent cruelty conceals the
more secret theme of the coldness of Nature, of the steppe,
of the icy image of the Mother wherein Cain discovers his own
destiny; the coldness of the stern mother is in reality a transmutation of cruelty from which the new man emerges. The
"mark" of Cain indicates how the "heritage" is to be used. Cain
and Christ bear the same mark, which leads to the crucifixion of
Man "who knows no sexual love, no property, no fatherland,
no cause, no work; who dies of his own willing, embodying the
idea of humanity...."

The work of Masoch draws on all the forces of German Romanticism. In our opinion, no other writer has used to such effect
the resources of fantasy and suspense. He has a particular way of
"desexualizing" love and at the same time sexualizing the entire
history of humanity.

*Venus in Furs* (*Venus im Pelz*, 1870) is one of Masoch's most famous
novels. It forms part of the first volume of *The Heritage of Cain*,
which deals with the subject of love. A translation by the econo-
mist R. Ledos de Beaufort appeared simultaneously in French and
in English in 1902, but it was extremely inaccurate. The present
version is a translation from the French of a subsequent translation by Aude Willm. The novel is followed by three appendices:
the first is a general statement by Masoch on the novel, followed
by an account of a scene from his childhood. The second con-

sists of the "love contracts" that Masoch signed with Fanny von Pistor and Wanda. The third appendix is Wanda Sacher-Masoch's account of the adventure with Ludwig II.

Masoch has been treated unjustly, not because his name was unfairly given to the perversion of masochism, but quite the reverse, because his work fell into neglect whereas his name passed into current usage. Although we occasionally find books written on Sade that show no knowledge of his work, this is increasingly rare. Sade is becoming more thoroughly known; clinical studies of sadism are considerably enriched by literary studies of the work of Sade, and vice versa. Even the best writings on Masoch, however, show a surprising ignorance of his work.

Sade and Masoch are not merely cases among others; they both have something essential to teach us, the one about masochism and the other about sadism. The second reason why Masoch's fate is unjust is that in clinical terms he is considered complementary to Sade. This may indeed be the reason why people who are interested in Sade show no particular interest in Masoch. It is too readily assumed that the symptoms only have to be transposed and the instincts reversed for Masoch to be turned into Sade, according to the principle of the unity of opposites. The theme of the unity of sadism and masochism and the concept of a sadomasochistic entity have done great harm to Masoch. He has suffered not only from unjust neglect but also from an unfair assumption of complementarity and dialectical unity with Sade.

As soon as we read Masoch we become aware that his universe has nothing to do with that of Sade. Their techniques differ, and their problems, their concerns and their intentions are entirely dissimilar. It is not valid to object that psychoanalysis has long shown the possibility and the reality of transformations between sadism and masochism; we are questioning the very concept of an entity known as sadomasochism. Medicine distinguishes between syndromes and symptoms, a symptom being the specific sign of an illness, and a syndrome the meeting-place or crossing-point of manifestations issuing from very different origins and arising within variable contexts. We would like to suggest that sado-masochism is a syndrome that ought to be split up into irreducible causal chains. It has been stated so often that sadism and masochism are found in the same person that we have come to believe it. We need to go back to the beginning and read Sade and Masoch. Because the judgment of the clinician is prejudiced, we must take an entirely different approach, the *literary approach*, since it is from literature that stem the original definitions of sadism and masochism. It is no accident that the names of two writers were used as labels for these two perversions. The critical (in the literary sense) and the clinical (in the medical sense) may be destined to enter into a new relationship of mutual learning. Symptomatology is always a question of art; the clinical specificities of sadism and masochism are not separable from the literary values peculiar to Sade and Masoch. In place of a dialectic which all too readily perceives the link between opposites, we should aim for a critical and clinical appraisal able to reveal the truly differential mechanisms as well as the artistic originalities.

CHAPTER I

# The Language of Sade and Masoch

"It is too idealistic...and therefore cruel."
Doestoevsky, *The Insulted and Injured*

What are the uses of literature? The names of Sade and Masoch
have been used to denote two basic perversions, and as such they
are outstanding examples of the efficiency of literature. Illnesses
are sometimes named after typical patients, but more often it is
the doctor's name that is given to the disease (Roger's disease,
Parkinson's disease, etc.). The principles behind this labeling
deserve closer analysis. The doctor does not invent the illness,
he dissociates symptoms that were previously grouped together,
and links up others that were dissociated. In short he builds up a
profoundly original clinical picture. The history of medicine can
therefore be regarded under at least two aspects. The first is the
history of illnesses, which may disappear, become less frequent,
reappear or alter their form according to the state of the society
and the development of therapeutic methods. Intertwined with
this history is the history of symptomatology, which sometimes
precedes and sometimes follows changes in therapy or in the
nature of diseases: symptoms are named, renamed and regrouped
in various ways. Progress from this point of view generally means

a tendency toward greater specificity, and indicates a refinement of symptomatology. (Thus the plague and leprosy were more common in the past not only for historical and social reasons but because one tended to group under these headings various types of diseases now classified separately.) Great clinicians are the greatest doctors: when a doctor gives his name to an illness this is a major linguistic and semiological step, inasmuch as a proper name is linked to a given group of signs, that is, *a proper name is made to connote signs.*

Should we therefore class Sade and Masoch among the great clinicians? It is difficult to treat sadism and masochism on a level with the plague, leprosy and Parkinson's disease; the word disease is clearly inappropriate. Nevertheless, Sade and Masoch present unparalleled configurations of symptoms and signs. In coining the term masochism, Krafft-Ebing was giving Masoch credit for having redefined a clinical entity not merely in terms of the link between pain and sexual pleasure, but in terms of something more fundamental connected with bondage and humiliation (there are limiting cases of masochism without algolagnia and even algolagnia without masochism).[1] Another question we should ask is whether Masoch does not present a symptomatology that is more refined than Sade's in that it enables us to discriminate between disturbances which were previously regarded as identical. In any case whether Sade and Masoch are "patients" or clinicians or both, they are also great anthropologists, of the type whose work succeeds in embracing a whole conception of man, culture and nature; they are also great artists in that they discovered new forms of expression, new ways of thinking and feeling and an entirely original language.

In principle, violence is something that does not speak, or speaks but little, while sexuality is something that is little spoken about. Sexual modesty cannot be related to biological fear, oth-

erwise it would not be formulated as it is: "I am less afraid of
being touched and even of being seen than of being put into
words." What is the meaning of the meeting of violence and sexuality in such excessive and abundant language as that of Sade and
Masoch? How are we to account for the violent language linked
with eroticism? In a text that ought to invalidate all theories relating Sade to Nazism, Georges Bataille explains that the language
of Sade is paradoxical *because it is essentially that of a victim.* Only
the victim can describe torture; the torturer necessarily uses the
hypocritical language of established order and power. "As a general rule the torturer does not use the language of the violence
exerted by him in the name of an established authority; he uses
the language of the authority.... The violent man is willing to
keep quiet and connives at cheating.... Thus Sade's attitude is dia-
metrically opposed to that of the torturer. When Sade writes he
refuses to cheat, but he attributes his own attitude to people who
in real life could only have been silent and uses them to make
self-contradictory statements to other people."[2]

Ought we to conclude that the language of Masoch is equally
paradoxical in this instance because the victim speaks the language of the torturer he is to himself, with all the hypocrisy of
the torturer?

What is known as pornographic literature is a literature reduced to a few imperatives (do this, do that) followed by obscene
descriptions. Violence and eroticism do meet, but in a rudimen-
tary fashion. Imperatives abound in the work of Sade and Masoch;
they are issued by the cruel libertine or by despotic woman.
Descriptions also abound (although the function of the descriptions as well as the nature of their obscenity are strikingly different in the two authors). It would appear that both for Sade and
for Masoch language reaches its full significance when it acts
directly on the senses. Sade's *The One Hundred and Twenty Days of*

*Sodom* hinges on tales told to the libertines by "women chroniclers," and in principle the heroes may not take any initiative in anticipation of these tales. Words are at their most powerful when they compel the body to repeat the movements they suggest, and "the sensations communicated by the ear are the most enjoyable and have the keenest impact." In Masoch's life as well as in his fiction, love affairs are always set in motion by anonymous letters, by the use of pseudonyms or by advertisements in newspapers. They must be regulated by contracts that formalize and verbalize the behavior of the partners. Everything must be stated, promised, announced and carefully described before being accomplished. However, the work of Sade and Masoch cannot be regarded as pornography; it merits the more exalted title of "pornology" because its erotic language cannot be reduced to the elementary functions of ordering and describing.

With Sade we witness an astonishing development of the demonstrative use of language. Demonstration as a higher function of language makes its appearance between sequences of description, while the libertines are resting, or in the interval between two commands. One of the libertines will read out a severe pamphlet, or expound inexhaustible theories, or draft a constitution. Alternatively he may agree to hold a conversation or a discussion with his victim. Such moments are frequent, particularly in *Justine*, where each of the heroine's torturers uses her as a listener and confidante. The libertine may put on an act of trying to convince and persuade; he may even proselytize and gain new recruits (as in *Philosophy in the Bedroom*). But the intention to convince is merely apparent, for nothing is in fact more alien to the sadist than the wish to convince, to persuade, in short to educate. He is interested in something quite different, namely to demonstrate that reasoning itself is a form of violence, and that he is on the side of violence, however calm and logical he may

18

be. He is not even attempting to prove anything to anyone, but to perform a demonstration related essentially to the solitude and omnipotence of its author. The point of the exercise is to show that the demonstration is identical to violence. It follows that the reasoning does not have to be shared by the person to whom it is addressed any more than pleasure is meant to be shared by the object from which it is derived. The acts of violence inflicted on the victims are a mere reflection of a higher form of violence to which the demonstration testifies. Whether he is among his accomplices or among his victims, each libertine, while engaged in reasoning, is caught in the hermetic circle of his own solitude and uniqueness — even if the argumentation is the same for all the libertines. In every respect, as we shall see, the sadistic "instructor" stands in contrast to the masochistic "educator."

Here, again, Bataille says of Sade: "It is a language which repudiates any relationship between speaker and audience." Now if it is true that this language is the supreme realization of a demonstrative function to be found in the relation between violence and eroticism, then the other aspect, the language of imperatives and descriptions, appears in a new light. It still remains, but in an entirely dependent role, steeped in the demonstrative element, as it were, floating in it. The descriptions, the attitudes of the bodies, are merely living diagrams illustrating the abominable descriptions; similarly the imperatives uttered by the libertines are like the statements of problems referring back to the more fundamental chain of sadistic theorems: "I have demonstrated it theoretically," says Noirceuil, "let us now put it to the test of practice."

We have therefore to distinguish two factors constituting a dual language. The first, the imperative and descriptive factor, represents the *personal* element; it directs and describes the personal violence of the sadist as well as his individual tastes; the second and higher factor represents the *impersonal* element in sadism and identifies the impersonal violence with an Idea of pure reason, with a terrifying demonstration capable of subordinating the first element. In Sade we discover a surprising affinity with Spinoza – a naturalistic and mechanistic approach imbued with the mathematical spirit. This accounts for the endless repetitions, the reiterated quantitative process of multiplying illustrations and adding victim upon victim, again and again retracing the thousand circles of an irreducibly solitary argument. Krafft-Ebing sensed the essential nature of such a process: "In certain cases the personal element is almost entirely absent. The subject gets sexual enjoyment from beating boys and girls, but the purely impersonal element of his perversion is much more in evidence.... While in most individuals of this type the feelings of power are experienced in relation to specific persons, we are dealing here with a pronounced form of sadism operating to a great extent in geographical and mathematical patterns."[3]

In the work of Masoch there is a similar transcendence of the imperative and the descriptive toward a higher function. But in this case it is all persuasion and education. We are no longer in the presence of a torturer seizing upon a victim and enjoying her all the more because she is unconsenting and unpersuaded. We are dealing instead with a victim in search of a torturer and who needs to educate, persuade and conclude an alliance with the torturer in order to realize the strangest of schemes. This is why advertisements are part of the language of masochism while they have no place in true sadism, and why the masochist draws up contracts while the sadist abominates and destroys them. The sadist is in need of institutions, the masochist of contractual relations. The middle ages distinguished with considerable insight between two types of commerce with the devil: the first resulted from possession, the second from a pact of alliance. The sadist thinks in terms of institutionalized possession, the masochist in

20

terms of contracted alliance. Possession is the sadist's particular
form of madness just as the pact is the masochist's. It is essential
to the masochist that he should fashion the woman into a despot,
that he should persuade her to cooperate and get her to "sign."
He is essentially an educator and thus runs the risk inherent in
educational undertakings. In all Masoch's novels, the woman,
although persuaded, is still basically doubting, as though she were
afraid: she is forced to commit herself to a role to which she may
prove inadequate, either by overplaying or by falling short of
expectations. In *The Divorced Woman*, the heroine complains: "Julian's ideal was a cruel woman, a woman like Catherine the Great,
but alas, I was cowardly and weak...." In *Venus*, Wanda says: "I
am afraid of not being capable of it, but for you, my beloved, I
am willing to try." Or again: "Beware, I might grow to enjoy it."

The educational undertaking of Masoch's heroes, their submission to a woman, the torments they undergo, are so many
steps in their climb toward the Ideal. *The Divorced Woman* is sub-
titled *The Calvary of an Idealist*. Severin, the hero of *Venus*, takes
as a motto for his doctrine of "supersensualism" the words of
Mephistopheles to Faust: "Thou sensual, supersensual libertine,
a little girl can lead thee by the nose." (*Ubersinnlich* in Goethe's
text does not mean "supersensitive" but "supersensual," "super-
carnal," in conformity with theological tradition, where *Sinn-
lichkeit* denotes the *flesh, sensualitas*). It is therefore not surprising
that masochism should seek historical and cultural confirmation
in mystical or idealistic initiation rites. The naked body of a
woman can only be contemplated in a mystical frame of mind,
as is the case in *Venus*. This fact is illustrated more clearly still in
*The Divorced Woman*, where the hero, Julian, under the disturbing influence of a friend, desires for the first time to see his mistress naked. He begins by invoking a "need" to "observe," but
finds that he is overcome by a religious feeling "without anything

sensual about it" (we have here the two basic stages of fetishism). The ascent from the human body to the work of art and from the work of art to the Idea must take place under the shadow of the whip. Masoch is animated by a dialectical spirit. In *Venus* the story is set in motion by a dream that occurs during an interrupted reading of Hegel. But the primary influence is that of Plato. While Sade is spinozistic and employs demonstrative reason, Masoch is platonic and proceeds by dialectical imagination. One of Masoch's stories is entitled *The Love of Plato* and was at the origin of his adventure with Ludwig II.[4] Masoch's relation to Plato is evidenced not only by the ascent to the realm of the intelligible, but by the whole technique of dialectical reversal, disguise and reduplication. In the adventure with Ludwig II Masoch does not know at first whether his correspondent is a man or a woman; he is not sure at the end whether he is one or two people, nor does he know during the episode what part his wife will play, but he is prepared for anything, a true dialectician who knows the opportune moment and seizes it. Plato showed that Socrates appeared to be the lover but that fundamentally he was the loved one. Likewise the masochistic hero appears to be educated and fashioned by the authoritarian woman whereas basically it is he who forms her, dresses her for the part and prompts the harsh words she addresses to him. It is the victim who speaks through the mouth of his torturer, without sparing himself. Dialectic does not simply mean the free interchange of discourse, but implies transpositions or displacements of this kind, resulting in a scene being enacted simultaneously on several levels with reversals and reduplications in the allocation of roles and discourse.

Pornological literature is aimed above all at confronting language with its own limits, with what is in a sense a "nonlanguage" (violence that does not speak, eroticism that remains unspoken). However this task can only be accomplished by an internal splitting of language: the imperative and descriptive function must transcend itself toward a higher function, the personal element turning by reflection upon itself into the impersonal. When Sade invokes a universal analytical Reason to explain that which is most particular in desire, we must not merely take this as evidence that he is a man of the eighteenth century; particularity and the corresponding delusion must also represent an Idea of pure reason. Similarly when Masoch invokes the dialectical spirit, the spirit of Mephistopheles and that of Plato in one, this must not merely be taken as proof of his romanticism; here too particularity is seen reflectively in the impersonal Ideal of the dialectical spirit. In Sade the imperative and descriptive function of language transcends itself toward a pure demonstrative, instituting function, and in Masoch toward a dialectical, mythical and persuasive function. These two transcendent functions essentially characterize the two perversions, they are twin ways in which the monstrous exhibits itself in reflection.

# CHAPTER II

# The Role of Descriptions

Since the transcendent function in Sade is demonstrative and in Masoch dialectical, the role and the significance of descriptions are very different in each case. Although Sade's descriptions are basically related to the function of demonstration, they are nevertheless relatively independent creations; they are obscene in themselves. Sade cannot do without this provocative element. The same cannot be said of Masoch, for while the greatest obscenity may undoubtedly be present in threats, advertisements or contracts, it is not a necessary condition. Indeed, the work of Masoch is on the whole commendable for its unusual decency. The most vigilant censor could hardly take exception to *Venus*, unless he were to question a certain atmosphere of suffocation and suspense which is a feature of all Masoch's novels. In many of his stories he has no difficulty in presenting masochistic fantasies as though they were instances of national custom and folklore, or the innocent games of children, or the frolics of a loving woman, or even the demands of morality and patriotism. Thus in the excitement of a banquet, the men, following an ancient custom, drink out of the women's shoes (*Sappho's Slipper*); young maidens ask their sweethearts to play at being bears or dogs, and harness them to little carts (*The Fisher of Souls*); a woman in love teasingly pretends

25

to use a document signed in blank by her lover (*The Blank Paper*). In a more serious vein, a woman patriot, in order to save her town, asks to be brought before the Turks, surrenders her husband to them as a slave and gives herself to the Pasha (*The Judith of Bialopol*). Undoubtedly in all these cases the man derives from his humiliation a "secondary gain" which is specifically masochistic. Nevertheless, Masoch succeeds in presenting a great part of his work on a "reassuring" note and finds justification for masochistic behavior in the most varied motivations or in the demands of fateful and agonizing situations. (Sade, on the other hand, could fool nobody when he tried this method.) Consequently Masoch was not a condemned author but a fêted and honored one. Even the blatantly masochistic elements in his work gained acceptance as the expression of Slavonic folklore or of the spirit of Little Russia. He was known as the Turgeniev of Little Russia: he could equally well have been compared to the Comtesse de Ségur! Masoch did of course produce a somber counterpart to these works: *Venus, The Mother of God, The Fountain of Youth, The Hyena of the Poussta*, restore the original rigor and purity of the masochistic motivation. But whether the descriptions are rosy or somber, they always bear the stamp of decency. We never see the naked body of the woman torturer; it is always wrapped in furs. The body of the victim remains in a strange state of indeterminacy except where it receives the blows.

How can we account for these two kinds of "displacement" in Masoch's descriptions? We are led back to the question: why does the demonstrative function of language in Sade imply obscene descriptions, while Masoch's dialectical function seems to exclude them or at least not to treat them as essential elements?

Underlying the work of Sade is negation in its broadest and deepest sense. Here we must distinguish between two levels of negation: negation (the negative) as a partial process and pure negation as a totalizing Idea. These two levels correspond to Sade's distinction between two *natures*, the importance of which was shown by Klossowski. Secondary nature is bound by its own rules and its own laws; it is pervaded by the negative, but not everything in it is negation. Destruction is merely the reverse of creation and change, disorder is another form of order, and the decomposition of death is equally the composition of life. The negative is all-pervasive, but the process of death and destruction that it represents is only a partial process. Hence the disappointment of the sadistic hero, faced with a nature which seems to prove to him that the perfect crime is impossible: "Yes, I abhor Nature." Even the thought that other people's pain gives him pleasure does not comfort him, for this ego-satisfaction merely means that the negative can be achieved only as the reverse of positivity. Individuation, no less than the preservation of a reign or a species are processes that testify to the narrow limits of secondary nature. In opposition to this we find the notion of primary nature and pure negation that override all reigns and all laws, free even from the necessity to create, preserve or individuate. Pure negation needs no foundation and is beyond all foundation, a primal delirium, an original and timeless chaos solely composed of wild and lacerating molecules. In the words of the Pope: "The criminal capable of overthrowing the three realms at once by annihilating them along with their productive capabilities, is the one who will have served Nature best." But in point of fact this original nature cannot be *given*: secondary nature alone makes up the world of experience, and negation is only ever given in the partial processes of the negative. Therefore original nature is necessarily the object of an Idea, and pure negation is a delusion; but it is a delusion of reason itself. Rationalism is not grafted onto the work of Sade; it is rather by an internal necessity that he evolves the idea of a delusion, an exorbitance specific to reason.

It is important to note that the distinction between the two natures corresponds to and is the foundation of the distinction between the two elements, the personal element which embodies the power of negativity and represents the way in which the sadistic ego still participates in secondary nature and reproduces its acts of violence, and the impersonal element which relates to primary nature and the delusional idea of negation, and represents the way in which the sadist negates secondary nature *along with his own ego*.

In *The One Hundred and Twenty Days of Sodom* the libertine states that he finds excitement not in "what is here," but in "what is not here," the absent Object, "the idea of evil." The idea of that which is not, the idea of the No or of negation which is not given and cannot be given in experience must necessarily be the object of a demonstration (in the sense that a mathematical truth holds good even when we are asleep and even if it does not exist in nature). Hence the rage and despair of the sadistic hero when he realizes how paltry his own crimes are in relation to the idea which he can only reach through the omnipotence of reasoning. He dreams of a universal, impersonal crime, or as Clairwil puts it, a crime "which is perpetually effective, even when I myself cease to be effective, so that there will not be a single moment of my life, even when I am asleep, when I shall not be the cause of some disturbance." The task of the libertine is to bridge the gulf between the two elements, the element at his actual disposal and the element in his mind, the derivative and the original, the personal and the impersonal. The system expounded by Saint-Fond (where Sade develops most fully the idea of a pure delirium of reason) asks under what conditions "a particular pain, $B$" produced in secondary nature *would necessarily reverberate and reproduce itself ad infinitum* in primary nature. This is the clue to the meaning of repetitiveness in Sade's writing and of the monotony

28

of sadism. In practice, however, the libertine is confined to illustrating his total demonstration with partial inductive processes borrowed from secondary nature. He cannot do more than accelerate and condense the motions of partial violence. He achieves the acceleration by multiplying the number of his victims and their sufferings. The condensation on the other hand implies that violence must not be dissipated under the sway of inspiration or impulse, or even be governed by the pleasures it might afford, since those pleasures would still bind him to secondary nature, but it must be exercised in cold blood, and condensed by this very coldness, the coldness of demonstrative reason. Hence the well-known *apathy* of the libertine, the self-control of the pornologist, with which Sade contrasts the deplorable "enthusiasm" of the pornographer. Enthusiasm is precisely what he dislikes in Rétif, and he could rightly say (as he always did when justifying himself publicly) that he at least had not depicted vice as pleasant or gay but as apathetic. This apathy does of course produce intense pleasure, but ultimately it is not the pleasure of an ego participating in secondary nature (even of a criminal ego participating in a criminal nature), but on the contrary the pleasure of negating nature within the ego and outside the ego, and negating the ego itself. It is in short the pleasure of demonstrative reason.

If we consider the means available to the sadist for conducting his demonstration, it appears that the demonstrative function subordinates the descriptive function, accelerates and condenses it in a controlled manner, but cannot by any means dispense with it. The descriptions must be precise both qualitatively and quantitatively and must bear on two areas: cruel actions and disgusting actions, both of which are for the cold-blooded libertine equal sources of pleasure. In the words of the monk Clement in *Justine*: "You have been arrested by two irregularities you have noticed in us: you are astonished that some of our companions should be pleasantly stimulated by matters commonly held to be fetid or impure, and you are similarly surprised that our voluptuous faculties can be powerfully excited by actions which, in your view, bear none but the emblem of ferocity...." In both cases it is through the intermediary of description and the accelerating and condensing effect of repetition that the demonstrative function achieves its strongest impact. Hence it would appear that the obscenity of the descriptions in Sade is grounded in his whole conception of the negative and of negation.

In *Beyond the Pleasure Principle* Freud distinguished between the life instincts and the death instincts, Eros and Thanatos. But in order to understand this distinction we must make a further and more profound distinction between the death or destructive instincts and the Death Instinct. The former are actually given or exhibited in the unconscious, but always in combination with the life instincts; this combination of the death instincts with Eros is as it were the precondition of the "presentation" of Thanatos. So that destruction, and the negative at work in destruction, always manifests itself as the other face of construction and unification as governed by the pleasure principle. This is the sense in which Freud is able to state that we do not find a No (pure negation) in the unconscious, since all opposites coincide there. By contrast when we speak of the Death Instinct, we refer to Thanatos, the absolute negation. Thanatos as such cannot be *given* in psychic life, even in the unconscious: it is, as Freud pointed out in his admirable text, essentially silent. And yet we must speak of it for it is a determinable principle, the foundation and even more of psychic life. Everything depends on it, though as Freud points out, we can only speak of it in speculative or mythical terms.

The distinction between the death or destructive instincts and the Death Instinct seems in fact to correspond to Sade's distinction between the two natures or the two elements. The sadistic hero appears to have set himself the task of thinking out the Death Instinct (pure negation) in a demonstrative form, and is only able to achieve this by multiplying and condensing the activities of component negative or destructive instincts. But the question now arises whether there is not yet another "method" besides the speculative sadistic one.

Freud has analyzed forms of resistance which in various ways imply a process of disavowal (*Verneinung, Verwerfung, Verleugnung*: Lacan has shown the significance of each of these terms). It might seem that a disavowal is, generally speaking, much more superficial than a negation or even a partial destruction. But this is not so, for it represents an entirely different operation. Disavowal should perhaps be understood as the point of departure of an operation that consists neither in negating nor even destroying, but rather in radically contesting the validity of that which is: it suspends belief in and neutralizes the given in such a way that a new horizon opens up beyond the given and in place of it. The clearest example given by Freud is fetishism: the fetish is the image or substitute of the female phallus, that is the means by which we deny that the woman lacks a penis. The fetishist's choice of a fetish is determined by the last object he saw as a child before becoming aware of the missing penis (a shoe, for example, in the case of a glance directed from the feet upward). The constant return to this object, this point of departure, enables him to validate the existence of the organ that is in dispute. The fetish is therefore not a symbol at all, but as it were a frozen, arrested, two-dimensional image, a photograph to which one returns repeatedly to exorcise the dangerous consequences of movement, the harmful discoveries that result from exploration; it represents the last point at which it was still possible to believe.... Thus it appears that fetishism is first of all a disavowal ("No, the woman does not

31

lack a penis"); secondly it is a defensive neutralization (since, contrary to what happens with negation, the knowledge of the situation as it is persists, but in a suspended, neutralized form); in the third place it is a protective and idealizing neutralization (for the belief in a female phallus is itself experienced as a protest of the ideal against the real; it remains suspended or neutralized in the ideal, the better to shield itself against the painful awareness of reality).

Fetishism, as defined by the process of disavowal and suspension of belief belongs essentially to masochism. Whether it also has a place in sadism is a very complex question. There is no doubt that many sadistic murders are accompanied by rituals, as when the victim's clothes are torn without any evidence of a struggle. But it is a mistake to think of the relation of the fetishist to the fetish in terms of sadomasochistic ambivalence; it leads too easily to the creation of a sadomasochistic entity. We should not confuse, as is so often done, two very different types of violence, a potential violence toward the fetish itself, and a violence which arises only in connection with the choice and constitution of the fetish (as in hair despoiling).[5] In our opinion fetishism only occurs in sadism in a secondary and distorted sense. It is divested of its essential relation to disavowal and suspense and passes into the totally different context of negativity and negation, where it becomes an agent in the sadistic process of condensation.

On the other hand there can be no masochism without fetishism in the primary sense. The way in which Masoch defines his idealism or "supersensualism" seems at first sight rather trivial. Why believe in the idea of a perfect world? asks Masoch in *The Divorced Woman*. What we need to do is to "put on wings" and escape into the world of dreams. He does not believe in negating or destroying the world nor in idealizing it: what he does is to disavow and thus to suspend it, in order to secure an ideal which is itself suspended in fantasy. He questions the validity of existing reality in order to create a pure ideal reality, an operation which is perfectly in line with the judicial spirit of masochism. It is not surprising that this process should lead straight into fetishism. The main objects of fetishism in Masoch's life and work are furs, shoes, the whip, the strange helmets that he liked to adorn women with, or the various disguises such as we find in *Venus*. The scene mentioned earlier from *The Divorced Woman* illustrates the split that occurs in fetishism and the corresponding double "suspension": on the one hand the subject is aware of reality but suspends this awareness; on the other the subject clings to his ideal. There is a desire for scientific observation, and subsequently a state of mystical contemplation. The masochistic process of disavowal is so extensive that it affects sexual pleasure itself; pleasure is postponed for as long as possible and is thus disavowed. The masochist is therefore able to deny the reality of pleasure at the very point of experiencing it, in order to identify with the "new sexless man."

In Masoch's novels, it is the moments of suspense that are the climactic moments. It is no exaggeration to say that Masoch was the first novelist to make use of suspense as an essential ingredient of romantic fiction. This is partly because the masochistic rites of torture and suffering imply actual physical suspension (the hero is hung up, crucified or suspended), but also because the woman torturer freezes into postures that identify her with a statue, a painting or a photograph. She suspends her gestures in the act of bringing down the whip or removing her furs; her movement is arrested as she turns to look at herself in a mirror. As we shall see, these "photographic" scenes, these reflected and arrested images are of the greatest significance both from the general point of view of masochism and from the particular point of view of the art of Masoch. They are one of his creative contributions to the novel. The same scenes are reenacted at various levels in a sort of frozen progression. Thus in *Venus* the key scene of the woman torturer is imagined, staged and enacted in earnest, the roles shifting from one character to another. The aesthetic and dramatic suspense of Masoch contrasts with the mechanical, cumulative repetition of Sade. We should note here that the art of suspense always places us on the side of the victim and forces us to identify with him, whereas the gathering momentum of repetition tends to force us onto the side of the torturer and make us identify with the sadistic hero. Repetition does occur in masochism, but it is totally different from sadistic repetition: in Sade it is a function of acceleration and condensation and in Masoch it is characterized by the "frozen" quality and the suspense.

We are now in a position to account for the absence of obscene descriptions in the work of Masoch. The function of the descriptions subsists, but any potential obscenity is disavowed or suspended, by displacing the descriptions either from the object itself to the fetish, or from one part of the object to another part, or again from one aspect of the subject to another. What remains is a strange and oppressive atmosphere, like a sickly perfume permeating the suspense and resisting all displacements. Of Masoch it can be said, as it cannot be of Sade, that no one has ever been so far with so little offense to decency. This leads us to another aspect of Masoch's art: he is a master of the atmospheric novel and the art of suggestion. The settings in Sade, the castles inhabited by his heroes are subject to the brutal laws of darkness and light that accelerate the gestures of their cruel occupants. The settings in Masoch, with their heavy tapestries, their cluttered intimacy, their boudoirs and closets, create a chiaroscuro where the only things that emerge are suspended gestures and suspended suffering. Both in their art and in their language Masoch and Sade are totally different. Let us try to summarize the differences so far: in the work of Sade, imperatives and descriptions transcend themselves toward the higher function of demonstration: the demonstrative function is based on universal negativity as an active process, and on universal negation as an Idea of pure reason; it operates by conserving and accelerating the descriptions, which are overlaid with obscenity. In the work of Masoch, imperatives and descriptions also achieve a transcendent function, but it is of a mythical and dialectical order. It rests on universal disavowal as a reactive process and on universal suspension as an Ideal of pure imagination; the descriptions remain, but they are displaced or frozen, suggestive but free from obscenity. The fundamental distinction between sadism and masochism can be summarized *in the contrasting processes of the negative and negation on the one hand, and of disavowal and suspense on the other.* The first represents a speculative and analytical manner of apprehending the Death Instinct – which, as we have seen, can never be given – while the second pursues the same object in a totally different way, mythically, dialectically and in the imaginary.

# CHAPTER III

# Are Sade and Masoch Complementary?

With Sade and Masoch the function of literature is not to describe the world, since this has already been done, but to define a counterpart of the world capable of containing its violence and excesses. It has been said that an excess of stimulation is in a sense erotic. Thus eroticism is able to act as a mirror to the world by reflecting its excesses, drawing out its violence and even conferring a "spiritual" quality on these phenomena by the very fact that it puts them at the service of the senses. (Sade, in *Philosophy in the Bedroom*, distinguishes between two kinds of wickedness, the one dull-witted and commonplace, the other purified, self-conscious and because it is sensualized, "intelligent.") Similarly the words of this literature create a counter-language which has a direct impact on the senses. It is as though Sade were holding up a perverse mirror in which the whole course of nature and history were reflected, from the beginning of time to the Revolution of 1789. In the isolation of their remote chateaux, Sade's heroes claim to reconstruct the world and rewrite the "history of the heart." They muster the forces of nature and tradition, from everywhere — Africa, Asia, the ancient world — to arrive at their tangible reality and the pure sensual principle underlying them. Ironically, they even strive toward a "republicanism" of which the French are not yet capable.

In Masoch we find the same ambition, to hold up a perverse mirror to all nature and all mankind, from the origins of history to the 1848 revolutions of the Austrian Empire — "The history of cruelty in love." For Masoch, the minorities of the Austrian Empire are an inexhaustible source of stories and customs (hence the Galician, Hungarian, Polish, Jewish and Prussian tales that form the main part of his work). Under the general title *The Heritage of Cain*, Masoch conceived of a "universal" work, the natural history of humanity in a cycle of stories with six main themes: love, property, money, the State, war and death. Each of these forces was to be restored to its cruel physical immediacy; under the sign of Cain, in the mirror of Cain, he was to show how monarchs, generals and diplomats deserved to be thrown in jail and executed along with murderers.[6] Masoch liked to imagine that the Slavs were in need of a beautiful female despot, a terrible Tsarina, to ensure the triumph of the revolutions of 1848 and to strengthen the Panslavic movement. "A further effort, Slavs, if you would become Republicans."

To what extent can we regard Sade and Masoch as accomplices or complementary forces? The sadomasochistic entity was not invented by Freud; we find it in the work of Krafft-Ebing, Havelock Ellis and Féré. The strange relationship between pleasure in doing and pleasure in suffering evil has always been sensed by doctors and writers who have recorded man's intimate life. The "meeting" of sadism and masochism, the affinity that exists between them, is apparent in the work of both Sade and Masoch. There is a certain masochism in Sade's characters: in *The One Hundred and Twenty Days of Sodom* we are told of the tortures and humiliations which the libertines deliberately undergo. The sadist enjoys being whipped as much as he enjoys whipping others. Saint-Fond in *Juliette* arranges for a gang of men to assail him with whips. La Borghèse cries: "I would wish that my aberrations lead me like the lowest of creatures to the fate which befits their wantonness: for me the scaffold would be a throne of exquisite bliss." Conversely, there is a certain sadism in masochism: at the end of his ordeals, Severin, the hero of *Venus in Furs*, declares himself cured and turns to whipping and torturing women. He sees himself no longer as the "anvil" but as the "hammer."

However, it is remarkable that in both instances the reversal should only occur at the end of the enterprise. Severin's sadism is a culmination; it is as though expiation and the satisfaction of the need to expiate were at last to permit the hero what his punishments were previously intended to deny him. Once they have been undergone, punishments and suffering allow the exercise of the evil they once prohibited. Likewise the "masochism" of the sadistic hero makes its appearance at the outcome of his sadistic exercises; it is their climax, the crowning sanction of their glorious infamy. The libertine is not afraid of being treated in the way he treats others. The pain he suffers is an ultimate pleasure, not because it satisfies a need to expiate or a feeling of guilt, but because it confirms him in his inalienable power and gives him a supreme certitude. Through insults and humiliations, in the throes of pain, the libertine is not expiating, but in Sade's words, "he rejoices in his inner heart that he has gone far enough to deserve such treatment." This kind of paroxysm in Sade's heroes is highly significant, for it means, as Maurice Blanchot points out, that "in spite of the similarity of the descriptions, it seems fair to grant the paternity of masochism to Sacher-Masoch and that of sadism to Sade. Pleasure in humiliation never detracts from the mastery of Sade's heroes; debasement exalts them; emotions such as shame, remorse or the desire for punishment are quite unknown to them."[7]

It would therefore be difficult to say that sadism turns into masochism and vice versa; what we have in each case is a para-

39

doxical by-product, a kind of sadism being the humorous outcome of masochism, and a kind of masochism the ironic outcome of sadism. But it is very doubtful whether the masochist's sadism is the same as Sade's, or the sadist's masochism the same as Masoch's. The masochist is able to change into a sadist by expiating, the sadist into a masochist on condition that he does not expiate. If its existence is too hastily taken for granted the sadomasochistic entity is liable to become a crude syndrome that fails to satisfy the demands of genuine symptomatology. It rather falls into the category of disturbances mentioned earlier which are coherent in appearance only and which must be broken down into discrete clinical entities. We should not deal with the problem of symptoms too lightly. It is sometimes necessary to start again from scratch and to break up a syndrome that blurs and arbitrarily unites radically dissimilar symptoms. Hence our suggestion that Masoch was perhaps an even greater clinician than Sade, in that he provided various elucidations and intuitions which help to break down the spurious sadomasochistic unity.

The belief in this unity is to a large extent the result of misunderstandings and careless reasoning. It may seem obvious that the sadist and the masochist are destined to meet. The fact that the one enjoys inflicting while the other enjoys suffering pain seems to be such striking proof of their complementarity that it would be disappointing if the encounter did not take place. A popular joke tells of the meeting between a sadist and a masochist; the masochist says: "Hurt me." The sadist replies: "No." This is a particularly stupid joke, not only because it is unrealistic but because it foolishly claims competence to pass judgment on the world of perversions. It is unrealistic because a genuine sadist could never tolerate a masochistic victim (one of the monks' victims in *Justine* explains: "They wish to be certain their crimes cost tears; they would send away any girl who was to come here voluntarily.") Neither would the masochist tolerate a truly sadistic torturer. He does of course require a special "nature" in the woman torturer, but he needs to mold this nature, to educate and persuade it in accordance with his secret project, which could never be fulfilled with a sadistic woman. Wanda Sacher-Masoch should not have been surprised that Sacher-Masoch failed to respond to one of their sadistic woman friends; conversely, the critics were wrong in suspecting Wanda of lying because she presented a vaguely innocent image of herself, however cunningly and clumsily. Sadistic characters do of course play a part in the masochistic situation as a whole, and the novels of Masoch, as we shall see, offer many examples of this. But their role is never a direct one, and it becomes significant only in the context of the situation that exists before their appearance. The female torturer regards with suspicion the sadist who proposes to help her, as though she sensed the incompatibility of their respective aims. In *The Fisher of Souls*, the heroine Dragomira expresses this feeling to the cruel count Boguslav Soltyk, who believes she is sadistic and cruel: "You make people suffer out of cruelty, but I castigate and kill in the name of God, without pity, but also without hatred."

We tend to ignore this obvious difference. The woman torturer of masochism cannot be sadistic precisely because she is *in* the masochistic situation, she is an integral part of it, a realization of the masochistic fantasy. She belongs in the masochistic world, not in the sense that she has the same tastes as her victim, but because her "sadism" is of a kind never found in the sadist; it is as it were the double or the reflection of masochism. The same is true of sadism. The victim cannot be masochistic, not merely because the libertine would be irked if she were to experience pleasure, but because the victim of the sadist belongs entirely in the world of sadism and is an integral part of the sadis-

41

tic situation. In some strange way she is the counterpart of the sadistic torturer (in Sade's two great novels which are like the reflections of each other, Juliette and Justine, the depraved and the virtuous girl, are sisters). Sadism and masochism are confused when they are treated like abstract entities each in isolation from its specific universe. Once they have been cut off from their *Umwelt* and stripped of their flesh and blood, it seems natural that they should fit in with each other.

This is not to say that the victim of the sadist is herself sadistic, nor that the torturer of masochism is masochistic. But equally unacceptable is Krafft-Ebing's view according to which the torturer of Masoch is either a true sadist or else pretends to be one. In our opinion the woman torturer belongs entirely to masochism; admittedly she is not a masochistic character, but she is a pure element of masochism. By distinguishing in a perversion between the subject (the person) and the element (the essence), we are able to understand how a person can elude his subjective destiny, but only with partial success, by playing the role of an element in the situation of his choice. The torturess escapes from her own masochism by assuming the active role in the masochistic situation. It is a mistake to think that she is sadistic or even pretending to be so. We must not imagine that it is a matter of the masochist encountering a sadist by a stroke of luck. Each subject in the perversion only needs the "element" of the same perversion and not a subject of the other perversion. Whenever the type of the woman torturer is observed in the masochistic setting, it becomes obvious that she is neither a genuine sadist nor a pseudosadist but something quite different. She does indeed belong essentially to masochism, but without realizing it as a subject; she incarnates instead the element of "inflicting pain" in an exclusively masochistic situation. Masoch and his heroes are constantly in search of a peculiar and extremely rare feminine

42

"nature." The subject in masochism needs a certain "essence" of masochism embodied in the nature of a woman who renounces her own subjective masochism; he definitely has no need of another subject, i.e., the sadistic subject.

Admittedly the term sadomasochism does not merely imply the external event of two persons meeting. Nevertheless the theme of an encounter often persists, if only in the form of a "witticism" floating in the unconscious. When Freud took up and reformulated the question of sadomasochism, he started with the consideration that sadomasochism operates *within one and the same individual*, involving opposite instincts and drives: "A person who feels pleasure in producing pain in someone else in a sexual relationship is also capable of enjoying as pleasure any pain which he may himself derive from sexual relations. A sadist is always at the same time a masochist, although the active or the passive aspect of the perversion may be the more strongly developed in him and may represent his predominant sexual activity."[8] His second consideration is that there is an *identity of experience*: the sadist, qua sadist, is only able to feel pleasure in inflicting pain because he has experienced in the past a link between his own pleasure and the pain he has suffered. This argument is all the more curious in that it is stated in the light of Freud's first thesis, where sadism is made to precede masochism. But Freud distinguishes two types of sadism: the first is purely aggressive and only aims at domination; the second is hedonistic and aims at producing pain in others. The masochistic experience of a link between one's own pleasure and one's own pain falls between these two forms of sadism. It would never occur to the sadist to find pleasure in other people's pain if he had not himself first undergone the masochistic experience of a link between pain and pleasure.[9] Thus Freud's first model is more complex than it seems, and suggests the following sequence: aggressive sadism — turning around

43

of sadism upon the self — masochistic experience — hedonistic sadism (by projection and regression). Note that the consideration of an identity of experience is invoked by Sade's libertines, who thus contribute to the idea of a sadomasochistic entity. Noirceuil explains that the libertine's experience of his own pain is related to a stimulation of his "nervous fluid"; it is therefore scarcely surprising that a man thus endowed should "imagine that he moves the object of his pleasure by the same means that affect him."

The third argument is concerned with *transformations*: it consists in showing that the sexual instincts are liable to merge into one another or to transform themselves directly with respect both to their aims and to their objects (reversal into the opposite, turning around upon the self). Again this argument is curious since Freud's attitude toward theories of transformation is extremely reserved. On the one hand he does not believe in an evolutionary tendency; on the other, the dualism which he always maintained in his theory of the instincts places a definite limitation on the possibility of transformations, since according to this theory they can never occur between one group of instincts and another. Thus, in *The Ego and the Id*, Freud explicitly rejects the hypothesis of a direct transformation of love into hate and vice versa, owing to the fact that these agencies depend on qualitatively differentiated instincts (Eros and Thanatos). In fact Freud shows a much greater affinity with Geoffroy Saint-Hilaire than with Darwin. When Freud says that we do not become perverse but simply fail to outgrow the perverse stage of infancy, he uses a formula which comes very close indeed to that used by Geoffroy in connection with freaks. The key concepts of fixation and regression are in direct line of descent from Geoffroy's teratology (arrested development and retrogradation). Geoffroy's point of view excludes all evolution by direct transformation: there is only

44

a hierarchy of possible types and forms, and development within this hierarchy stops at a more or less early stage, or "retrogradation" sets in more or less severely. We find the same conception in Freud: the various combinations of the two types of instincts make up a whole hierarchy of forms at which the individual may become fixated or to which he may regress. It is all the more remarkable that in his treatment of perversions Freud seems to admit of a polymorphous system with possibilities of evolution and direct transformation, which he regards as unacceptable in the field of neurotic and cultural formations.

Therefore if we are to view the concept of a sadomasochistic entity in the light of Freud's arguments we are faced with a problem. Even the notion of a component instinct is a dangerous one in this context since it tends to make us ignore the specificity of types of sexual behavior. We tend to forget that all the available energy of the subject becomes mobilized at the service of his particular perversion. The sadist and the masochist might well be enacting separate dramas, each complete in itself, with different sets of characters and no possibility of communication between them, either from inside or from outside. Only the normal "communicate" — more or less. In the sphere of perversions, it is a mistake to confuse the formations, the concrete and specific manifestations, with an abstract "grid," as though a common libidinal substance flowed now into one form, now into another. We are told that some individuals experienced pleasure both in inflicting pain and in suffering it. We are told furthermore that the person who enjoys inflicting pain experiences in his innermost being the link that exists between the pleasure and the pain. But the question is whether these "facts" are not mere abstractions, whether the pleasure–pain link is being abstracted from the concrete formal conditions in which it arises. The pleasure–pain complex is regarded as a sort of neutral substance common to both sadism

45

and masochism. The link is even further specified by being ascribed to a particular subject, and it is supposed to be experienced equally and identically by the sadistic and the masochistic subject, regardless of the concrete forms *from which it results* in each case. To assume that there is an underlying common "substance" which explains in advance all evolutions and transformations is surely to proceed by abstraction. Even though the sadist may definitely enjoy being hurt, it does not follow that he enjoys it in the same way as the masochist; likewise the masochist's pleasure in inflicting pain is not necessarily the same as the sadist's. We are inevitably led back to the problem of syndromes: some syndromes merely attach a common label to irreducibly different disturbances. Biology warns us against over-hasty acceptance of the existence of an uninterrupted evolutionary chain. The fact that two organs are *analogous* need not mean that there is an evolutionary link between them. We should avoid falling into "evolutionism" by aligning in a single chain results which are approximately continuous but which imply irreducible and heterogeneous formations. An eye, for example, could be produced in several independent ways, as the outcome of different sequences, the analogous product of completely different mechanisms. I suggest that this is also true of sadism and masochism and of the pleasure–pain complex as their allegedly common organ. The concurrence of sadism and masochism is fundamentally one of analogy only; their processes and their formations are entirely different; their common organ, their "eye," squints and should therefore make us suspicious.

46

CHAPTER IV

# The Three Women in Masoch

The heroines of Masoch have in common a well-developed and muscular figure, a proud nature, an imperious will and a cruel disposition even in their moments of tenderness and naiveté. The oriental courtesan, the awe-inspiring Tsarina, the Hungarian or the Polish revolutionary, the servant-mistress, the Sarmatian peasant girl, the cold mystic, the genteel girl, all share these basic traits: "Whether she is a princess or a peasant girl, whether she is clad in ermine or sheepskin, she is always the same woman: she wears furs, she wields a whip, she treats men as slaves and she is both my creation and the true Sarmatian Woman."[10] But beneath this apparent uniformity we may distinguish three very different types of women.

The first type is that of the Grecian woman, the pagan, hetaera or Aphrodite, the generator of disorder. Her life, in her own words, is dedicated to love and beauty; she lives for the moment. She is sensual; she loves whoever attracts her and gives herself accordingly. She believes in the independence of woman and in the fleeting nature of love; for her the sexes are equal: she is hermaphrodite. But it is Aphrodite, the female principal, that triumphs – as Omphale unmans Hercules with woman's attire. She conceives equality merely as the critical moment at which she

47

gains dominance over man, for "man trembles as soon as woman becomes his equal." She is modern, and denounces marriage, morality, the Church and the State as the inventions of man, which must be destroyed. She is the dream character who appears in the opening chapter of *Venus*; we meet her again at the beginning of *The Divorced Woman*, where she makes a lengthy profession of faith; in *The Siren* she is the "imperious and coquettish" Zenobia who creates havoc in the patriarchal family, inspires the women of the household with the desire to dominate, subjugates the father, cuts the hair of the son in a curious ritual of baptism and causes everyone to dress in clothes of the opposite sex.

At the other extreme we find the sadistic woman. She enjoys hurting and torturing others, but it is significant that her actions are prompted by a man or otherwise performed in concert with a man, whose victim she is always liable to become. It is as though the primitive Grecian woman had found her Grecian man or Apollonian element, her virile sadistic impulse. Masoch often introduces a character which he calls the Greek, or indeed Apollo, who intervenes as a third party to incite the woman to sadistic behavior. In *The Fountain of Youth*, Countess Elizabeth Nadasdy tortures young men in collaboration with her lover, the fearful Ipolkar; to this end they invent one of the rare machines to be found in Masoch's writing (a steel woman in whose arms the victim is held fast: "The lovely inanimate creature began her work; thousands of blades shot out of her chest, her arms, her legs and her feet"). In *The Hyena of the Poussta*, Anna Klauer performs her sadistic acts in league with a brigand chief. Even the heroine of *The Fisher of Souls*, Dragomira, in charge of the chastisement of the sadistic Boguslav Soltyk, is swayed by his argument that they are both "of the same race" and concludes an alliance with him.

In *Venus* the heroine, Wanda, sees herself at first as a Grecian woman and ends up believing she is a sadist. At the beginning

48

she identifies with the woman in the dream, the Hermaphrodite. In a fine speech, she declares: "I admire the serene sensuality of the Greeks — pleasure without pain; it is the ideal I strive to realize. I do not believe in the love preached by Christianity and our modern knights of the spirit. Take a look at me: I am worse than a heretic, I am a pagan.... Despite holy ceremonies, oaths and contracts, no permanence can ever be imposed on love; it is the most changeable element in our transient lives. Can you deny that our Christian world is falling into decay?" But at the end of the novel she behaves like a sadist; under the influence of the Greek she has Severin whipped by him: "I was dying of shame and despair. What was most humiliating was that I felt a wild and supersensual pleasure in my pitiful situation, lashed by Apollo's whip and mocked by the cruel laughter of my Venus. But Apollo whipped all poetry from me as one blow followed the next, until finally, clenching my teeth in impotent rage, I cursed myself and my voluptuous imagination, and above all woman and love." Thus the novel culminates in sadism: Wanda goes off with the cruel Greek toward new cruelties, while Severin himself turns sadist or, as he puts it, becomes the "hammer."

It is clear, however, that neither the hermaphroditic nor the sadistic type represents Masoch's ideal. In *The Divorced Woman* the egalitarian pagan woman is not the heroine but the friend of the heroine, the two friends being like "two extremes." In *The Siren* the imperious Zenobia, the hetaera who spreads havoc everywhere, is finally defeated by the young Natalie who is just as domineering but in an altogether different way. The opposite pole, the sadistic woman, is equally unsatisfactory. Dragomira, in *The Fisher of Souls*, is not truly sadistic in the first place; moreover, in forming an alliance with Soltyk, she degrades herself and loses all significance; she is finally defeated and killed by the young Anitta, whose type is more truly in keeping with Masoch's idea.

49

In *Venus* the adventure begins with the theme of the hetaera and ends with the sadistic theme; yet the essential part of the story is enacted in between these two extremes, in another element. The two themes do not represent the masochistic ideal but rather the end points between which this ideal swings, like the span of the pendulum. At one extreme masochism has yet to come into operation, and at the other it has already lost its *raison d'être*. The character of the woman torturer regards these outer limits with a mixture of fear, revulsion and attraction, since she never quite knows whether she will be able to maintain her prescribed role, and fears that she might at any moment fall back into primitive hetaerism or forward into the other extreme of sadism. Anna, in *The Divorced Woman*, declares that she is too weak, too capricious – the capriciousness of the hetaera – to incarnate Julian's ideal. In *Venus*, Wanda only becomes sadistic because she can no longer maintain the role that Severin has imposed on her ("It was you who stifled my feelings with your romantic devotion and insane passion").

What is the essential masochistic element, the scene between the two boundaries where the crucial action takes place? What is the intermediate feminine type between the hetaera and the sadist? Only by piecing together the various descriptions of her in Masoch's writings can we hope to arrive at this fantastic character, this fantasy. In a "*conte rose,*" *The Aesthetics of Ugliness*, he describes the mother of the family: "an imposing woman, with an air of severity, pronounced features and cold eyes, who nevertheless cherishes her little brood." Martscha is described as being "like an Indian woman or a Tartar from the Mongolian desert"; she has "the tender heart of a dove together with the cruel instincts of the feline race." Lola likes to torture animals and dreams of witnessing or even taking part in executions, but "in spite of her peculiar tastes, the girl was neither brutal nor eccentric; on the

contrary, she was reasonable and kind, and showed all the tenderness and delicacy of a sentimental nature." In *The Mother of God*,
Mardona is gentle and gay, and yet she is stern, cold and a master
torturer: "Her lovely face was flushed with anger, but her large
blue eyes shone with a gentle light." *Niera Baranoff* is a haughty
nurse with a heart of stone, but she becomes the tender fiancée
of a dying man, and eventually meets her own death in the snow.
In *Moonlight* we finally come upon the secret of Nature: Nature
herself is cold, maternal and severe. The trinity of the masochistic dream is summed up in the words: cold — maternal — severe,
icy — sentimental — cruel. These qualities point to the difference
between the woman torturer and her "counterparts," the hetaera
and the sadist; their sensuality is replaced by her supersensuous
sentimentality, their warmth and their fire by her icy coldness,
their confusion by her rigorous order.

The sadistic hero, just as much as the feminine ideal of Masoch,
professes an essential coldness which Sade calls "apathy." But one
of our main problems is precisely to ascertain whether, with
respect to cruelty, the apathy of the sadist is not completely different from the coldness of the ideal masochistic type. There is
once more a danger of merely reinforcing the sadomasochistic
abstraction by equating what are in fact two very different kinds
of coldness. The "apathy" of the sadist is essentially directed
against feeling: all feelings, even and especially that of doing evil,
are condemned on the grounds that they bring about a dangerous dissipation which prevents the condensation of energy and
its precipitation into the pure element of impersonal and demonstrative sensuality. "Try to turn into pleasure all things that alarm
your heart." All enthusiasm, even and especially the enthusiasm
for evil, is condemned because it enchains us to secondary nature
and is still a residue of goodness within us. In the novels of Sade,
the true libertines mistrust those characters who are still subject

to emotional outbursts, and who show that, even in the midst of evil and for evil's sake, they are liable to be "converted to the first misfortune." The coldness of the masochistic ideal has a quite different meaning: it is not the negation of feeling but rather the disavowal of sensuality. It is as if sentimentality assumed in this instance the superior role of the impersonal element, while sensuality held us prisoner of the particularities and imperfections of secondary nature. The function of the masochistic ideal is to ensure the triumph of ice-cold sentimentality by dint of coldness; the coldness is used here, as it were, to suppress pagan sensuality and keep sadistic sensuality at bay. Sensuality is disavowed, and no longer exists in its own right; thus Masoch can announce the birth of the new man "devoid of sexual love." Masochistic coldness represents the freezing point, the point of dialectical transmutation, a divine latency corresponding to the catastrophe of the Ice Age. But under the cold remains a supersensual sentimentality buried under the ice and protected by fur; this sentimentality radiates in turn through the ice as the generative principle of new order, a specific wrath and a specific cruelty. The coldness is both protective milieu and medium, cocoon and vehicle: it protects supersensual sentimentality as inner life, and expresses it as external order, as wrath and severity.

Masoch was acquainted with the work of his contemporary Bachofen, an eminent ethnologist and Hegelian jurist. Is not Bachofen, as much as Hegel, the inspiration behind the dream at the beginning of *Venus*? Bachofen distinguished three eras in the evolution of humanity. The first is the hetaeric or Aphroditic era, born in the lustful chaos of primeval swamps: woman's relations with man were many and fickle, the feminine principle was dominant and the father was "Nobody" (this phase, typified by the ruling courtesans of Asia, has survived in such institutions as temple prostitution). The second, or Demetrian era, dawned

among the Amazons and established a strict gynocratic and agricultural order; the swamps were drained; the father or husband
now acquired a certain status but he still remained under the
domination of the woman. Finally the patriarchal or Apollonian
system established itself, matriarchy surviving in degenerate
Amazonian or even Dionysian forms.[11] Masoch's three feminine
types can easily be recognized in these three stages, the first and
third eras being the limits between which the second oscillates
in its precarious splendor and perfection. Here the fantasy finds
what it needs, namely a theoretical and ideological structure
which transforms it into a general conception of human nature
and of the world. Talking about the art of the novel, Masoch
remarked that we must proceed from the "schema" to the "problem"; from our starting point in the obsessive fantasy we must
progress to the theoretical framework where the problem arises.[12]

How does the Greek ideal become transformed into the masochistic ideal, the chaotic sensuality of the hetaeric era into the
new order of gynocratic sentimentality? Obviously through the
catastrophe of the glacial epoch, which accounts for both the
repression of sensuality and the triumphant rise of severity.

In the masochistic fantasy, fur retains its utilitarian function;
it is worn less for the sake of modesty than from fear of catching
cold. "Venus must hide herself in a vast fur lest she catch cold in
our abstract northern clime, in the icy realm of Christianity."
Masoch's heroines frequently sneeze. Everything is suggestive of
coldness: marble body, women of stone, Venus of ice, are favorite expressions of Masoch; his characters often serve their amorous
apprenticeship with a cold statue, by the light of the moon. The
woman in the dream, at the beginning of *Venus*, expresses in her
speech a romantic nostalgia for the lost world of the Greeks: "You
cannot begin to appreciate love as pure bliss and divine serenity...
you modern men, you children of reason...as soon as you try to

be natural you become vulgar.... Stay in your northern mists and Christian incense.... You do not need the gods — they would freeze to death in your climate." That is indeed the essence of the matter: the catastrophe of the Ice Age having engulfed the world of the Greeks and with it the type of the Grecian woman, both sexes found themselves impoverished. Man became coarse and sought a new dignity in the development of consciousness and thought; as a reaction to man's heightened consciousness woman developed sentimentality, and toward his coarseness, severity. The glacial cold was wholly responsible for the transformation: sentimentality became the object of man's thought, and cruelty the punishment for his coarseness. In the coldhearted alliance between man and woman, it is this cruelty and sentimentality in woman that compel man to thought and properly constitute the masochistic ideal.

Like Sade, Masoch distinguishes two natures, but he characterizes them differently. Coarse nature is ruled by individual arbitrariness: cunning and violence, hatred and destruction, disorder and sensuality are everywhere at work. Beyond this lies the great primary nature, which is impersonal and self-conscious, sentimental and supersensual. In the prologue to Masoch's *Galician Tales* a character known as "the wanderer" indicts Nature for being evil. Nature replies in her own defense that she is not hostile and does not hate us, even when she deals death, but always turns to us a threefold face: cold, maternal, severe.... Nature is the steppe. Masoch's descriptions of the steppe are of great beauty, especially the one that appears at the beginning of *Frinko Balaban*; the representation of nature by the identical images of the steppe, the sea and the mother aims to convey the idea that the steppe buries the Greek world of sensuality and rejects at the same time the modern world of sadism. It is like a cooling force which transforms desire and transmutes cruelty. This is the messianic idealism of the steppe. It does not follow that the cruelty of the masochistic ideal is any the lesser than primitive or sadistic cruelty, than the cruelty of whims or that of wickedness. Although masochism always has a theatrical quality that is not to be found in sadism, the sufferings it depicts are not, for all that, simulated or slight, neither is the ambient cruelty less great (the stories of Masoch record excruciating tortures). What characterizes masochism and its theatricality is a peculiar form of cruelty in the woman torturer: the cruelty of the Ideal, the specific freezing point, the point at which idealism is realized.

Masoch's three women correspond to three fundamental mother images: the first is the primitive, uterine, hetaeric mother, mother of the cloaca and the swamps; the second is the Oedipal mother, the image of the beloved, who becomes linked with the sadistic father as victim or as accomplice; and in between these two, the oral mother, mother of the steppe, who nurtures and brings death. We call her intermediate, but she may also come last of all, for she is both oral and silent and therefore has the last word. Freud saw her thus in *The Theme of the Three Caskets*, in agreement with many themes from mythology and folklore. "The mother herself, the beloved who is chosen after her pattern, and finally the Mother Earth who receives him again...the third of the Fates alone, the silent goddess of Death, will take him into her arms." Her true place, however, is between the two others, although she is displaced by an inevitable illusion of perspective. In this connection we feel that Bergler's general thesis is entirely sound: the specific element of masochism is the oral mother,[13] the ideal of coldness, solicitude and death, between the uterine mother and the Oedipal mother. We must wonder all the more why so many psychoanalysts insist on discovering a disguised father-image in the masochistic ideal, and on detecting the presence of the father behind the woman torturer.

# CHAPTER V

## Father and Mother

It is argued that the overtness of the masochist's conflict with the mother, his readiness to incriminate her, should convince us that it is not the mother but the father who plays the central role. But this is to assume that all resistances spring from repression; and in any case the masochist's alleged resistance might just as easily take the form of a displacement from one mother figure to another. It is not enough either to point to the muscular build and the furs of the torturess as evidence of a composite image. The "father" hypothesis stands in need of serious phenomenological or symptomatological support and cannot be made to rest on a line of reasoning which already presupposes an etiology, and with it the fallacious concept of a sadomasochistic entity. It is assumed that since the father-image is a determinant in sadism, this must also be true for masochism, the same factors operating in both cases, once one allows for the inversions, projections and blurring characteristic of masochism. From this viewpoint the masochist would start by wishing to take the place of the father and steal his potency (the sadistic stage); a feeling of guilt would then arise, and with it the fear of castration, leading him to renounce the active aim and take the place of the mother in soliciting the father's love. But in order to avoid the new onset of guilt and castration fear to which the passive role gives rise, he would now replace the desire to be loved by the father with the "desire to be beaten," which not only represents a lesser form of punishment, but is a substitute for the love relationship itself. But why is it the mother who does the beating and not, as we should expect, the father? We are given various reasons for this: first the need to avoid a choice which is too blatantly homosexual; second the need to preserve the first stage where the mother was the desired object, and graft onto it the punishing action of the father; finally the need to present the whole process as a kind of demonstration or plea addressed solely to the father: "You see, it is not I who wanted to take your place, it is she who hurts, castrates and beats me...."

If the father appears to play the decisive role throughout these successive stages, it is because masochism is treated as a combination of highly abstract elements subject to various transformations. There is a failure to appreciate the total concrete situation, the specific world of the perversion: we are not given a genuinely differential diagnosis because the symptoms themselves have been obscured by a preconceived etiology. Even such notions as castration and guilt lose their explanatory force when they are used to show that situations that are fundamentally unrelated nevertheless reverse into one another and are thus related after all. Modes of equivalence and translation are mistaken for systems of transition and transformation. Even a psychoanalyst of Reik's insight can say: "Whenever we had the opportunity to study a case we found the father or his representative hidden behind the figure of the beating woman." In making such a statement we need to be far more specific about the meaning of "hidden," and to explain under what conditions someone or something can be said to be hidden in the relation between symptoms and causes. The same author adds: "After having considered, tested, and put all this in the balance, there yet remains a doubt...does not the oldest stratum of masochism as phantasy and action regress after all to the mother–child relationship as to a historical reality?" And yet he upholds what he calls his "impression" concerning the essential and constant role of the father.[14] Is he speaking about symptoms or offering an etiology based on combinations of abstractions? We are again faced with the question whether the belief in the determinant role of the father in masochism is not simply the result of the preconceived notion of a sadomasochistic entity.

The paternal and patriarchal theme undoubtedly predominates in sadism. There are many heroines in Sade's novels, but their actions, the pleasures they enjoy together and their common projects are all in imitation of man; man is the spectator and presiding genius to whom all their activities are dedicated. Sade's androgynous creations are the product of an incestuous union of father and daughter. Although parricide occurs as frequently as matricide in the work of Sade, the two forms of crime are far from equivalent. Sade equates the mother with secondary nature, which is composed of "soft" molecules and is subject to the laws of creation, conservation and reproduction; the father by contrast only belongs to this nature through social conservatism. Intrinsically he represents primary nature, which is beyond all constituted order and is made up of wild and lacerating molecules that carry disorder and anarchy: *pater sive Natura prima.* Therefore the father is murdered only insofar as he departs from his true nature and function, while the mother is murdered because she remains faithful to hers. As Klossowski has shown with the greatest insight, the sadistic fantasy ultimately rests on the theme of the father destroying his own family, by inciting the daughter to torture and murder the mother.[15] In sadism the Oedipal image of woman is made, as it were, to explode: the mother becomes the victim *par excellence*, while the daughter is elevated to the position of incestuous accomplice. For since the institution of the family and even the law are affected by the maternal character of secondary nature, the father can only be a father by overriding the law, by dissolving the family and prostituting its members. The father represents nature as a primitive anarchic force that can only be restored to its original state by destroying the laws and the secondary beings that are subject to them. The ultimate aim of the sadist is to put an effective end to all procreation, since it competes with primary nature. What makes Sade's heroines sadistic is their sodomitic union with the father in a fundamental alliance against the mother. Sadism is in every sense an active negation of the mother and an exaltation of the father who is beyond all laws.

In "The Passing of the Oedipus Complex," Freud points to two possible outcomes: the active-sadistic, where the child identifies with the father, and the passive-masochistic, where he takes instead the place of the mother and desires to be loved by the father. The theory of partial impulses allows for the coexistence of these two entities and thus lends support to the belief in the unity of sadism and masochism. Freud says of the Wolf Man: "In his sadism he maintained his ancient identification with his father; but in his masochism he chose him as a sexual object." So when we are told that the character who does the beating in masochism is the father, we are entitled to ask: Who in reality is being beaten? Where is the father hidden? Could it not be in the person who is being beaten? The masochist feels guilty, he asks to be beaten, he expiates, but why and for what crime? Is it not precisely the father-image in him that is thus miniaturized, beaten, ridiculed and humiliated? What the subject atones for is his resemblance to the father and the father's likeness in him: the formula of masochism is the humiliated father. Hence the father is not so much the beater as the beaten. A point of great significance in the fantasy of the three mothers is the symbolic transfer or redistribution of all paternal functions to the threefold feminine figure: the father is excluded and completely nullified. Most of Masoch's novels contain a hunting scene which is described in minute detail: the ideal woman hunts a bear or a wolf and despoils it of its fur. We could interpret this symbolically as the struggle of woman against man, from which woman emerges triumphant. But this would be a mistake, since woman has already triumphed when masochism begins, the bear and the fur have already been invested with an exclusively feminine significance. The animal stands for the primitive hetaeric mother, the pre-birth mother, it is hunted and despoiled for the benefit of the oral mother, with the aim of achieving a rebirth, a parthenogenetic second birth in which, as we shall see, the father has no part. It is true that man reappears at the opposite pole, on the side of the Oedipal mother: an alliance is contracted between the third woman and the sadistic man (Elizabeth and Ipolkar in *The Fountain of Youth*, Dragomira and Boguslav in *The Fisher of Souls*, and Wanda and the Greek in *Venus*). But this reappearance of man is compatible with masochism only to the extent that the Oedipal mother maintains her rights and her integrity; not only does the man appear in effeminate, transvestite form (the Greek in *Venus*), but in contrast to what happens in sadism, the mother-representative is the accomplice and the young girl is the victim. (In *The Fountain of Youth*, the masochistic hero allows Elizabeth to murder Gisèle, the young girl he loves.) Where the sadistic man happens to triumph, as he does at the end of *Venus*, all masochistic activity ceases; like the Forms in Plato, it withdraws or perishes rather than unite with its opposite, sadism.

However, the transfer of the functions of the father onto the three mother-images is only one aspect of the fantasy. The main significance of the fantasy lies in the concentration of all the maternal functions in the person of the second mother, the oral or "good" mother. It is a mistake to relate masochism to the theme of the bad mother. There are of course bad mothers in masochism (the two extremes of the uterine mother and the Oedipal mother) but this is because the whole tendency of masochism is to idealize the functions of the bad mother and transfer them onto the good mother. The function of prostitution belongs specifically to the uterine, hetaeric mother, and is transformed by the sadistic hero into an institution designed to destroy the Oedipal mother and make the daughter into an accomplice. Although we find in Masoch and masochism a similar propensity to prostitute the woman, we should not regard this as proof that sadism and masochism share in a common nature. The important difference in this case is that in masochism the woman assumes the function of prostitution in her capacity as honest woman, the mother in her capacity as the good oral mother. Wanda relates how Masoch persuaded her to look for lovers, to answer advertisements and to prostitute herself. But he justified this desire as follows: "How delightful to find in one's own respectable, honest and good wife a voluptuousness that must usually be sought among women of easy virtue." The mother, insofar as she is oral, respectable and pure, must assume the function of prostitute normally reserved for the uterine mother. The same is true of the sadistic functions of the Oedipal mother: the administration of cruelty is taken over by the good mother and is thus profoundly transformed and put to the service of the masochistic ideal of expiation and rebirth. Prostitution should not therefore be regarded as a common feature that links up the two perversions. The dream of universal prostitution, as it appears in Sade's "society of the friends of crime," is embodied in an *objective institution* that aims to destroy the mother and give preferment to the daughter (the mother becomes an outcast and the daughter a partner). In Masoch on the contrary the ideal form of prostitution is based on a *private* contract whereby the masochist persuades his wife, in her capacity as good mother, to give herself to other men.[16] Thus the oral mother as the ideal of masochism is expected to assume all the functions of the other female figures; in taking on these functions, she transforms and sublimates them. This is why we feel that psychoanalytic interpretations relating masochism to the "bad mother" are of very limited applicability.

This concentration of functions in the person of the good oral mother is one of the ways in which the father is cancelled out, and his parts and functions distributed among the three women. The way is thus made clear for the struggle and the epiphany of the three women, which will eventually result in the triumph of the oral woman. In short the three women constitute a symbolic order in which and through which the father is abolished in advance − for all time. This eternal, timeless supremacy of the mother can only be expressed in the language of myths, which is therefore essential to masochism: everything has already happened, and the entire action takes place between the mother images (thus the hunt and the conquest of the fur). It is therefore surprising that even the most enlightened psychoanalytic writers link the emergence of a symbolic order with the "name of the father." This is surely to cling to the singularly unanalytical conception of the mother as the representative of nature and the father as sole principle and representative of culture and law. The masochist experiences the symbolic order as an intermaternal order in which the mother represents the law under certain prescribed conditions; she generates the symbolism through which the masochist expresses himself. It is not a case of identification with the mother, as is mistakenly believed. The threefold division of the mother literally expels the father from the masochistic universe. In *The Siren*, Masoch tells the story of a young boy who allows people to believe that his father is dead merely because he finds it easier and more polite not to dispel a misunderstanding. There is a disavowal of the mother by magnifying her ("symbolically the mother lacks nothing") and a corresponding disavowal of the father by degrading him ("the father is nothing," in other words he is deprived of all symbolic function).

We need therefore to examine more closely the way in which man, the third element, is introduced or reintroduced in the masochistic fantasy. The life and work of Masoch were dominated by the quest for this third party whom he calls "the Greek." However, in *Venus* the character has two aspects. The first or fantasy aspect is effeminate: the Greek is "like a woman.... In Paris he has been seen dressed up as a woman, and men were showering him with love letters." The second aspect is virile and marks on the contrary the end of the fantasy and of the masochistic exercise. When the Greek takes up the whip and thrashes Severin the supersensual charm quickly dissolves: "voluptuous dream, woman and love," all melt away. The novel has a sublime and humorous ending, with Severin giving up masochism and turning sadist. We may therefore conclude that the father, though abolished in the symbolic order, nevertheless continues to act in the order of the real,[17] or of experience. There is a fundamental law, first formulated by Jacques Lacan, according to which an object which has been abolished on the symbolic plane resurges in "the real" in a hallucinatory form.[18] The final episode of *Venus* is a typical instance of the aggressive and hallucinatory return of the father in a world that has symbolically abolished him. Everything in the text suggests that the full "reality" of the scene can only be experienced in a hallucinatory manner: the hallucination in return makes the pursuit or continuance of the fantasy impossible. It would therefore be thoroughly misleading to confuse the fantasy that comes into play in the symbolic order and the hallucination that represents the return of what had been symbolically abolished. Theodor Reik quotes a case where all the "magic" vanishes from the masochistic scene because the subject thinks he recognizes in the woman about to strike him a trait that reminds him of the father.[19] (The same thing happens at the end of *Venus*, and even more strikingly, since here, as a result of the actual substitution of a father figure, the Greek, for the torturess, Severin is moved to give up the masochistic aim altogether.) Reik seems to regard the case quoted above as proof that the torturess essentially represents the father and that the mother-image is the father in disguise – an argument once again in favor of a sadomasochistic entity. In our opinion the conclusion should be quite the reverse; Reik maintains that the subject is "disillusioned," but we ought rather to say that he is "disfantasized," fantasy giving way to hallucination and a hallucinatory state. Far from being the truth behind masochism and the confirmation of its connection with sadism, the aggressive return of the father disrupts the masochistic situation; it represents the constant threat from the side of reality to the masochist's world and to the defenses that condition and limit the symbolic world of his perversion. It would be "wild" psychoanalysis to favor this breakdown of his defenses by mistaking the "protest" from external reality for the expression of an inner reality.

What are the masochistic defenses against both the reality and the hallucination of the father's aggressive return? The masochistic hero must evolve a complex strategy to protect his world of fantasy and symbols, and to ward off the hallucinatory inroads of reality (or to put it differently, the real attacks of hallucination). This procedure which, as we shall see, is constantly used in masochism, is the *contract*. A contract is established between the hero and the woman, whereby at a precise point in time and for a deter-

minate period she is given every right over him. By this means
the masochist tries to exorcise the danger of the father and to
ensure that the temporal order of reality and experience will be
in conformity with the symbolic order, in which the father has
been abolished for all time. Through the contract, that is through
the most rational and temporarily determinate act, the masochist
reaches toward the most mythical and the most timeless realms,
where the three mother-images dwell. Finally, he ensures that he
will be beaten; we have seen that what is beaten, humiliated and
ridiculed in him is the image and the likeness of the father, and
the possibility of the father's aggressive return. *It is not a child but
a father that is being beaten.* The masochist thus liberates himself
in preparation for a rebirth in which the father will have no part.

But how shall we account for the fact that even in the contract the masochist requires a third party, the Greek? Why should
he so ardently desire this third party? The answer is that the
Greek, while he undoubtedly evokes the danger of the aggressive
return of the father, also stands for something more — something
of an entirely different kind, namely the hope of a rebirth, the
projection of the new man that will result from the masochistic
experiment. The Greek is a compound figure combining various
elements: when he is idealized he foreshadows the outcome of
masochism and stands for the new man; in his sadistic role, by
contrast, he represents the dangerous father who brutally interrupts the experiment and interferes with the outcome. Let us
remind ourselves of the fundamental structure of fantasy in general, for the art of masochism is the art of fantasy. Fantasy plays
on two series, two opposite "margins," and the resonance thus
set up gives life to and creates the heart of the fantasy. In masochism the two symbolic margins are the uterine mother and the
Oedipal mother; between them and moving from one to the other
is the oral mother, the core of the fantasy. The masochist plays

on the two extremes and causes them to produce a resonance in the oral mother. He thereby invests her with an amplitude which repeatedly brings her very close to the figures of her rivals. The oral mother must wrest from the uterine mother her hetaeric functions (prostitution) and from the Oedipal mother her sadistic functions (punishment). At either end of her pendulumlike motion, the good mother must confront the third party: the anonymous uterine mother and the sadistic Oedipal mother. But in point of fact (unless things take a turn for the worse as a result of the hallucinatory return of the father) the third party is never invited or sought after for its own sake, but to be neutralized by the substitution of the good mother for the uterine and the Oedipal mother. The adventure with Ludwig II admirably illustrates this: its comic effect is due to the parries put up by the two characters in confrontation.[20] When Masoch receives the first letters from "Anatole" he sincerely hopes that his correspondent is a woman. But he has already planned his parry in case it should be a man: he will introduce Wanda into the affair and in collusion with the third party will get her to perform a hetaeric or sadistic function, but in her capacity as good mother. Whereupon Anatole, who has other plans, replies with an unexpected parry, and introduces his hunchbacked cousin who is intended to neutralize Wanda herself, contrary to all Masoch's intentions. The question whether masochism is feminine and passive and sadism virile and active is only of secondary importance. In any case it arises from the presupposition that sadism and masochism are complementary, the one being the reverse of the other. But sadism and masochism do not together constitute a single entity; they are not respectively made up of partial impulses, but each is complete in itself. The masochist's experience is grounded in an alliance between the son and the oral mother; the sadist's in the alliance of father and daughter. In both cases this alliance is confirmed by the respective disguises. In masochism the masculine impulse is embodied in the role of the son, while the feminine impulse is projected in the role of the mother; but in point of fact the two impulses constitute one single figure; femininity is posited as lacking in nothing and placed alongside a virility suspended in disavowal (just as the absence of a penis need not indicate lack of the phallus, its presence likewise need not indicate possession of the phallus). Hence in masochism a girl has no difficulty in assuming the role of son in relation to the beating mother who possesses the ideal phallus and on whom rebirth depends. Similarly, in sadism, it becomes possible for the boy to play the role of a girl in relation to a projection of the father. We might say that the masochist is hermaphrodite and the sadist androgynous.... They represent parallel worlds, each complete in itself, and it is both unnecessary and impossible for either to enter the other's world. We cannot at any rate say that they are exact opposites, except insofar as opposites avoid each other and must either do so or perish. This very opposition tends unfortunately to suggest possibilities of transformation, reversal and combination. Yet there is between sadism and masochism an irreducible dissymmetry: sadism stands for the active negation of the mother and the inflation of the father (who is placed above the law); masochism proceeds by a twofold disavowal, a positive, idealizing disavowal of the mother (who is identified with the law) and an invalidating disavowal of the father (who is expelled from the symbolic order).

CHAPTER VI

# The Art of Masoch

There is a fundamental aesthetic or plastic element in the art of
Masoch. It has been said that the senses become "theoreticians"
and that the eye, for example, becomes a human eye when its
object itself has been transformed into a human or cultural object,
fashioned by and intended solely for man. Animal nature is profoundly hurt when this transmutation of its organs from the animal to the human takes place, and it is the experience of this
painful process that the art of Masoch aims to represent. He calls
his doctrine "supersensualism" to indicate this cultural state of
transmuted sensuality; this explains why he finds in works of art
the source and the inspiration of his loves. The lover embraces a
marble woman by way of initiation; women become exciting
when they are indistinguishable from cold statues in the moonlight or paintings in darkened rooms. *Venus* is set under the sign
of Titian, with its mystical play of flesh, fur and mirror, and the
conjunction of cold, cruelty and sentiment. The scenes in Masoch
have of necessity a frozen quality, like statues or portraits; they
are replicas of works of art, or else they duplicate themselves in
mirrors (as when Severin catches sight of his own reflection
in the mirror).

Sade's heroes, by contrast, are not art lovers, still less collectors. In *Juliette*, Sade explains why: "Ah, if only an engraver could record for posterity this divine and voluptuous scene! But lust, which all too quickly crowns our actors, might not have allowed the artist time to portray them. It is not easy for art, which is motionless, to depict an activity the essence of which is movement." Sensuality is movement. In order to convey the immediacy of this action of one soul against another, Sade chooses to rely on the quantitative techniques of accumulation and acceleration, mechanically grounded in a materialistic theory: reiteration and internal multiplication of the scenes, precipitation, over-determination. (The subject is at once parricide, incestuous, murderer, prostitute and sodomite.) We have seen why number, quantity and quantitative precipitation were the specific obsessions of sadism. Masoch, on the contrary, has every reason to rely on art and the immobile and reflective quality of culture. In his view the plastic arts confer an eternal character on their subject because they suspend gestures and attitudes. The whip or the sword that never strikes, the fur that never discloses the flesh, the heel that is forever descending on the victim, are the expression, beyond all movement, of a profound state of waiting closer to the sources of life and death. The novels of Masoch display the most intense preoccupation with arrested movement; his scenes are frozen, as though photographed, stereotyped or painted. In *Venus* it is a painter who says: "Woman, goddess...do you not know what it is to love, to be consumed by longing and passion?" And Wanda looms with her furs and her whip, adopting a suspended posture, like a *tableau vivant*: "I want to show you another portrait of me, one that I painted myself. You shall copy it." "You shall copy it" suggests both the sternness of the order and the reflection in the mirror.

Waiting and suspense are essential characteristics of the masochistic experience. Hence the ritual scenes of hanging, cruci-

70

fixion and other forms of physical suspension in Masoch's novels. The masochist is morose: but his moroseness should be related to the experience of waiting and delay. It has often been pointed out that the pleasure–pain complex is insufficient to define masochism; but humiliation, expiation, punishment and guilt are not sufficient either. It is argued, justifiably, that the masochist is not a strange being who finds pleasure in pain, but that he is like everyone else, and finds pleasure where others do, the simple difference being that for him pain, punishment or humiliation are necessary prerequisites to obtaining gratification. However, this mechanism remains incomprehensible if it is not related to the form and in particular to the temporal form that makes it possible. Thus it is a mistake to treat the pleasure–pain complex as a raw material able intrinsically to lend itself to any transformation, beginning with the alleged transformation of sadism into masochism. Formally speaking, masochism is a state of waiting; the masochist experiences waiting in its pure form. Pure waiting divides naturally into two simultaneous currents, the first representing what is awaited, something essentially tardy, always late and always postponed, the second representing something that is expected and on which depends the speeding up of the awaited object. It is inevitable that such a form, such a rhythmic division of time into two streams, should be "filled" by the particular combination of pleasure and pain. For at the same time as pain fulfills what is expected, it becomes possible for pleasure to fulfill what is awaited. The masochist waits for pleasure as something that is bound to be late, and expects pain as the condition that will finally ensure (both physically and morally) the advent of pleasure. He therefore postpones pleasure in expectation of the pain which will make gratification possible. The anxiety of the masochist divides therefore into an indefinite awaiting of pleasure and an intense expectation of pain.

71

Disavowal, suspense, waiting, fetishism and fantasy together make up the specific constellation of masochism. Reality, as we have seen, is affected not by negation but by a disavowal that transposes it into fantasy. Suspense performs the same function in relation to the ideal, which is also relegated to fantasy. Waiting represents the unity of the ideal and the real, the form or temporality of the fantasy. The fetish is the object of the fantasy, the fantasized object par excellence. Consider the following masochistic fantasy: a woman in shorts is pedaling energetically on a stationary bicycle; the subject is lying under the bicycle, the whirring pedals almost brushing him, his palms pressed against the woman's calves. All the elements are conjoined in this image, from the fetishism of the woman's calf to the twofold waiting represented by the motion of the pedals and the immobility of the bicycle. We should say, however, that there is no such thing as a specifically masochistic kind of waiting, but rather that the masochist is morose, by which we mean that he experiences waiting in its pure form. For example, Masoch arranged to have a healthy tooth pulled out while his wife, dressed in furs, stood before him with a threatening air. What is true of masochistic writing is equally true of masochistic fantasy: there is no specifically masochistic fantasy, but rather a masochistic art of fantasy.

The masochist needs to believe that he is dreaming even when he is not; sadism offers no such discipline in the art of the fantasy. Maurice Blanchot has given an excellent analysis of the position of Sade (and of his characters) in relation to fantasy: "His own erotic dream consists in projecting the unreal dynamic of his sensuous enjoyment on to characters who are not dreaming but acting.... Therefore the more this eroticism is *dreamt*, the more it requires a fiction from which dreams are excluded and where debauchery is fully actualized."[21] In other words, Sade needs to believe that he is not dreaming even when he is. In sadism a powerful force of paranoid projection transforms the fantasy into the instrument of a fundamental and sudden change in the objective world. Clairwil dreams that her wickedness never ceases to impinge on the world even while she is asleep. Hence the pleasure–pain potential characteristic of the fantasy requires for its realization that real characters should experience actual pain, while pleasure accrues to the sadist inasmuch as he can continue to dream that he is not dreaming.

Juliette gives the following advice: "For a whole fortnight abstain from all lustful behavior; distract and entertain yourselves with other things.... Then lie down in the dark and little by little imagine different wanton acts. One of these will affect you more powerfully and become like an obsession, and you must then note it down and promptly put it into action." In this way the fantasy acquires maximum aggressive power, systematization and capacity of intervention in the real world: the Idea is projected with extraordinary violence. The masochistic use of fantasy is totally different: it consists in neutralizing the real and containing the ideal within the fantasy. In our opinion the difference in the use of the fantasy determines to a certain extent the difference in content. The sadist's destructive relation to the fetish must be interpreted in the light of his projective use of fantasy. To say that the destruction of the fetish implies a belief in the fetish (as profanation is said to imply a belief in the sacred) is to indulge in meaningless generalities. The destruction of the fetish is a measure of the speed with which projection takes place, and of the way in which the dream as such is eliminated and the Idea erupts into the real waking world. By contrast, the constitution of the fetish in masochism points to the inner force of the fantasy, its characteristic of patient waiting, its suspended and static power, and the way in which the ideal and the real are together absorbed by it.

It would seem that the contents of sadism and masochism are each intended to fulfill a form. Variations in the distribution of the pleasure–pain complex as well as variations in the content of the fantasy (whether the mother or the father is the determinant image) depend on the specific requirements of the form. If we take the material content as our starting point, we solve everything and we arrive besides at the supposed unity of sadism and masochism, but at the price of total confusion. Any given formula for the association of pleasure and pain must take into account certain specific formal conditions (e.g., the form of waiting, the form of projection). "Material" definitions of masochism based on the pleasure–pain complex are insufficient: as the logician would say, they are purely nominal, they do not indicate the possibility of what they define, they do not show that particular conditions must follow. But worse still, they lack distinctive features, and open up the way to all sorts of confusions between sadism and masochism such as the possibility of their reversing into each other. "Moral" definitions based on the concepts of guilt and expiation are no better, since they are based on the alleged communication between sadism and masochism (in this sense they are even more moral than they seem). Fundamentally, masochism is neither material nor moral, but essentially formal. We need, for the understanding of the world of perversions in general, a genuinely formal, almost deductive psychoanalysis which would attend first of all to the formal patterns underlying the processes, viewed as formal elements of fictional art.

In the field of formal psychoanalysis as applied to masochism, the work of Theodore Reik deserves special credit. He distinguished four basic characteristics of masochism:

1. The "special significance of fantasy," that is the form of the fantasy (the fantasy experienced for its own sake, or the scene

74

which is dreamed, dramatized, ritualized and which is an indispensable element of masochism).

2. The "suspense factor" (the waiting, the delay, expressing the way in which anxiety affects sexual tension and inhibits its discharge).

3. The "demonstrative" or, more accurately, the persuasive feature (the particular way in which the masochist exhibits his suffering, embarrassment and humiliation).

4. The "provocative fear" (the masochist aggressively demands punishment since it resolves anxiety and allows him to enjoy the forbidden pleasure).[22]

It is curious that Reik, no less than other analysts, neglects a fifth factor which is very important: the form of the contract in the masochistic relationship. In Masoch's personal adventures as well as in his fiction, and in his particular case as well as in the structure of masochism in general, the contract represents the ideal form of the love-relationship and its necessary precondition. A contract is drawn up between the subject and the tortureress, giving a new application to the idea of the jurists of antiquity that slavery itself is based on a contract. The masochist appears to be held by real chains, but in fact he is bound by his word alone. The masochistic contract implies not only the necessity of the victim's consent, but his ability to persuade, and his pedagogical and judicial efforts to train his torturer. In the two contracts of Masoch reproduced here (see Appendix II) it is interesting to note how the conditions alter from the first to the second contract in the direction of greater strictness: the first contract retains a degree of reciprocity of duties, a time limit, a preservation of inalienable rights (the right of work or the subject's honor); the second confers more and more rights on the woman at the expense of the subject, who loses the right to his name, his honor and his life.[23] (The contract in *Venus* changes Severin's name.) The tightening of the contractual bond indicates that the function of the contract is to lay down the law, which, once established, becomes increasingly cruel and restrictive toward one of the parties (in this case the initiator of the contract). The function of the masochistic contract is to invest the mother-image with the symbolic power of the law. The question remains why a contract is necessary, and why it develops as it does toward extreme severity. In any case there is no doubt that masochism cannot do without a contract, either actual or in the mind of the masochist (as in the phenomenon of *pagisme*[24]).

We have now seen the two aspects of the "culturism" of Masoch, the aesthetic aspect which is expressed in the model of art and suspense, and the juridical aspect which is expressed in the model of the contract and of submission. By contrast, Sade is not only supremely indifferent to the resources of the work of art, but he regards the contract and any appeal to its authority, or indeed any idea or theory connected with it, with the deepest hostility. The sadist heaps derision on the principle of the contract. But having said this, we should not simply oppose the culturalism of Masoch to the naturalism of Sade. Both authors exhibit a form of naturalism and both distinguish between two natures, but they do not make the same kind of distinction, and above all they have very different views on how the passage from one nature to the other is accomplished. According to Masoch, it is essentially the work of art and the contract that makes possible the transition from a lower nature to the great Nature, which is sentimental and self-conscious. For Sade, on the contrary, the transition from secondary nature to primary nature implies no suspense or system of aesthetics, but an attempt to establish a *mechanism* of perpetual motion, and with it *institutions* of perpetual motion. Sade's secret societies, his societies of libertines, are institutional societies; in a word, Sade thinks in terms of "institutions," Masoch in terms of "the contract." The juridical distinction between contract and institution is well known: the contract presupposes in principle the free consent of the contracting parties and determines between them a system of reciprocal rights and duties; it cannot affect a third party and is valid for a limited period. Institutions, by contrast, determine a long-term state of affairs which is both involuntary and inalienable; it establishes a power or an authority which takes effect against a third party. But even more significant is the difference between the contract and the institution with respect to what is known as a *law*: the contract actually generates a law, even if this law oversteps and contravenes the conditions which made it possible; the institution is of a very different order in that it tends to render laws unnecessary, to replace the system of rights and duties by a dynamic model of action, authority and power. Saint-Just accordingly demanded that there should be many institutions and few laws, and proclaimed that the Republic could not be a republic so long as laws had the supremacy over institutions....[25] In short, the specific impulse underlying the contract is toward the creation of a law, even if in the end the law should take over and impose its authority upon the contract itself; whereas the corresponding impulse at work in the case of the institution is toward the degradation of all laws and the establishment of a superior power that sets itself above them.

The affinity of Sade's theorizing with the theme of the institution (as well as with certain aspects of Saint-Just's thinking) has often been pointed out. But it is not enough to say that Sade's heroes put institutions at the service of their abnormality, or need them as the limits that give full value to their transgressions. Sade's conception of institutions is more positive and profound, and his relation to revolutionary ideology is accordingly a complex one: he rejects any contractual conception of the republican regime

and is even more strongly against the idea of the law. He found in
the Revolution what he hated most: the law and the contract,
which he regards as the two main obstacles that still prevent the
French from achieving a true republic. The crux of Sade's political thinking is the contrast he draws between the institution and
the law, between a republic based on institutions and one based
on contractual relations. Saint-Just pointed out the following
inverse relation: the fewer institutions, the greater the number
of laws (as in monarchy and despotism); the fewer laws, the
greater the number of institutions (the republic). Sade seems to
have developed this idea to its ironic and perhaps also its most
serious conclusion; he asked which institutions would require the
fewest possible laws, and ultimately no laws at all (laws "so leni-
ent and so few..."). Laws bind actions; they immobilize and mor-
alize them. Pure institutions without laws would by definition
be models of free, anarchic action, in perpetual motion, in permanent revolution, in a constant state of immorality. "Insurrection... is not a moral state of affairs; it has nevertheless to be the
permanent condition in a republic. It would be both absurd and
dangerous to require that those who are to ensure the perpetual
subversion of the established machinery should be moral, for the
state of a moral man is one of peace and tranquillity, while the
state of immorality is one of perpetual unrest resembling the necessary state of insurrection in which the republican must always
keep the government of which he is a member." It would be a
mistake to regard the famous text from *Philosophy in the Bedroom*,
"Yet another effort, Frenchmen, if you wish to become Republicans," merely as a paradoxical application of sadian fantasies in
the field of politics. The problem that it raises, both on the formal and on the political level, is far more serious and original. It is
this: Granted that both the contract and the law are in the nature
of mystifications, the law being used by despotism for its own

78

purposes, and granted that the institution is the only form of political organization that differs essentially from both law and contract, where should we look to for the perfect institution — the one that banishes contracts and allows only the barest minimum of laws? In reply, Sade points to the ironic possibility, under these conditions, of making atheism, calumny, theft, prostitution, incest and sodomy — even murder — into institutions, and shows furthermore that they are necessarily the types of the ideal institution, the institution in perpetual motion. He stresses in particular the possibility of *instituting* universal prostitution and he attempts to refute the "contractual" objection to such "universalization."

In any case those who contrast Sade's extreme theoretical pronouncements with his very moderate personal stand during the Revolution fail to do justice to his political thought. The opposition that he established between the institution and the contract and its corollary, the opposition between institutions and laws, have become juridical platitudes of positivist thinking. But this is because their original significance and their revolutionary character have been obscured by uneasy compromises. If we wish to recover the original meaning of these oppositions and of the choices and directions they imply, we must return to Sade (and to Saint-Just, who does not give quite the same answers as Sade). There is a profound political insight in Sade's conception of the revolutionary republic as an institution based on opposition to both law and contract; but this conception is ironic through and through because it is sexual and sexualized, as if deliberately to challenge any attempt to think of politics in legalistic or contractual terms. We should expect to find in Masoch a comparable tour de force, the *humorous* converse of Sade's. As against the latter's *ironic* conception of the institution based on the rejection of law and contract, and in the context of the Revolution of 1789, we have to consider the *humorous* contribution of Masoch and his conception of the relationship between the contract and the law, in the context of the 1848 Revolution. As a result, fundamental problems of rights begin to emerge in their true light even as they become perverted in the work of Sade and Masoch and turned into literary elements in a parody of the philosophy of history.

The classical conception of the law found its perfect expression in Plato and in that form gained universal acceptance throughout the Christian world. According to this conception, the law may be viewed either in the light of its underlying principles or in the light of its consequences. From the first point of view, the law itself is not a primary but only a secondary or delegated power dependent on a supreme principle which is the Good. If men knew what the Good was, or knew how to conform to it, they would not need laws: the law is only a representative of the Good in a world that the Good has more or less forsaken. Hence, from the point of view of its consequences, obedience to the law is "best," the best being in the image of the Good. The righteous man obeys the laws of the country of his birth or residence, and in so doing acts for the best, even though he retains his freedom of thought, freedom to think of the Good and for the sake of the Good.

This conception, which is seemingly so conventional, nevertheless conceals elements of irony and humor which made political philosophy possible, for it allows the free play of thought at the upper and lower limits of the scale of the law. The death of Socrates is an exemplary illustration of this: the laws place their fate in the hands of the condemned man, and ask that he should sanction their authority by submitting to them as a rational man. There is indeed a great deal of irony in the operation that seeks to trace the laws back to an absolute Good as the necessary principle of their foundation. Equally, there is considerable humor in the attempt to reduce the laws to a relative Best in order to persuade us that we should obey them. Thus it appears that the notion of law is not self-sufficient unless backed by force; ideally it needs to rest on a higher principle as well as on a consideration of its remote consequences. This may be why, according to the mysterious text in the *Phaedo*, the disciples present at the death of Socrates could not help laughing. Irony and humor are the essential forms through which we apprehend the law. It is in this essential relation to the law that they acquire their function and their significance. Irony is the process of thought whereby the law is made to depend on an infinitely superior Good, just as humor is the attempt to sanction the law by recourse to an infinitely more righteous Best.

The final overthrow of the classical conception of the law was certainly not the result of the discovery of the relativity and variability of laws, since these were fully recognized and understood in this conception and were indeed an integral part of it. The true cause must be sought elsewhere. In the *Critique of Practical Reason* Kant gave a rigorous formulation of a radically new conception, in which the law is no longer regarded as dependent on the Good, but on the contrary, the Good itself is made to depend on the law. This means that the law no longer has its foundation in some higher principle from which it would derive its authority, but that it is self-grounded and valid solely by virtue of its own form. For the first time we can now speak of THE LAW, regarded as an absolute, without further specification or reference to an object. Whereas the classical conception only dealt with *the laws* accord-

ing to the various spheres of the Good or the various circumstances attending the Best, Kant can speak of the moral law, and
of its application to what otherwise remains totally undetermined. The moral law is the representation of a pure form and is
independent of content or object, spheres of activity or circumstances. The moral law is THE LAW, the form of the law and as
such it cannot be grounded in a higher principle. In this sense
Kant is one of the first to break away from the classical conception of the law and to give us a truly modern conception. The
Copernican revolution in Kant's *Critique of Pure Reason* consisted
in viewing the objects of knowledge as revolving around the
subject; but the *Critique of Practical Reason*, where the Good is
conceived as revolving around the Law, is perhaps even more revolutionary. It probably reflected major changes in the world. It
may have been the expression of the ultimate consequences of a
return beyond Christianity to Judaic thought, or it may even have
foreshadowed a return to the pre-Socratic (Oedipal) conception
of the law, beyond to the world of Plato. However that may be,
Kant, by establishing that THE LAW is an ultimate ground or principle, added an essential dimension to modern thought: the
object of the law is by definition unknowable and elusive.[26]

But there is yet a further dimension. We are not concerned
here with the architectonics of Kant's system (and the manner
in which he salvages the Good in the system), but with a second
discovery which is correlated with and complementary to the
first. The law can no longer be grounded on the superior principle of the Good, but neither can it be sanctioned any more by
recourse to the idea of the Best as representing the good will of
the righteous. Clearly THE LAW, as defined by its pure form, without substance or object or any determination whatsoever, is such
that no one knows nor can know what it is. It operates without
making itself known. It defines a realm of transgression where

one is already guilty, and where one oversteps the bounds without knowing what they are, as in the case of Oedipus. Even guilt and punishment do not tell us what the law is, but leave it in a state of indeterminacy equaled only by the extreme specificity of the punishment. This is the world described by Kafka. The point is not to compare Kant and Kafka, but to delineate two dimensions of the modern conception of the law.

If the law is no longer based on the Good as a preexisting, higher principle, and it is valid by virtue of its form alone, the content remaining entirely undetermined, it becomes impossible to say that the righteous man obeys the law for the sake of the Best. In other words, the man who obeys the law does not thereby become righteous or feel righteous; on the contrary, he feels guilty and is guilty in advance, and the more strict his obedience, the greater his guilt. This is the process by which the law manifests itself in its absolute purity, and proves us guilty. The two fundamental propositions of the classical conception are overthrown together: the law as grounded in the further principle of the Good; the law as sanctioned by righteousness. Freud was the first to recognize the extraordinary paradox of the conscience. It is far from the case that obedience to the law secures a feeling of righteousness, "for the more virtuous a man is, the more severe and distrustful" is the behavior of his conscience toward him; Freud goes on to remark on "the extraordinary severity of conscience in the best and most tractable people."[27]

Freud resolved the paradox by showing that the renunciation of instinctual gratification is not the product of conscience, but on the contrary that conscience itself is born of such renunciation. Hence it follows that the strength and severity of conscience increases in direct proportion to the strength and severity of the renunciation. Conscience is heir to the repressed instinctual drives. "The effect of instinctual renunciation on the conscience

then is that every piece of aggression whose satisfaction the subject gives up is taken over by the superego and increases the latter's aggressiveness (against the ego)." We are now in a position to
unravel the second paradox concerning the fundamentally undetermined character of the law. In Lacan's words, the law is the
same as repressed desire. The law cannot specify its object without self-contradiction, nor can it define itself with reference to
a content without removing the repression on which it rests. The
object of the law and the object of desire are one and the same,
and remain equally concealed. When Freud shows that the essential nature of the object relates to the mother while that of desire
and the law relates to the father, he does not thereby try to restore
a determinate content to the law; he does indeed almost the
opposite, he shows how the law, by virtue of its Oedipal origins,
must of necessity conceal its content in order to operate as a pure
form which is the result of a renunciation both of the object (the
mother) and of the subject (the father).

The classical irony and humor of Plato that had for so long
dominated all thinking on the subject of the law are thus turned
upside down. The upper and lower limits of the law, that is to
say the superior principle of the Good and the sanction of the
righteous in the light of the Best are reduced to nothingness. All
that remains is the indeterminate character of the law on the one
hand and the specificity of the punishment on the other. Irony
and humor immediately take on a different, modern aspect. They
still represent a way of conceiving the law, but the law is now
seen in terms of the indeterminacy of its content and of the guilt
of the person who submits to it. Kafka gives to humor and irony
their full modern significance in agreement with the transformed
character of the law. Max Brod recalls that when Kafka gave a reading of *The Trial*, everyone present, including Kafka himself, was
overcome by laughter – as mysterious a phenomenon as the laugh-

ter that greeted the death of Socrates. A spurious sense of tragedy dulls our intelligence; how many authors are distorted by placing a childishly tragic construction on what is more often the expression of an aggressively comic force! The comic is the only possible mode of conceiving the law, in a peculiar combination of irony and humor.

In modern thought irony and humor take on a new form: they are now directed at a subversion of the law. This leads us back to Sade and Masoch, who represent the two main attempts at subversion, at turning the law upside down. Irony is still in the process or movement which bypasses the law as a merely secondary power and aims at transcending it toward a higher principle. But what if the higher principle no longer exists, and if the Good can no longer provide a basis for the law or a justification of its power? Sade's answer is that in all its forms — natural, moral and political — the law represents the rule of secondary nature which is always geared to the demands of conservation; it is a usurpation of true sovereignty. It is irrelevant whether we see the law as the expression of the rule of the strongest or as the product of the self-protective union of the weak. Masters and slaves, the strong and the weak, all are creatures of secondary nature; the union of the weak merely favors the emergence of the tyrant; his existence depends on it. In every case the law is a mystification; it is not a delegated but a usurped power that depends on the infamous complicity of slaves and masters. It is significant that Sade attacks the regime of laws as being the regime of the tyrannized and of the tyrants. Only the law can tyrannize: "I have infinitely less reason to fear my neighbor's passions than the law's injustice, for my neighbor's passions are contained by mine, whereas nothing stops or contains the injustices of the law." Tyrants are created by the law alone: they flourish by virtue of the law. As Chigi says in *Juliette*, "Tyrants are never born in anarchy, they only flour-

86

ish in the shadow of the laws and draw their authority from them." Sade's hatred of tyranny, his demonstration that the law enables the tyrant to exist, form the essence of his thinking. The tyrant speaks the language of the law, and acknowledges no other, for he lives "in the shadow of the laws." The heroes of Sade are inspired with an extraordinary passion against tyranny; they speak as no tyrant ever spoke or could ever speak; theirs is the counter-language of tyranny.

We now note a new attempt to transcend the law, this time no longer in the direction of the Good as superior principle and ground of the law, but in the direction of its opposite, the Idea of Evil, the supreme principle of wickedness, which subverts the law and turns Platonism upside down. Here, the transcendence of the law implies the discovery of a primary nature which is in every way opposed to the demands and the rule of secondary nature. It follows that the idea of absolute evil embodied in primary nature cannot be equated either with tyranny — for tyranny still presupposes laws — or with a combination of whims and arbitrariness; its higher, impersonal model is rather to be found in the anarchic institutions of perpetual motion and permanent revolution. Sade often stresses the fact that the law can only be transcended toward an institutional model of anarchy. The fact that anarchy can only exist in the interval between two regimes based on laws, abolishing the old to give birth to the new, does not prevent this divine interval, this vanishing instant, from testifying to its fundamental difference from all forms of the law. "The reign of laws is pernicious; it is inferior to that of anarchy; the best proof of this is that all governments are forced to plunge into anarchy when they wish to remake their constitutions." The law can only be transcended by virtue of a principle that subverts it and denies its power.

While the sadian hero subverts the law, the masochist should not by contrast be regarded as gladly submitting to it. The element of contempt in the submission of the masochist has often been emphasized: his apparent obedience conceals a criticism and a provocation. He simply attacks the law on another flank. What we call humor – in contradistinction to the upward movement of irony toward a transcendent higher principle – is a downward movement from the law to its consequences. We all know ways of twisting the law by excess of zeal. By scrupulously applying the law we are able to demonstrate its absurdity and provoke the very disorder that it is intended to prevent or to conjure. By observing the very letter of the law, we refrain from questioning its ultimate or primary character; we then behave as if the supreme sovereignty of the law conferred upon it the enjoyment of all those pleasures that it denies us; hence, by the closest adherence to it, and by zealously embracing it, we may hope to partake of its pleasures. The law is no longer subverted by the upward movement of irony to a principle that overrides it, but by the downward movement of humor which seeks to reduce the law to its furthest consequences. A close examination of masochistic fantasies or rites reveals that while they bring into play the very strictest application of the law, the result in every case is the opposite of what might be expected (thus whipping, far from punishing or preventing an erection, provokes and ensures it). It is a demonstration of the law's absurdity. The masochist regards the law as a punitive process and therefore begins by having the punishment inflicted upon himself; once he has undergone the punishment, he feels that he is allowed or indeed commanded to experience the pleasure that the law was supposed to forbid. The essence of masochistic humor lies in this, that the very law which forbids the satisfaction of a desire under threat of subsequent punishment is converted into one which demands the punishment first and then orders that the satisfaction of the desire should necessarily follow upon the punishment. Once more, Theodor Reik gives an excellent analysis of this process: masochism is not pleasure in pain, nor even in punishment; at most, the masochist gets a preliminary pleasure from punishment or discomfort; his real pleasure is obtained subsequently, in that which is made possible by the punishment. The masochist must undergo punishment before experiencing pleasure. It would be a mistake to confuse this temporal succession with logical causality: suffering is not the cause of pleasure itself but the necessary precondition for achieving it. "The temporal reversal points at a reversal of the contents.... The previous 'You must not do that' has been transmuted into 'You have to do that!'... What else but a demonstration of absurdity is aimed at, when the punishment for forbidden pleasure brings about this very same pleasure?"[28] The same process is reflected in the other features of masochism, such as disavowal, suspense and fantasy, which should be regarded as so many forms or aspects of humor. The masochist is insolent in his obsequiousness, rebellious in his submission; in short, he is a humorist, a logician of consequences, just as the ironic sadist is a logician of principles.

From the idea that the law should not be based on the principle of the Good but on its form alone, the sadist fashions a new method of ascending from the law to a superior principle; this principle, however, is the informal element of a primary nature which aims at the subversion of all laws. In the other modern discovery that the law increases the guilt of the person who submits to it, the masochist in his turn finds a new way of descending from the law to its consequences: he stands guilt on its head by making punishment into a condition that makes possible the forbidden pleasure. In so doing he overthrows the law as radically as the sadist, though in a different way. We have seen how these methods proceed, ideologically speaking. The Oedipal content, which always remains concealed, undergoes a dual transformation — as though the mother–father complementarity had been shattered twice and asymmetrically. In the case of sadism the father is placed above the laws; he becomes a higher principle with the mother as his essential victim. In the case of masochism the totality of the law is invested upon the mother, who expels the father from the symbolic realm.

CHAPTER VIII

# From Contract to Ritual

Some authors have stressed the importance of anxiety in masochism (cf. Reik, Nacht). Punishment, in their view, would only figure so prominently because of its function in resolving anxiety
and thereby making pleasure possible. But this explanation fails to
determine under what particular conditions punishment assumes
this anxiety-resolving function, nor especially how anxiety and
the guilt it implies are not only "resolved" but, on a more subtle
level, are distorted and parodied to serve the aims of masochism.
We must analyze what seems to us the essence of the formal process, namely the transference of the law onto the mother and
the identification of the law with the image of the mother. It is
only under these conditions that punishment acquires its original function and that guilt is transformed into triumph. At first
sight, however, the transference onto the mother would hardly
seem to account for the feeling of "relief" inherent in masochism,
for there is no reason to expect greater leniency from the side of
the sentimental, icy and cruel mother.

It is already apparent that in his attempt to derive the law from
the contract, the masochist aims not to mitigate the law but on
the contrary to emphasize its extreme severity. For while the contract implies in principle certain conditions like the free accept-

ance of the parties, a limited duration and the preservation of inalienable rights, the law that it generates always tends to forget its own origins and annul these restrictive conditions. Thus the contract–law relationship involves in a sense a mystification. To imagine that a contract or quasi contract is at the origin of society is to invoke conditions which are necessarily invalidated as soon as the law comes into being. For the law, once established, violates the contract in that it can apply to a third party, is valid for an indeterminate period and recognizes no inalienable rights. This process of invalidation of the contract by the law is reflected, as we have seen, in the peculiar progression of Masoch's successive love-contracts, the terms of which become increasingly strict, as if to prepare the way for the law that will eventually override them. Since the law results in our enslavement, we should place enslavement first, as the dreadful object of the contract. One could even say, as a general rule, that in masochism the contract is caricatured in order to emphasize its ambiguous destination. The contract may indeed be said to exemplify the very type of a culture-bound relationship that is artificial, Apollonian and virile, as opposed to the natural, chthonic relations which bind us to the mother and the woman. In the contractual relation the woman typically figures as an object in the patriarchal system. The contract in masochism reverses this state of affairs by making the woman into the party with whom the contract is entered into. Its paradoxical intention extends even further in that it involves a master–slave relationship, and one furthermore in which the woman is the master and torturer. The contractual basis is thereby implicitly challenged, by excess of zeal, a humorous acceleration of the clauses and a complete reversal of the respective contractual status of man and woman. Hence we have once more a sort of demystification of the contract, inasmuch as it is made deliberately to promote slavery and even death at the service of the woman and the mother. The ultimate paradox is that such a contract should be initiated, and the power conferred, by the victim himself, that is to say the male party. Sade's ironic attitude to the 1789 Revolution is that the Revolution would remain sterile unless it gave up making laws and set up institutions of perpetual motion; it is paralleled by Masoch's humorous attitude to the revolutions of 1848 and the Panslavic movement: he suggests that contracts should be drawn up with a terrible Tsarina, thus ensuring the most sentimental but at the same time the coldest and severest law. (In *Live Stories*, Masoch considers the problems discussed by the Panslavic congresses and he asks: Will the Slavs achieve unity for Russia by getting rid of the Tsarist regime or should they aim for a strong State under the rule of a Tsarina of genius?)[29]

What does the victim expect by entering into this extreme form of contract with the mother? The aim is seemingly naive and straightforward. The masochistic contract excludes the father and displaces onto the mother the task of exercising and applying the paternal law. But we have seen that the mother is both stern and cruel. The problem, however, should be stated differently: the same threat which, when experienced as coming from the father and linked to his image, has the effect of preventing incest, has the reverse effect when entrusted to the mother and associated with her image: it then makes incest possible and ensures its success. Here the transference is very effective. As a general rule castration acts as a threat preventing incest or a punishment that controls it; it is an obstacle to or a chastisement of incest. But when it is linked with the image of the mother, the castration of the son becomes the very condition of the success of incest: incest is assimilated by this displacement to a second birth which dispenses with the father's role. "Interrupted love" is an important feature of masochism to which many authors have

93

drawn attention; its function is to facilitate the masochist's identification of sexual activity with both incest and second birth, a process which not only saves him from the threat of castration but actually turns castration into the symbolic condition of success.

The masochistic contract generates a type of law which leads straight into ritual. The masochist is obsessed; ritualistic activity is essential to him, since it epitomizes the world of fantasy. Three main types of rite occur in Masoch's novels: hunting rites, agricultural rites and rites of regeneration and rebirth. They echo the three fundamental elements: the cold, that requires the conquest of the fur, the trophy of the hunt; the buried sentimentality and sheltered fecundity which agriculture demands, together with the strictest organization of work; and finally that very element of strictness, that cruel rigor which regeneration and rebirth demand. The coexistence and interaction of these three rites sum up the mythical complex of masochism. We find it again and again, variously embodied throughout the work of Masoch: the ideal woman hunts the bear or the wolf; she organizes or presides over an agricultural community; she makes man undergo a process of rebirth. The last would appear to be the essential rite in which the other two culminate and from which they derive their function in the totality of the myth.

In *Wolf and She-wolf* the heroine asks her suitor to let himself be sewn into a wolf's skin and to live and howl and be hunted like a wolf. The ritual hunt is instrumental to rebirth; by taking possession of the trophy of the primitive, uterine mother, the second mother, that is to say the oral mother, acquires the power to bring about a rebirth. This second birth is independent both of the father and of the uterine mother; it is a parthenogenesis. *Venus* gives a detailed description of an agrarian rite: the Negresses "led me to a vineyard that lay along the south side of the garden. Maize had been planted between the vines and a few dry heads

94

were still standing; a plough had been left there. The blackamoors tied me to a stake and amused themselves by pricking me with golden hairpins. But this did not last long, for Wanda appeared with her ermine toque, her hands in the pockets of her jacket. She told them to untie me and fasten my hands behind my back. Then she had a yoke laid on my shoulders and I was harnessed to the plough. The black demons pushed me into the field; one drove the plough, the other led me on a leash, and the third goaded me with the whip, while Venus in Furs stood by watching the scene."

The three Negresses stand for the three mother images; we notice, however, that the oral mother is split: she occurs twice, once as an element in the triad, on a par with the other women, and afterward outside the triad, presiding over it, having appropriated and transformed all the functions of the other women in order to serve the theme of rebirth. Everything points to a parthenogenesis: the marriage of the vine and the maize (the Dionysian element and the female agrarian community); the plough, representing union with the mother; the pinpricking and the whipping, representing parthenogenetic stimulation; the new birth of the son drawn out by the rope.[30] We have once more the theme of the choice between the three mothers, the oscillating movement of the pendulum, and the final absorption of both the uterine and the Oedipal mothers by the triumphant oral mother. She is mistress of the Law — what Masoch calls the law of the commune, in which the hunting, the agrarian and the matriarchal elements become fully integrated. The uterine mother, the hunter, is herself hunted down and despoiled; the Oedipal mother, or mother of the shepherd, already integrated in the patriarchal system (as victim or as accomplice) is likewise sacrificed. The oral mother alone remains triumphant; she is the common essence of agriculture, matriarchy and rebirth. Hence the dream

95

of agrarian communism which recurs throughout the work of Masoch and underlies his "blue tales of happiness" (*Marcella, The Paradise on the Dniestr, The Aesthetics of Ugliness*). A deep bond is forged between the commune, the law of the commune embodied in the oral mother, and the man of the commune, who can only be born by being reborn of the oral mother.

The two principle male figures in Masoch's work are Cain and Christ. Their sign is the same, the sign of Cain prefiguring the sign of the cross which used to be written as X or as +. That Cain should occupy such an important place in the work of Masoch has a very wide range of significance. He symbolizes in the first place the omnipresence of crime in nature and history, and the immensity of man's sufferings ("My punishment is more than I can bear"). But beyond this, there is the fact that Cain is a "tiller of the ground" and the favorite of the mother: Eve greeted his birth with cries of joy, but did not rejoice at the birth of Abel, the "keeper of sheep," who is on the father's side. The mother's favorite went so far as to commit a crime to sever the alliance between the father and the other son: he killed his father's likeness and made Eve into the goddess-mother. (Herman Hesse's strange novel, *Demian*, interweaves Nietzschean and masochistic themes: the mother-goddess is identified with Eve, a female giant who bears on her forehead the mark of Cain.) Masoch is attracted to Cain not only because of the torments he suffers but also by the very crime that he commits. His crime should not be regarded as a sadomasochistic archetype, for the entire project falls squarely within the world of masochism, with its attendant features of loyalty to the maternal rule, dedication to the oral mother, expulsion of the father, and its elements of humor and provocation. Cain's "heritage" is a "mark"; his punishment by the Father represents the aggressive, hallucinatory return of the latter: so much for the first episode. The second episode is the story of Christ: the likeness of the father is once more abolished. ("Why hast thou forsaken me?"), but here it is the Mother who crucifies the Son; in the masochistic elaboration of the Marian fantasy, the Virgin in person puts Christ on the cross; this is Masoch's version of "the death of God." By putting him on the cross and thus placing him under the same sign as the son of Eve, the Virgin carries on the aim of the mother-goddess, the great oral mother: she ensures the parthenogenetic second birth of the son in his resurrection. But again, it is not the son who dies so much as God the Father, that is the likeness of the father in the son. The cross represents the maternal image of death, the mirror in which the narcissistic self of Christ (Cain) apprehends his ideal self (Christ resurrected).

But we may wonder why there should be so much pain in both cases and why expiation should be the necessary precondition of the second birth. Why should such a terrible punishment be inflicted upon Cain, and why should Christ's torture be so unbearable? Why is Christology an all-pervasive element in the work of Masoch? While Sade was concerned above all with rationalistic and atheistic, masonic and anarchistic societies, Masoch gave his attention to the mystical agrarian sects of his day (such as those found in the Austrian Empire). Two of his novels, *The Fisher of Souls* and *The Mother of God* actually deal with these sects; they are among his finest. Their rarefied and stifling atmosphere, their intense portrayal of willingly accepted torture is unparalleled except in the best works of H.H. Ewers, who also specialized in sects (*The Sorcerer's Apprentice*). The story of *The Mother of God* is as follows: The heroine, Mardona, rules over her sect or commune in a manner that combines the qualities of tenderness, severity and coldness. She is wrathful and orders people to be whipped or stoned; yet she is gentle. Indeed the whole sect is gentle and gay, though intolerant of sinfulness and hostile to disorder. Mardona has a servant girl, Nimfodora, a graceful, melancholy maiden who gashes her arm so that the Mother of God may bathe in the blood, drink of it and thus gain eternal youth. Sabadil loves Mardona, but he loves Nimfodora too, though in a different way. Mardona is disturbed by this, and speaking as the Mother of God, she says to Sabadil: "It is the love of the Mother of God that brings redemption and gives new birth to man.... I have not succeeded in changing your flesh and transforming your carnal love into divine affection.... I have become to you nothing more than a judge." She asks that he consent to be tortured, and orders him to be nailed to the cross. Nimfodora nails down his hands and Mardona his feet. Mardona then enters into a painful ecstasy, while at nightfall Sabadil enacts the Passion of Christ. To Mardona he cries, "Why has thou forsaken me?" and to Nimfodora, "Why has thou betrayed me?" The Mother of God must crucify her son in order that he should truly become her son and enjoy the privilege of a rebirth from her alone.

In *The Siren*, Zenobia cuts off Theophan's hair and exclaims: "At last I have succeeded in making a man of you." Similarly, in *The Divorced Woman*, Anna longs to be worthy of her task, to whip Julian and to be able at last to say to him: "You have been through the ordeal, now you are a man." The theme recurs again in a fine short story where Masoch recounts the life of a seventeenth-century Messiah, Sabattai Zwi. Sabattai Zwi is a cabbalist and fanatic given to self-mortification: he marries Sarah, but does not consummate the union; he tells her, "You will be by my side, like a gentle torture." On the order of the rabbis he leaves her for Hannah, and repeats his previous behavior with her. He finally marries Miriam, a young Polish Jewess, but she anticipates him and forbids him to touch her. In love with Miriam, he leaves for Constantinople, where he tries to convince the Sultan of his Messianic mission. Meanwhile, whole cities are swept with enthusiasm; he has already won over Salonika, Smyrna, Cairo; his fame has even spread as far as Europe. He leads a determined battle against the rabbis, and announces to the Jews the return to Judea. The Sultana is displeased and informs Miriam that she will have Sabattai put to death if he does not mend his ways. Miriam then orders him to bathe at the confluence of the three rivers, Arda, Tuntcha and Narisso. One cannot help recognizing in the three rivers and in the three wives of Sabattai the three mother-images, and in Miriam the oral mother, who triumphs over them. Miriam makes him confess to her, crowns him with thorns and whips him, and finally consummates the marriage. "Woman, what have you done to me?" "I have made a man of you." The next day, summoned by the Sultan, he recants and becomes a Muslim. Thereupon, his numerous followers, even among the Turks, declare that the Messiah can only appear in a perfectly virtuous world or else in a totally evil one, and since apostasy is the worst of all crimes, they declare that they will all become apostates to hasten the coming of the Messiah.[31]

But what is the significance of this constantly recurring theme: "You are not a man, I am making a man of you?" What does "becoming a man" signify? Clearly it does not mean *to be like the father*, or to take his place. On the contrary, it consists in obliterating his role and his likeness in order to generate the new man. The tortures are in effect directed at the father, or at his likeness in the son. We argued earlier that the masochistic fantasy is less an instance of "a child being beaten" than of *a father being beaten*: in many of Masoch's tales, it is the master who undergoes the tortures; thus in *Theodora* or *The Living Bench*, in the course of a peasant revolt led by the women of the commune, the master is harnessed to the plough side by side with the ox, or is used as a bench to sit upon. When the torture is inflicted upon the hero, that is to say the son, the lover or the child, we should conclude that what is beaten, foresworn and sacrificed, what is ritually expiated, is the father's likeness, the genital sexuality inherited from the father — however miniaturized he may be. This is the real "Apostasy." To become a man is to be reborn from the woman alone, to undergo a second birth. This is why castration, and the "interrupted love" which represents castration, cease to be an obstacle to or a punishment of incest, and become instead a precondition of its success with the mother, since it is then equated with a second, autonomous and parthenogenetic rebirth. The masochist practices three forms of disavowal at once: the first magnifies the mother, by attributing to her the phallus instrumental to rebirth; the second excludes the father, since he has no part in this rebirth; and the third relates to sexual pleasure, which is interrupted, deprived of its genitality and transformed into the pleasure of being reborn.

The final objective of Masoch's work expresses itself in the myth that embraces both Cain and Christ: Christ is not the son of God, but the new Man; his likeness to the father is abolished, he is "Man on the Cross, who knows no sexual love, no property, no fatherland, no cause, no work...."[32]

We were not able to give material definitions of masochism, since the combinations of pleasure and pain in a specific sensual experience imply certain formal conditions which cannot be ignored without confusing everything, especially sadism and masochism. Nor is a moral definition of masochism in terms of guilt any more adequate. Guilt and expiation (no less than a particular pleasure–pain combination) are genuinely and deeply experienced by the masochist, but here again the important point is to know in what form guilt is experienced. The depth and intensity of a feeling is not affected by the uses which it may be made to serve, including even parody; the nature of the feeling, however, will alter correspondingly. The psychoanalytic statement to the effect that the masochist experiences guilt in relation to the father (in Reik's words, since the punishment comes from the father, the crime must have been committed against the father), clearly leads to the creation of an arbitrary etiology which is solely determined by the tendency to derive masochism from sadism. There is no doubt that the masochist lives in the very depths of guilt; but far from feeling that he has sinned against the father, it is the father's likeness in him that he experiences as a sin which must be atoned for. Hence guilt is turned completely upside down: it is both at its deepest and its most absurd. It is an integral part of the masochist's triumph, and ensures his liberation. Indeed it is indistinguishable from humor. It is quite inadequate to say, as Reik does, that the punishment resolves the anxiety arising from guilt, and makes possible the forbidden pleasure. The humor which characterizes the masochist's predicament is already at work in the very intensity of his sense of guilt, no less than in the severity of the punishment, for it is the father who is guilty in the son, not the son in relation to the father. Masochism in its material aspects is a phenomenon of the senses (i.e., a certain combination of pain and pleasure); in its moral aspects it is a function of feeling or sentiment. But beyond all sensation or feeling there is a third aspect, a superpersonal element that animates the masochist: this is the story in which he relates the triumph of the oral mother, the abolition of the father's likeness and the consequent birth of the new man. Of course the masochist must use his body and his soul to write this story, but there is nevertheless a formal masochism which preexists physical, sensual or material masochism, just as there is a dramatic masochism before any moral or sentimental masochism. Hence the theatrical impression which is conveyed at the point where the masochist's feelings are at their deepest and his pain and sensation most intensely experienced.

We have traced a progression from the contract to the myth, through the intermediary of the law; for the law transcends the contract but leads us straight into ritual and myth. By means of the contract the paternal function of applying the law was transferred to the mother, resulting in the most radical transformation of the law. The law now ordains what it was once intended to forbid; guilt absolves instead of leading to atonement, and punishment makes permissible what it was intended to chastise. The law has become essentially maternal, leading into those regions of the unconscious where the three images of the mother hold supreme sway. The contract represents a personal act of will on the part of the masochist, but through the contract, and the vicissitudes of the law that issues from it, the masochist is led back into the impersonal realm of fate, which finds expression in the myth and in the rites that we have described. The situation that the masochist establishes by contract, at a specific moment and for a specific period, is already fully contained timelessly and ritually in the symbolic order of masochism. For the masochist, the modern contract as it is elaborated in the bedroom corresponds to the oldest rites once enacted in the swamps and the steppes. The novels of Masoch reflect this twofold history and bring out the identity between its most modern and its most ancient forms.

CHAPTER IX

# Psychoanalysis and the Problem

# of Masochism

Freud gave two successive accounts of sadomasochism, the first
in relation to the duality of the sexual and the ego-instincts,
the second in relation to the duality of the life and the death
instincts. Both accounts tend to treat sadomasochism as a particular entity within which transitions occur from one component to the other. We want to examine to what extent these two
accounts are really different, to what extent they both imply a
"transformist" attitude on the part of Freud, and finally to what
extent the hypothesis of a duality of instincts limits in both cases
the "transformist" argument.

In the first account, masochism is seen as deriving from sadism by a process of reversal. Every instinct is thought to include
aggressive components which are directed upon its object and
necessary to the realization of its aim; sadism would, in this view,
have its origin in the aggressive component of the sexual instincts.
In the course of its development the aggressive–sadistic component may become conditioned in such a way that it is turned
around against the subject's own self. The factors determining this
turning around are of two main types: aggression against the father
and mother may be turned around upon the self either under the
effect of "fear of loss of love" or as the result of guilt-feelings

(linked with the formation of the superego). These two conditions of masochistic "turning around" are quite distinct — as
B. Grunberger pointed out — the first having a pregenital and the
second an Oedipal source.[33] But in either case the father-image
and the mother-image have very unequal roles, for even though
the transgression bears on the person of the mother, its essential
object must still be the father: he is the one who possesses the
penis, the one whom the child wishes to castrate or to kill; he is
the one who punishes, and who must be placated by this process
of turning around. Hence, in every case, the father-image seems
to have a pivotal role.

It soon becomes apparent, for a variety of reasons, that masochism cannot simply be defined as a form of sadism turned
around upon the self. The first reason is that the process of turning around is necessarily accompanied by a *desexualization* of libidinal aggression, that is the relinquishing of specifically sexual aims.
Freud shows in particular that the formation of the superego or
conscience, which marks the resolution of the Oedipus complex,
implies the desexualization of the latter. In this sense it is possible to conceive of a reversal of sadism, with the superego acting
sadistically upon the ego without the ego itself being masochistic. There is no masochism proper without a reactivation of the
Oedipus complex, hence without a "resexualization" of the conscience. Masochism is characterized not by guilt-feelings but by
the desire to be punished, the purpose of masochism being to
resolve guilt and the corresponding anxiety and make sexual gratification possible. Hence masochism should be defined less by
the process of turning around itself than by the resexualization of
the aggression turned upon the self in this process.

The second reason is concerned with another and quite distinct aspect of masochistic sexualization, namely its specific
"erogenicity." We may well grant that punishment should resolve

or satisfy feelings of guilt, but this only constitutes a preliminary pleasure of a *moral* nature that merely prepares for sexual pleasure or makes it possible; it does not explain how sexual pleasure actually occurs in association with the *physical* pain of punishment. The fact is that the process of sexualization could never culminate without a particular masochistic erogenicity. For this we require some material basis, some peculiar link which the masochist experiences between his pain and his sexual pleasure. Freud suggested the hypothesis of "libidinal sympathetic coexcitation," according to which processes and excitations overstepping certain quantitative limits become erotically charged. Such a hypothesis recognizes the existence of an irreducible masochistic basis. This is why Freud, even in his first interpretation, is not content with saying that masochism is a reversed form of sadism; he also maintains that sadism is a projected form of masochism, since the sadist can only take pleasure in the pain he inflicts upon others to the extent that he has himself experienced "masochistically" the link between pleasure and pain. Freud nevertheless maintains the primacy of sadism, while distinguishing between (1) a purely aggressive sadism, (2) a turning around of sadism upon the self, (3) the masochistic experience and (4) a hedonistic sadism. But even if one maintains that the intermediary masochistic experience presupposes a turning around of aggression upon the self, this turning around must be regarded as one of the conditions for discovering the masochistic experience of a link between pain and pleasure, and cannot be said to constitute this link — the very possibility of which must point to a specific masochistic basis.[34]

There is yet a third reason: the process of turning around upon the self may be regarded as a *reflexive* stage, as in obsessional neurosis ("I punish myself"), but since masochism implies a passive stage ("I am punished, I am beaten"), we must infer the existence in masochism of a particular mechanism of projection through which an external agent is made to assume the role of the subject. This third reason is clearly connected with the first: resexualization is inseparable from projection (conversely the reflexive stage is indicative of a sadistic superego which remains desexualized). It is in terms of this projection that psychoanalysis tries to account for the role played by the mother-image. Since, according to the theory, the masochist's aim is to escape from the consequences of the transgression against the father, he proceeds to identify with the mother and offers himself to the father as a sexual object; however, since this would in turn renew the threat of castration which he is trying to avert, he chooses "being beaten" both as exorcism of "being castrated" and as a regressive substitute of "being loved"; at the same time the mother takes on the role of the person who beats, as a result of repression of the homosexual choice. Alternatively, the subject shifts the blame on the mother ("It is not I, it is she who wishes to castrate the father"), either in order to identify with the bad mother under the cover of projection and thus take possession of the father's penis (perverse masochism); or else, on the contrary, to make any such identification impossible by maintaining the projection and substituting himself as the victim (moral masochism: "It is not the father, it is I who am castrated").[35]

For these various reasons we must reject as inadequate the formula "sadism turned around upon the self" as a definition of masochism. It needs to be supplemented by three other considerations: the sadism must be (1) resexualized, (2) the resexualization must be grounded in a new erogenicity and (3) the sadism must be projected. These three determinations correspond to the three aspects of masochism which Freud distinguishes even in his first interpretation: an erotogenic aspect, as a basis for sexual excitation, a passive aspect, accounting in a very complex manner both for the projection onto the woman and for the identification with her, and a moral aspect or sense of guilt, to which the process of resexualization is related.[36] But the question is whether we save the Freudian theory by supplementing it in this way or whether on the contrary we severely affect its validity. Reik, who maintains throughout the idea that masochism is derived from sadism, nevertheless points out that masochism "springs from the denial that meets the sadistic instinctual impulse and develops from the sadistic, aggressive or defiant phantasy which replaces reality. It remains incomprehensible as long as one assumes its derivation directly from sadism by a facing about against the ego. Much as psychoanalysts and sexologists may oppose such an opinion, I maintain that the birthplace of masochism is phantasy."[37] In other words, the masochist has renounced his sadistic impulse, even turned around upon himself. What he does is to neutralize his sadism in fantasy, substituting his dream for action; hence the primary importance of fantasy. Given these conditions, the violence that the masochist inflicts or causes to be inflicted upon himself can no longer be called sadistic, since it is based on his particular type of suspension. The question, once more, is whether we can still affirm the principle of a derivation when the derivation has ceased to be direct and therefore disproves the hypothesis of a straightforward turning around.

Freud maintains that no direct transformation can take place between impulses or instincts that are qualitatively distinct; their qualitative difference precludes any transition from one to the other. This is certainly true of the sexual and the ego instincts. Undoubtedly sadism and masochism, like any other psychic formations, represent particular combinations of the two instincts, but any "passage" from one combination to the other as, for instance, from sadism to masochism, can only occur by a process of desexualization and resexualization. In masochism the locus or theater of this process is fantasy. Are we to say that the same subject participates in both sadistic and masochistic sexuality, given that the one implies the desexualization of the other? Is this desexualization an actual process experienced by the masochist (in which case a transition could be said to occur, however indirectly), or is it on the contrary a structural presupposition of masochism which severs it from all communication with sadism? When we are given two stories, it is always possible to bridge the gaps that separate them, but in the process we arrive at a third story of a different quality from the other two. The psychoanalytical theory of sadomasochism appears to be doing just this: for instance, the image of the father, in view of its importance in sadism, is regarded as still continuing to operate in masochism, disguised under the mother-image and determining its role. This method has a serious drawback in that it displaces the emphasis and gives crucial importance to secondary factors. For example, the theme of the bad mother does indeed appear in masochism, but only as a marginal phenomenon, the central position being occupied by the good mother; it is the good mother who possesses the phallus, who beats and humiliates the subject or even prostitutes herself. If we ignore this and give prominence to the bad mother, it is all too easy to reestablish the link with the father, and the corresponding link between sadism and masochism. The existence of the good mother, on the other hand, implies the existence of a gap or blank which stands for the abolition of the father in the symbolic order. Again, while the sense of guilt has great importance in masochism, it acts only as a cover, as the humorous outcome of a guilt that has already been subverted; for it is no longer the guilt of the child toward the father, but that of the father himself, and of his likeness in the child. Here again we come across a "blank" which is hurriedly filled in by psychoanalysis for the purpose of deriving masochism from sadism. The fallacy is to treat as an ongoing process a state of affairs which must already obtain, which must already be presupposed for masochism to be possible. When guilt is experienced "masochistically," it is already distorted, artificial and ostentatious; similarly, the father is experienced as already abolished symbolically. In trying to fill in the gaps between masochism and sadism, we are liable to fall into all kinds of misapprehensions, both theoretical and practical or therapeutic. Hence our contention that masochism can be defined neither as erotogenic and sensuous (pleasure–pain), nor as moral and sentimental (guilt–punishment): each of these definitions implies the possibility of any manner of transformation. Masochism is above all formal and dramatic; this means that its peculiar pleasure–pain complex is determined by a particular kind of formalism, and its experience of guilt by a specific story. In the field of pathology every disturbance is characterized by "gaps" and it is only by grasping at the structures demarcated by these gaps and taking the greatest care not to fill them in that we may hope to avoid the illusions of "transformism," and to make progress in our analysis of the disturbance.

Doubts about the unity and intercommunication of sadism and masochism are further reinforced when we come to Freud's second interpretation. The qualitative duality is now that of the life and the death instincts, Eros and Thanatos. Let us immediately note, however, that the Death Instinct, which is a pure principle, can never be given as such; all that is given or can be given are combinations of the two instincts. Accordingly, the Death Instinct manifests itself in two different ways, depending on whether, under the action of Eros, it is turned outward (sadism) or whether part of it remains as a residue libidinally "bound" within the organism (masochism). In the latter case we have masochism of the erotogenic type, which is primary and no longer derived from sadism. Nevertheless, we reencounter the previous theory in terms of "turned around" sadism which produces the other types of masochism (the passive and the moral), and we are faced once again, even more starkly, with our previous doubts. For it now appears that the passage from sadism to masochism implies not only the process of desexualization and resexualization but equally a defusion of instincts as well as their combination. Both sadism and masochism imply that a particular quantity of libidinal energy be neutralized, desexualized, displaced and put at the service of Thanatos. Thus we never have a direct transformation of one instinct into another, but a "displacement of cathectic energy." This is what Freud means by "defusion." He isolated two fundamental occurrences of defusion, narcissism and the formation of the superego. The whole problem lies in the nature of these processes of defusion and in how they are related to the combination of the instincts (fusion). Everywhere we meet with a combination of the two instincts, but at the same time defusion is at work everywhere.

# CHAPTER X

# The Death Instinct

Of all the writings of Freud, the masterpiece which we know as *Beyond the Pleasure Principle* is perhaps the one where he engaged most directly – and how penetratingly – in specifically philosophical reflection. Philosophical reflection should be understood as "transcendental," that is to say concerned with a particular kind of investigation of the question of principles. It soon becomes apparent that in *Beyond the Pleasure Principle*, Freud is not really preoccupied with the exceptions to that principle; they are not what he means by the "beyond" of the title. All the apparent exceptions which he considers, such as the unpleasure and the circuitousness which the reality principle imposes on us, the conflicts which cause what is pleasurable to one part of us to be felt as unpleasure by another, the games by means of which we try to reproduce and to master unpleasant experiences, or even those functional disturbances or transference phenomena from which we learn that wholly and unequivocally unpleasurable events are nevertheless reproduced with obstinate regularity – all these are treated by Freud as merely apparent exceptions which could still be reconciled with the pleasure principle. In other words there are no exceptions to the principle – though there would indeed seem to be some rather strange complications in the workings of pleasure. This is precisely where the problem arises, for though nothing contradicts the pleasure principle and everything can always be reconciled with it, it is far from obvious that it can account for all the various elements and processes which go to make its application so complicated. Everything might well be governed by the pleasure principle without therefore being finally dependent on it, and since the demands of the reality principle are no more adequate to account for the complications involved, these being more often the products of fantasy, we must conclude that the pleasure principle, though it may rule over all, does not have the final or highest authority over all. There are no exceptions to the principle but there is a residue that is irreducible to it; nothing contradicts the principle, but there remains something which falls outside it and is not homogeneous with it — something, in short, *beyond*....

At this point we need to resort to philosophical reflection. What we call a principle or law is, in the first place, that which governs a particular field; it is in this sense that we speak of an empirical principle or a law. Thus we say that the pleasure principle governs life universally and without exception. But there is another and quite distinct question, namely in virtue of what is a field governed by a principle; there must be a principle of another kind, a second-order principle, which accounts for the necessary compliance of the field with the empirical principle. It is this second-order principle that we call transcendental. Pleasure is a principle insofar as it governs our psychic life. But we must still ask what is the highest authority which subjects our psychic life to the dominance of this principle. Already Hume had remarked that though psychic life clearly exhibits and distinguishes between pleasures and pains, we could never, no matter how exhaustively we examined our ideas of pain and pleasure, derive from them a *principle* in accordance with which we seek pleasure and avoid pain. We find Freud saying much the same: we continually encounter pleasures and pains in psychic life, but they are found scattered here and there in a free state, "unbound." That the pleasure principle should nevertheless be so organized that we systematically seek pleasure and avoid pain makes it imperative that we should look for a higher type of explanation. For there is in short *something* that the pleasure principle cannot account for and that necessarily falls outside it, namely its own particular status, the fact that it has dominance over the whole of psychic life. In virtue of what higher connection – what "binding" power – is pleasure a principle, with the dominance that it has? Freud's problem, we may say, is the very opposite of what it is often supposed to be, for he is concerned not with the exceptions to the principle but with its *foundation*. His problem is a transcendental one: the discovery of a transcendental principle – a problem, as Freud puts it, for "speculation."

Freud's answer is that the binding of excitation alone makes it "resolvable" into pleasure, that is to say makes its discharge possible. Without the process of binding, discharges and pleasures would still no doubt occur but only in a scattered, haphazard manner, with no systematic value. It is the binding process which makes pleasure as the principle of mental life possible. Eros thus emerges as the foundation of the pleasure-principle behind the twin aspects of the binding process – the energetic which binds excitation, and the biological which binds the cells (the first being perhaps dependent on, or at least helped by specially favorable conditions obtaining in the second). The "binding" action of Eros, which is constitutive of the pleasure principle may, and indeed must, be characterized as "repetition" – repetition in respect of excitation, and repetition of the *moment* of life, and the necessary union – necessary indeed even in the case of unicellular organisms.

It is in the nature of a transcendental inquiry that we cannot break it off when we please. No sooner have we reached the condition or ground of our principle than we are hurled headlong beyond to the absolutely unconditioned, the "ground-less" from which the ground itself emerged. Musil wrote: "What fearful power, what awesome divinity is repetition! It is the pull of the void that drags us deeper and deeper down like the ever-widening gullet of a whirlpool.... For we knew it well all along: it was none other than the deep and sinful fall into a world where repetition drags one down lower and lower at each step...."[38] We remarked earlier that repetition characterized the binding process inasmuch as it is repetition of the very moment of excitation, the moment of the emergence of life; repetition is what holds together the instant; it constitutes *simultaneity*. But inseparable from this form of the repetition we must conceive of another which in its turn repeats *what was before the instant* — before excitation disturbed the indifference of the inexcitable and life stirred the inanimate from its sleep. How indeed could excitation be bound and thereby discharged except by this double action of repetition, which on the one hand binds the excitation and on the other tends to eliminate it? Beyond Eros we encounter Thanatos; beyond the ground, the abyss of the groundless; beyond the repetition that links, the repetition that erases and destroys. It is hardly surprising that Freud's writings should be so complex; sometimes he suggests that repetition is one and the same agency, acting now demonically, how beneficiently, in Thanatos and in Eros; elsewhere he contradicts this by insisting on the strictest qualitative difference between Eros and Thanatos, the difference being that between union, the construction of ever larger units, and destruction; elsewhere again he tones down the strictly dualistic hypothesis by suggesting that what probably underlies the qualitative difference is a difference in rhythm and amplitude, a difference on a time-scale — according as repetition is repetition *at* the origination of life, or before. It should be understood that repetition as conceived by Freud's genius is in and of itself a synthesis of time — a "transcendental" synthesis. It is at once repetition of *before*, *during* and *after*, that is to say it is a constitution in time of the past, the present and even the future. From a transcendental viewpoint, past, present and future are constituted in time *simultaneously*, even though, from the natural standpoint, there is between them a qualitative difference, the past following upon the present and the present upon the future. Hence the threefold determination which we brought out in Freud's treatment: a monism, a qualitative dualism and a difference in rhythm. If it is possible to add the future (i.e., *after*) to the other two dimensions of repetition (i.e., *before* and *during*), it is because these two correlative structures cannot constitute the synthesis of time without immediately opening up to and making for the possibility of a future in time. To repetition that binds — constituting the present — and repetition that erases — constituting the past — we must add a third, that saves or fails to save, depending on the modes of combination of the other two. (Hence the decisive role of transference as a progressive repetition which liberates and saves — or fails.)

We saw that repetition came before the pleasure principle as the unconditioned condition of the principle. If we now return to experience, we find that the order is reversed, and repetition subordinated to the principle; it is now at the service of the pleasure, since we tend to repeat what has been found to be pleasurable, or is anticipated to be. Our transcendental inquiry showed that while Eros is what makes possible the establishment of the empirical pleasure principle, it is always necessarily and inseparably linked with Thanatos. Neither Eros nor Thanatos can be given in experience; all that is given are combinations of both — the role of Eros being to bind the energy of Thanatos and to subject these combinations to the pleasure principle in the id. This is why Eros, although it is no more given in experience than Thanatos, at least makes its presence felt; it is an active force. Whereas Thanatos, the ground-less, supported and brought to the surface by Eros, remains essentially silent and all the more terrible. Thanatos *is*; it is an absolute. And yet the "no" does not exist in the unconscious because destruction is always presented as the other side of a construction, as an instinctual drive which is necessarily combined with Eros.

What then is the meaning of *defusion* of the instincts? We may put it differently and ask what becomes of the combination of the instincts when we no longer consider the id but the ego, the superego and their complementarity. Freud showed how the formation of the narcissistic ego and of the superego both implied a "desexualization." A certain quantity of libido (Eros-energy) is neutralized, and becomes undifferentiated and freely mobile. The desexualization process would seem to be profoundly different in each case: in the first it is the equivalent of a process of *idealization*, which can perhaps constitute the power of the imagination in the ego; in the second it is the equivalent of *identification*, which would constitute the power of thought in the superego. Desexualization has two possible effects on the workings of the pleasure principle: either it introduces functional disturbances which affect the application of the principle, or else it promotes a sublimation of the instincts whereby pleasure is transcended in favor of gratifications of a different kind. In any case it would be a mistake to view defusion in terms of invalidation of the pleasure principle, as though the combinations that are subject to it were destroyed in favor of the emergence of Eros and Thanatos in their pure form. Defusion, with respect to the ego and the superego, simply means the formation of this freely mobile energy within the various combinations. The pleasure principle in itself is not in the least invalidated, however serious the disturbances which may affect the function responsible for its application. (Thus Freud could still maintain his wish-fulfillment theory of the dream, even in those cases of traumatic neurosis where the dream function is most seriously perturbed.) Nor is the pleasure principle over-turned by the renunciations which reality imposes upon it, or by the spiritual extensions brought about by sublimation. We may never encounter Thanatos; its voice is never heard; for life is lived through and through under the sway of the empirical pleasure principle and the combinations that are subject to it — though the formulae governing the combinations may vary considerably.

Is there no other solution besides the functional disturbance of neurosis and the spiritual outlet of sublimation? Could there not be a third alternative which would be related not to the functional interdependence of the ego and the superego, but to the structural split between them? And is not this the very alternative indicated by Freud under the name of perversion? It is remarkable that the process of *desexualization* is even more pronounced than in neurosis and sublimation; it operates with extraordinary coldness; but it is accompanied by a *resexualization* which does not in any way cancel out the desexualization, since it operates in a new dimension which is equally remote from functional disturbances and from sublimations: it is as if the desexualized element were resexualized but nevertheless retained, in a different form, the original desexualization; the desexualized has become in itself the object of sexualization. This explains why coldness is the essential feature of the structure of perversion; it is present both in the apathy of the sadist, where it figures as theory, and in the ideal of the masochist, where it figures as fantasy. The deeper the coldness of the desexualization, the more powerful and extensive the process of perverse resexualization; hence we cannot define perversion in terms of a mere failure of integration. Sade tried to demonstrate that no passion, whether it be political ambition, avariciousness, etc., is free from "lust" — not that lust is their mainspring but rather that it arises at their culmination, when it becomes the agent of their instantaneous resexualization. (Juliette, when she discoursed on how to maximize the power of sadistic projection, began by giving the following advice: "For a whole fortnight abstain from all lustful behaviour; distract and entertain yourselves with other things....") Although the coldness of the masochist is totally different from the sadist's, the desexualization process in masochism is equally the precondition of instantaneous resexualization, as a result of which all the passions of man, whether they concern property, money, the State, etc., are transformed and put at the service of masochism. The crucial point is that resexualization takes place instantaneously, in a sort of leap. Here again, the pleasure principle is not overthrown, but retains its full empirical dominance. The sadist derives pleasure from other people's pain, and the masochist from suffering pain himself as a necessary precondition of pleasure. Nietzsche stated the essentially religious problem of the meaning of pain and gave it the only fitting answer: if pain and suffering have any meaning, it must be that they are enjoyable to someone. From this viewpoint there are only three possibilities: the first, which is the "normal" one, is of a moral and sublime character; it states that pain is pleasing to the gods who contemplate and watch over man; the other two are perverse and state that pain is enjoyable either to the one who inflicts it or to the one who suffers it. It should be clear that the normal answer is the most fantastic, the most psychotic of the three. So far as the structure of perversion is concerned, given that the pleasure principle must retain its dominance here as elsewhere, we must ask what has happened to the combinations which are normally subject to the principle. What is the significance of the resexualization, the *leap*? Earlier we became aware of the particular role played by the function of *reiteration* in masochism no less than in sadism: it takes the form of quantitative accumulation and precipitation in sadism and qualitative suspense and "freezing" in masochism. In this respect the manifest content of the perversion is liable to obscure the deeper issues, for the apparent link of sadism with pain and the apparent link of masochism with pain are in fact subordinate to the function of reiteration. Evil as defined by Sade is indistinguishable from the perpetual movement of raging molecules; the crimes imagined by Clairwil are so intended as to ensure perpetual repercussions and liberate repetition from all constraints. Again, in Saint-Fond's system, the value of punishment lies solely in its capacity for infinite reproduction through the agency of destructive molecules. In another context we noted that masochistic pain depends entirely on the phenomenon of waiting and on the functions of repetition and reiteration which characterize waiting. This is the essential point: *pain only acquires significance in relation to the forms of repetition which condition its use.* This is pointed out by Klossowski, when he writes with reference to the monotony of Sade: "The carnal act can only constitute a transgression if it is experienced as a spiritual event; but in order to apprehend its object it is necessary to circumscribe and reproduce that event in a reiterated description of the carnal act. This reiterated description not only accounts for the transgression but it is in itself a transgression of language by language." Or again when he emphasizes the role of repetition, in relation this time to masochism and the frozen scenes of masochism: "Life reiterating itself in order to recover itself in its fall, as if holding its breath in an instantaneous apprehension of its origin."[39]

Such a conclusion would nevertheless seem to be disappointing, insofar as it suggests that repetition can be reduced to a pleas-

urable experience. There is a profound mystery in the *bis repetita*.
Beneath the sound and fury of sadism and masochism the terrible force of repetition is at work. What is altered here is the normal function of repetition in its relation to the pleasure principle:
instead of repetition being experienced as a form of behavior
related to a pleasure already obtained or anticipated, instead of
repetition being governed by the idea of experiencing or reex-
periencing pleasure, repetition runs wild and becomes independent of all previous pleasure. It has itself become an idea or ideal.
Pleasure is now a form of behavior related to repetition, accom-
panying and following repetition, which has itself become an
awesome, independent force. Pleasure and repetition have thus
exchanged roles, as a consequence of the instantaneous leap, that
is to say the twofold process of desexualization and resexualization. In between the two processes the Death Instinct seems
about to speak, but because of the nature of the leap, which is
instantaneous, it is always the pleasure principle that prevails.
There is a kind of mysticism in perversion: the greater the renunciation, the greater and the more secure the gains; we might compare it to a "black" theology where pleasure ceases to motivate
the will and is abjured, disavowed, "renounced," the better to be
recovered as a reward or consequence, and as a law. The formula
of perverse mysticism is coldness and comfort (the coldness of
desexualization, on the one hand, and the comfort of resexualization, on the other, the latter being clearly illustrated by Sade's
characters). As for the anchoring of sadism and masochism in pain,
this cannot really be understood so long as it is considered in isolation: pain in this case has no sexual significance at all; on the
contrary it represents a desexualization which makes repetition
autonomous and gives it instantaneous sway over the pleasures of
resexualization. Eros is desexualized and humiliated for the sake
of a resexualized Thanatos. In sadism and masochism there is no

mysterious link between pain and pleasure; the mystery lies in the desexualization process which consolidates repetition at the opposite pole to pleasure, and in the subsequent resexualization which makes the pleasure of repetition seemingly proceed from pain. In sadism no less than in masochism, there is no direct relation to pain: pain should be regarded as an *effect* only.

CHAPTER XI

# Sadistic Superego and

# Masochistic Ego

If we consider the psychoanalytic interpretation of the derivation of masochism from sadism (there being in this respect no great difference between Freud's two interpretations: in the first the existence of primary masochism is implied, despite his assertion to the contrary; in the second Freud recognizes the existence of this primary masochism, but goes on to maintain that for a complete account of masochism we need the hypothesis of the turning around of sadism upon the subject), it would appear that the sadist's superego is singularly weak, while the masochist suffers from an overwhelming superego which causes sadism to be turned against the ego. Other psychoanalytic interpretations which do not link the process of turning around with the superego should nevertheless be seen either as attempts to complement the Freudian theory, or as variants of it, insofar as they retain the general hypothesis of a reversal of sadism and with it that of a sadomasochistic entity. To simplify matters, we may therefore consider the theory which posits an original aggressive instinct followed by the turning around of aggression upon the subject through the agency of the superego. The transformation into masochism would take place by a transfer of the aggressive component to the superego, which would then cause sadism to be turned around upon the ego. This is essentially the kind of etiology which leads to the assumption of a sadomasochistic entity. But the line of progression is far from direct: it is broken at many points and maps out the various symptoms very imperfectly.

The masochistic ego is only apparently crushed by the superego. What insolence and humor, what irrepressible defiance and ultimate triumph lie hidden behind an ego that claims to be so weak. The weakness of the ego is a strategy by which the masochist manipulates the woman into the ideal state for the performance of the role he has assigned to her. If the masochist is lacking in anything, it would be a superego and not an ego at all. In projecting the superego onto the beating woman, the masochist appears to externalize it merely in order to emphasize its derisory nature and make it serve the ends of the triumphant ego. One could say almost the opposite of the sadist: he has a powerful and overwhelming superego and nothing else. The sadist's superego is so strong that he has become identified with it; he is his own superego and can only find an ego in the external world. What normally confers a moral character on the superego is the internal and complementary ego upon which it exerts its severity, and equally the maternal element which fosters the close interaction between ego and superego. But when the superego runs wild, expelling the ego along with the mother-image, then its fundamental immorality exhibits itself as sadism. The ultimate victims of the sadist are the mother and the ego. *His ego exists only in the external world*: this is the fundamental significance of sadistic apathy. *The sadist has no other ego than that of his victims*; he is thus monstrously reduced to a pure superego which exercises its cruelty to the fullest extent and instantaneously recovers its full sexuality as soon as it diverts its power outward. The fact that the sadist has no other ego than that of his victims explains the apparent paradox of sadism, its pseudomasochism. The libertine enjoys

124

suffering the pain he inflicts upon others; when the destructive madness is deflected outward it is accompanied by an identification with the external victim. The irony of sadism lies in the two-fold operation whereby he necessarily projects his dissolved ego outward and as a result experiences what is outside him as his only ego. There is no real unity with masochism here, nor any common cause, but a process which is quite specific to sadism – a pseudomasochism which is entirely and exclusively sadistic and which is only apparently and crudely similar to masochism. Irony is in fact the operation of an overbearing superego, the art of expelling or negating the ego, with all its sadistic consequences.

In order to interpret masochism it is not sufficient to reverse the pattern obtaining in sadism. It is true that in masochism the ego triumphs and the superego can only appear from outside, in the form of the torturess. But there are significant differences: in the first place the superego is not negated as the ego is in the sadistic operation; the superego retains in appearance its power to pass judgment. Furthermore, the more power it retains, the more this power appears derisory, a mere disguise for something else; the beating woman embodies the superego but only in an utterly derisory capacity, as one might display the hide of an animal or a trophy after the hunt. For in reality the superego is dead – not, however, as the result of an active negation but of a "disavowal." The beating woman represents the superego superficially and in the external world, and she also transforms the superego into the recipient of the beating, the essential victim. This explains the conspiracy of the mother-figure and the ego against the father's likeness. *The father's likeness represents both genital sexuality and the superego as an agent of repression: the one is expelled with the other.*[40] Therein lies the humor which is not merely the opposite of irony but has its own autonomous function. Humor is the triumph of the ego over the superego, to which it seems to say: "You see, whatever you do, you are already dead; you only exist as a caricature; the woman who beats me supposedly stands for you, and yet it is in fact you yourself who are being beaten in me.... I disavow you since you negate yourself." The ego triumphs, and asserts its autonomy in pain, its parthenogenetic rebirth from pain, pain being experienced as inflicted upon the superego. We do not believe, as Freud did, that humor is the expression of a strong superego. Freud recognized that humor inevitably brings about a secondary gain for the ego, and spoke of the defiance and invulnerability of the ego and of the triumph of narcissism, with the complicity of the superego. But the ego-gain is not "secondary," as Freud thought, but primary or essential. We should be falling into the trap of humor if we were to take literally the picture it gives of the superego, for this picture is intended to laugh away and disavow the superego, the very prohibitions of the superego becoming the preconditions for obtaining the forbidden pleasure. Humor is the operation of a triumphant ego, the art of deflecting and disavowing the superego, with all its masochistic consequences. Thus there is a pseudosadism in masochism, just as there is a pseudomasochism in sadism. This specifically masochistic sadism, which attacks the superego in the ego and outside it is not in any way related to the sadism of the sadist.

There is a progression in sadism from the negative to negation, that is, from the negative as a partial process of destruction endlessly reiterated, to negation as an absolute idea of reason. It is indeed the vicissitudes of the superego in sadism which account for this progression. Insofar as the sadistic superego expels the ego and projects it into its victims, it is always faced with the task of destroying something outside itself again and again; insofar as it specifies or determines a peculiar "ego-ideal" – identification with its victims – it must add up and totalize all the partial processes in an attempt to transcend them toward an Idea of pure negation which constitutes the cold purity of thought in the superego. Thus the superego represents the apex of the desexualization process specific to sadism: the operation of totalizing extracts a neutral or displaceable energy from the combinations in which the negative only features as partial process. But at the culmination of desexualization a total resexualization takes place, which now bears on the neutral energy or pure thought. This is why the demonstrative impetus, and the speculative speeches and statements which embody this energy are not extraneous complications of Sade's novels, but the essential components of the instantaneous operation on which the whole of sadism is based. The essential operation of sadism is the sexualization of thought and of the speculative process as such, insofar as these are the product of the superego.

In masochism we find a progression from disavowal to suspense, from disavowal as a process of liberation from the pressures of the superego to suspense as incarnation of the ideal. Disavowal is a qualitative process that transfers to the oral mother the possession and privileges of the phallus. Suspense points to the new status of the ego and to the ideal of rebirth through the agency of the maternal phallus. From the interplay of disavowal and suspense there arises in the ego a qualitative relation of imagination, which is very different from the quantitative relation of thought in the superego. Disavowal is a reaction of the imagination, as negation is an operation of the intellect or of thought. Disavowal challenges the superego and entrusts the mother with the power to give birth to an "ideal ego" which is pure, autonomous and independent of the superego. The process of disavowal is linked to castration not contingently but essentially and originally; the expression of fetishistic disavowal, "No, the mother does not lack a phallus," is not one particular form of disavowal among others, but formulates the very principle from which the other manifestations of disavowal derive, namely the abolition of the father and the rejection of sexuality. Nor is disavowal in general just a form of imagination; it is nothing less than the foundation of imagination, which suspends reality and establishes the ideal in the suspended world. Disavowal and suspense are thus the very essence of imagination, and determine its specific object: the ideal. Hence disavowal should be regarded as the form of desexualization particular to masochism. The maternal phallus does not have a sexual character, but is rather the ideal organ of a neutral energy which in its turn generates the ideal ego of parthenogenetic rebirth, the "new Man devoid of sexual love." It is because of this split in the ego of the masochist and in view of the superpersonal element which produces it, that we were able earlier to speak of the impersonal element in masochism while nevertheless maintaining the primacy of the ego. But even as masochistic desexualization reaches its highest point, resexualization proceeds simultaneously in the narcissistic ego, which contemplates its image in the ideal ego through the agency of the oral mother. The cold purity of thought in sadism stands in contrast to the iciness of imagination in masochism. As Reik indicated, it is fantasy which must be regarded as the primary theater of masochism. In sadism the dual process of desexualization and resexualization manifests itself in thought and finds expression in the demonstrative thrust; in masochism, on the other hand, the twofold process manifests itself in the imagination and finds expression in the dialectical movement (the dialectical element is in the relation between the narcissistic ego and the ideal ego, this relation itself being conditioned by the image of the mother, which introduces the mythical dimension).

The etiological fallacy of the unity of sadism and masochism may perhaps be due to an erroneous interpretation of the nature of the ego and the superego and of their interrelations. The superego is in no way an agency that turns sadism into masochism. The structure of the superego falls essentially within sadism. Desexualization or even defusion are not by any means modes of transition (as implied by the sequence of a sadism of the ego followed by desexualization in the superego, followed in turn by resexualization in the masochistic ego). Sadism and masochism both possess their integral and particular form of desexualization and resexualization. Their respective connections with pain are a function of formal conditions which are entirely different in each case. Nor can it be said that the Death Instinct ensures the unity and intercommunication of the two perversions. It is undoubtedly the common mold in which both sadism and masochism present themselves, but it remains external and transcendent to them, a limiting agency which can never be given in experience. However, while the Death Instinct is never actually "given," it becomes an object for thought in the superego in sadism and for the imagination in the ego in masochism. This corresponds to Freud's observation that it is only possible to speak of a Death Instinct in speculative or in mythical terms. With regard to the Death Instinct sadism and masochism are differentiated in every possible way: they have intrinsically different structures and are not functionally related; they cannot be transformed into each other. In short, the true nature of sadism and of masochism is revealed not in any supposed genetic derivation but in the structural ego–superego split, which occurs differently in each of them. Daniel Lagache recently emphasized the possibility of such a split between the ego and the superego: he distinguishes and even contrasts the *narcissistic ego–ideal ego* system and the *superego–ego ideal* system. Either the ego undertakes a mythical operation of *idealization*, in which the mother-image serves as a mirror to reflect and even produce the "ideal ego" as a narcissistic ideal of omnipotence, or else it launches into speculative *identification* and uses the father-image to produce a superego which in turn appoints an "ego-ideal" as an ideal of authority which brings into play forces from outside the subject's narcissistic ego.[41] Of course, the polarity of ego and superego, ideal ego and ego ideal and the types of desexualization corresponding to them may occur together in a structural whole, where they give rise not only to a great variety of forms of sublimation, but equally to the most serious functional disturbances (thus Lagache can interpret mania in terms of the functional dominance of the superego–ego ideal). But even more significant is the possibility that these two poles of desexualization should operate within the differentiated or dissociated structures of perversions and bring about a perverse resexualization which confers upon each a complete structural self-sufficiency.

Masochism is a story that relates how the superego was destroyed and by whom, and what was the sequel to this destruction. Sometimes the story is misunderstood and one is led to think that the superego triumphs at the very point when it is dying. This is the danger in any story, with its unavoidable "gaps." The masochist is saying, with all the weight of his symptoms and his fantasies: "Once upon a time there were three women. . . ." He tells of the war they wage on one another, resulting in the triumph of the oral mother. He introduces himself into this age-old story by means of a very specific act, the instrument of which is the modern contract – with the most curious consequences, for he abjures the father's likeness and the sexuality which it confers, and at the same time challenges the father-image as the repressive authority which regulates this sexuality and which is constitutive of the superego. In opposition to the institutional superego he now establishes the contractual partnership between the ego and the oral mother. Intermediate between the first mother and the third mother, or lover, the oral mother functions as an image of death, holding up to the ego the cold mirror of its twofold rejection. But death can only be imagined as a second birth, a parthenogenesis from which the ego reemerges, liberated from the superego as well as from sexuality. The reflection of the ego in and through death produces the ideal ego in the conditions of independence and autonomy which obtain in masochism. The narcissistic ego contemplates the ideal ego in the maternal mirror of death: such is the story begun by Cain with the aid of Eve, continued by Christ with the aid of the Virgin Mary, and revived by Sabattai Zwi with the help of Miriam, and such is the masochistic visionary, with his prodigious vision of "the death of God." But the narcissistic ego benefits from this split in that it becomes resexualized in proportion as the ideal ego becomes desexualized. This is why the most extreme punishments and the most intense pains acquire in this context such a very peculiar erotic function in relation to the death-image. They represent on the one hand, in the ideal ego, the desexualization process which liberates it both from the superego and from the father's likeness, and on the other hand, in the narcissistic ego, the resexualization that allows it to enjoy the pleasures that the superego forbids.

Sadism likewise tells a story. It relates how the ego, in an entirely different context and in a different struggle, is beaten and expelled; how the unrestrained superego assumes an exclusive role, modeled on an inflated conception of the father's role – the mother and the ego becoming its choice victims. Desexualization, now represented by the superego, ceases to be of a moral or moralizing character, since it is no longer directed upon an inner ego but is turned outward, upon external victims who take on the quality of the rejected ego. The Death Instinct now assumes the character of a Thought of a fearful nature, an idea of demonstrative reason, and resexualization bears on the "ego ideal" of the sadistic "thinker," who thus turns out to be in every way the opposite of the masochistic visionary. Indeed, he recounts a different story altogether.

We have merely been trying to demonstrate the following: it is always possible to speak of violence and cruelty in sexual behavior and to show that these phenomena can be combined with sexuality in different ways; it is always possible, furthermore, to contrive means of passing from one combination to another. It is assumed that the *same person* enjoys both undergoing pain and inflicting it, and imaginary points of turning back and turning around are accordingly set up and applied to an extensive and ill-defined whole. On the strength of transformist presuppositions, the unity of sadism and masochism is simply taken for granted. Our intention has been to show that this approach only leads to very crude and ill-differentiated concepts. In order to prove the unity of sadism and masochism one proceeds as follows. From the point of view of etiology, sadism and masochism are each deprived of some of their components in order to ensure that the two types of perversion can transform into each other (thus the superego, which is an essential component of sadism, is actually treated as the point where sadism reverses into masochism; similarly for the ego, which is an essential component of masochism). From the symptomatological viewpoint, crude common symptoms, vaguely analogous manifestations and approximate "coincidences" are treated as proof of the existence of a sadomasochistic entity (for example, the "masochism" of the sadist and the "sadism" of the masochist). And yet no doctor would treat a fever as though it were a definite symptom of a specific disease; he views it rather as an indeterminate syndrome common to a number of possible diseases. The same is true of sadomasochism: it is a syndrome of perversion in general which must be broken down to make way for a differential diagnosis. The belief in a sadomasochistic entity is not really grounded in genuine psychoanalytic thinking but in pre-Freudian thinking which relied on hasty assimilations and faulty etiological interpretations that psychoanalysis merely helped to make more convincing, instead of questioning their reality.

This is why it is necessary to read Masoch. His work has suffered from unfair neglect, when we consider that Sade has been the object of such penetrating studies both in the field of literary criticism and in that of psychoanalytic interpretation, to the benefit of both. But it would be equally unfair to read Masoch with Sade in mind, and with the intention of finding in his work a proof or verification that sadism effectively reverses into masochism, even if masochism in turn evolves toward a form of sadism. The genius of Sade and that of Masoch are poles apart; their worlds do not communicate, and as novelists their techniques are totally different. Sade expresses himself in a form which combines obscenity in description with rigor and apathy in demonstration, while the art of Masoch consists in multiplying the disavowals in order to create the coldness of aesthetic suspense. There is no reason to suppose that Masoch would suffer from such a confrontation. Influenced by his Slavic background and by German Romanticism, Masoch makes use of all the resources of fantasy and suspense rather than of the romantic dream. By his techniques alone he is a great writer; by his use of folklore he manages to tap the forces of the myth, just as Sade was able to achieve the full power of demonstration by his use of descriptions. The fact that their names have been linked with two basic perversions should remind us that diseases are named after their symptoms rather than after their causes. Etiology, which is the scientific or experimental side of medicine, must be subordinated to symptomatology, which is its literary, artistic aspect. Only on this condition can we avoid splitting the semiological unity of a dis-

turbance, or uniting very different disturbances under a misbegotten name, in a whole arbitrarily defined by nonspecific causes.

Sadomasochism is one of these misbegotten names, a semiological howler. We found in every case that what appeared to be
a common "sign" linking the two perversions together turned out
on investigation to be in the nature of a mere syndrome which
could be further broken down into irreducibly specific symptoms
of the one or the other perversion. Let us now try to summarize
the results of our inquiry. (1) Sadism is speculative-demonstrative,
masochism dialectical-imaginative; (2) sadism operates with the
negative and pure negation, masochism with disavowal and suspension; (3) sadism operates by means of quantitative reiteration,
masochism by means of qualitative suspense; (4) there is a masochism specific to the sadist and equally a sadism specific to the
masochist, the one never combining with the other; (5) sadism
negates the mother and inflates the father, masochism disavows
the mother and abolishes the father; (6) the role and significance
of the fetish, and the function of the fantasy are totally different
in each case; (7) there is an aestheticism in masochism, while sadism is hostile to the aesthetic attitude; (8) sadism is institutional,
masochism contractual; (9) in sadism the superego and the process of identification play the primary role, masochism gives primacy to the ego and to the process of idealization; (10) sadism
and masochism exhibit totally different forms of desexualization
and resexualization; (11) finally, summing up all these differences,
there is the most radical difference between sadistic *apathy* and
masochistic *coldness*.

These eleven propositions taken together should account not
only for the differences between sadism and masochism, but
equally for the differences in the literary techniques and in the
art of Sade and Masoch.

# Notes

1. Krafft-Ebing himself points out the existence of "passive flagellation" independently from masochism. Cf. *Psychopathia Sexualis* (revised by Moll, 1963).

2. Georges Bataille, *Eroticism*, Engl. tr. M. Dalwood (Calderbooks, 1965), pp. 187, 188, 189.

3. Krafft-Ebing, *Psychopathia Sexualis*, pp. 208-9.

4. Cf. Appendix III.

5. To cut off a pigtail would not seem in this instance to imply any hostility toward the fetish; it is merely the necessary condition of its constitution. We cannot allude to hair despoilers without drawing attention to a psychiatric problem of historical importance. Krafft-Ebing's *Psychopathia Sexualis*, revised by Moll, is a compendium of cases of the most abominable perversions for the use of doctors and jurists, as the subtitle indicates. Assault, crime, bestiality, disembowelling, necrophilia, etc., are all treated with the appropriate scientific detachment, without passion or value-judgment. With case 396, however, the tone changes abruptly: "a dangerous pigtail fetishist was spreading anxiety in Berlin...." And this comment follows: "These people are so dangerous that they ought definitely to be subject to long-term confinement in an asylum until their eventual recovery. They do not by any means deserve unqualified leniency.... When I think of the immense sorrow caused to a family in which a young girl is thus deprived of her beautiful hair, I find it quite impossible to understand that such people are not confined indefinitely in an asy-

lum.... Let us hope that the new penal law will remedy this situation." Such an indignant explosion against a relatively harmless perversion seems to indicate that powerful personal motivations lay behind the author's departure from his usual scientific objectivity. When he reached case 396, the psychiatrist allowed his feelings to get the better of him — let this be a lesson to us all.

6. Letter to his brother Charles on 5th January 1869 (quoted by Wanda).

7. Maurice Blanchot, *Lautréamont et Sade* (Minuit, Collection "Arguments," 1963), p. 30.

8. *Three Essays on the Theory of Sexuality*, The Complete Psychological Works (Hogarth, 1955-64), Vol. VII, p. 159.

9. "The instincts and their vicissitudes," in *Papers on Metapsychology*, Collected Papers (1946), Vol. IV, p. 71.

10. Cf. Appendix I.

11. Cf. Bachofen, *Das Muterrecht* (1861). An example of a work owing much to Bachofen's ideas is the excellent book *L'initiation sexuelle et l'évolution religieuse*, by Pierre Gordon (P.U.F., 1946).

12. Cf. Appendix I.

13. E. Bergler, *The Basic Neurosis* (New York: Grune, 1949).

14. Theodore Reik, *Masochism in Sex and Society*, Engl. tr. M.H. Beigel and G.M. Kurth (Grove Press, 1962), pp. 21, 209.

15. Pierre Klossowski, "Elements d'une étude psychanalytique sur le Marquis de Sade," *Revue de Psychanalyse*, 1933.

16. An illustration of the difference in nature between the two prostitution fantasies, the sadistic and the masochistic, may be found in Klossowski's tale *Le Souffleur*: cf. the contrast between "L'Hôtel de Longchamp" and "les lois de l'hospitalité."

17. The author's use of "*the symbolic* (order)" or (the order of) *the real* should be understood in the context of the fundamental distinction established by Jacques Lacan between three "orders" or dimensions: the Symbolic, the Imaginary and the Real. (Translators' note.)

18. Cf. Jacques Lacan, *La Psychanalyse*, I, pp. 48 ff. As defined by Lacan, the mechanism of repudiation or foreclosure, *Verwerfung*, operates in the sym-

bolic dimension and in connection with the father, more specifically "the name of the father." Lacan appears to look upon this as a primary and irreducible operation which is independent of all maternal influence; the distortion of the mother's role would on the contrary arise *as a result* of the symbolic "repudiation" of the father. Cf. however the article by a follower of Lacan, Piera Aulagnier, "Remarques sur la structure psychotique," *La Psychanalyse*, VIII, which would seem to restore to some extent to the mother an active role as symbolic agent.

19. Reik, *Masochism*, p. 18.

20. Cf. Appendix III.

21. Maurice Blanchot, *Lautréamont et Sade*, p. 35.

22. Reik, *Masochism*, pp. 44-91.

23. Cf. Appendix II.

24. *Pagisme*: form of masochism where the subject imagines he is a pageboy attending the woman.

25. This is the essential thesis of *Institutions Republicaines*.

26. On the elusive character of the object of the law, cf. J. Lacan's commentaries relating both to Kant and to Sade: *Kant avec Sade* (Critique, 1963).

27. *Civilization and its Discontents*, Complete Psychological Works, Vol. XXI, pp. 125, 128.

28. Theodore Reik, *Masochism*. "The masochist exhibits the punishment but also its failure. He shows his submission certainly, but he also shows his invincible rebellion, demonstrating that he gains pleasure despite the discomfort.... He cannot be broken from outside. He has an inexhaustible capacity for taking a beating and yet knows unconsciously he is not licked" (pp. 145, 163).

29. Revue Bleue, 1888.

30. On the link between agrarian and incestuous themes and the role of the plough, cf. Salvador Dali's brilliant text in *Mythe tragique de l'Angélus de Millet*, Pauvert.

31. Masoch's tale is a relatively accurate account of the life of Sabattai Zwi. Another account may be found in Grätz, *History of the Jews*, where the hero's historical importance is emphasized.

32. Letter to his brother Charles on January 8, 1869.

33. B. Grunberger, in "Esquisse d'une théorie psychodynamique du masochisme," *Revue Française de Psychanalyse* (1954), disagrees with Oedipal interpretations of masochism, but he replaces the "murder of the Oedipal father" by a pre-genital wish to castrate the father, regarded as the true source of masochism. In any case, he does not accept the maternal–oral etiology.

34. "The instincts and their vicissitudes" in *Papers on Metapsychology*.

35. This second explanation, which was offered by Grunberger, traces masochism back to a pre-Oedipal source.

36. These three aspects are formally distinguished in an article written in 1924, "The economic problem of masochism," but they are already indicated in the first interpretation.

37. Reik, p. 186.

38. Musil, *The Man without Qualities*. (Translator's note: this passage does not seem to be included in the English translation of this work.)

39. Klossowski, *Un si funeste désir* (N.R.F.), p. 127, and *La révolution de l'Edit de Nantes* (Minuit), p. 15.

40. *Jokes and their Relation to the Unconscious*, Complete Psychological Works, Vol. VIII.

41. Cf. Daniel Lagache, "La psychanalyse et la structure de la personalité," *La Psychanalyse*, 6, pp. 36-47.

# Venus in Furs

Leopold von Sacher-Masoch

*The Lord hath smitten him by the hand of a woman.*
— Book of Judith, 16.7

I was in delightful company: the lady who sat facing me across the massive Renaissance fireplace was none other than Venus; she was no *demi-mondaine* who had taken a pseudonym to wage war upon the masculine sex, but the goddess of Love in person.

She had lit a crackling fire and was settled in a comfortable armchair; the firelight flickered over her pale face, her white eyes and from time to time her feet when she sought to warm them.

Her head was magnificent in spite of the stony, lifeless eyes, but this was the only part of her that I was able to see, for the sublime creature had wrapped her marble body in a great fur beneath which she was huddled like a shivering cat.

"I do not understand, madam," I ventured. "It is no longer cold; in fact the past two weeks have been delightfully springlike. It must be your nerves."

"You may keep your spring," she replied in a toneless voice, and then sneezed divinely twice over. "I cannot stand it here, and I am beginning to see why. . . ."

"What, my dear?"

143

"I am beginning to believe the incredible and understand the incomprehensible, namely the philosophy of the German people and the qualities of their womenfolk. It no longer surprises me in the least that you northerners are unable to love, for you have not an inkling what love is about."

"I beg your pardon, madam," I replied, my blood rising, "I have really given you no reason to speak in this way."

"No, it is true, you have not." The Divine One sneezed for the third time and shrugged her shoulders with inimitable grace. "That is why I have always been kind to you, and have even paid you a visit now and then although I invariably catch cold in spite of my furs. Do you remember the first time we met?"

"How could I forget it?" I said. "You had thick brown curls then, brown eyes and rosy lips, but I recognized you at once by the outline of your face and its marble pallor. You always wore a jacket trimmed with squirrel."

"Yes, you were truly in love with that jacket; and what an attentive suitor!"

"You taught me the meaning of love. Worshiping you made me forget two thousand years of history."

"How incomparably faithful I was!"

"Oh, as for faithfulness...."

"You ungrateful man!"

"I do not wish to reproach you. You are undoubtedly a divine woman, but above all you are a woman and, like every member of your sex, cruel in matters of love."

"What you call cruelty," the goddess of Love retorted, "is the very substance of sensual and natural love. It is woman's true nature to give herself wherever she loves and to love whatever pleases her."

"But can there be greater cruelty for a lover than a beloved's infidelity?"

"Alas," she replied, "woman is faithful as long as she loves, but you demand that she be faithful without love and give herself without enjoyment. Who is cruel then, woman or man? You northerners take love too seriously. You speak of duty where it is purely a question of pleasure."

"Yes, madam, as far as love is concerned our feelings are honorable and virtuous and our relations are durable."

"And yet," interrupted the lady, "you nurse a secret craving for a life of sheer paganism. You modern men, you children of reason, cannot begin to appreciate love as pure bliss and divine serenity; indeed this kind of love is disastrous for men like you, for as soon as you try to be natural you become vulgar. To you Nature is an enemy. You have made devils of the smiling gods of Greece and you have turned me into a creature of evil. You may cast anathemas on me, curse me or offer yourself in sacrifice like frenzied bacchantes at my altar, but if one of you so much as dares to kiss my crimson lips, he must make a barefoot pilgrimage to Rome in sackcloth and ashes, and pray until the cursed staff grows green again, while all around me roses, violets and myrtle bloom everlastingly. Their fragrance is not for you. Stay in your northern mists and Christian incense and leave our pagan world to rest under the lava and the rubble. Do not dig us up; Pompeii was not built for you, nor were our villas, our baths and our temples. You do not need the gods — they would freeze to death in your climate!"

The lovely marble creature coughed and rearranged the sable around her shoulders.

"Thank you for the lesson in classics," I replied, "but I cannot deny that in your peaceful and sunny world just as in our misty climate man and woman are natural enemies. Love may unite them briefly to form one mind, one heart, one will, but all too soon they are torn asunder. And this you know better than I:

either one of them must bend the other to his will, or else he must let himself be trampled underfoot."

"Under the woman's foot, of course," said Lady Venus impertinently. "And that you know better than I."

"Of course, that is why I have no illusions."

"In other words you are now my slave without illusions, and I shall trample you mercilessly."

"Madam!"

"You do not know me yet. I admit that I am cruel — since the word gives you so much delight — but am I not entitled to be so? It is man who desires, woman who is desired; this is woman's only advantage, but it is a decisive one. By making man so vulnerable to passion, nature has placed him at woman's mercy, and she who has not the sense to treat him like a humble subject, a slave, a plaything, and finally to betray him with a laugh — well, she is a woman of little wisdom."

"My dear, your principles..." I protested.

"Are founded on the experience of a thousand years," she replied mischievously, running her white fingers through the dark fur. "The more submissive woman is, the more readily man recovers his self-possession and becomes domineering; but the more cruel and faithless she is, the more she ill-treats him, the more wantonly she toys with him and the harsher she is, the more she quickens his desire and secures his love and admiration. It has always been so, from the time of Helen and Delilah all the way to Catherine the Great and Lola Montez."

"I cannot deny it," I said. "Nothing could be more attractive to man than the idea of a beautiful tyrant, both voluptuous and cruel, who insolently and inconsistently changes her favorite to suit her humor."

"And wears furs," said the goddess.

"What made you think of that?"

"I know your tastes."

"Are you aware," I said, "that you have become quite a coquette since we last met?"

"What do you mean by that?"

"I mean that I can think of nothing more extravagantly flattering to your white skin than these dark furs...."

The goddess laughed.

"You are dreaming," she cried. "Wake up!" She grasped my arm with her marble hand. "Wake up!" she repeated, this time in a low, gruff voice. I strained to open my eyes. I could see the hand that was shaking me, but suddenly it turned a tawny brown, and the voice became the husky alcoholic voice of my Cossack, who stood towering above me.

"Do get up," said the good fellow, "this is disgraceful."

"What is disgraceful?"

"To fall asleep with your clothes on and a book in your hand." He snuffed the candles which had burned right down and picked up the volume that had fallen from my hand. He looked at the title page: "Aha, Hegel. Besides, it is time we left for Mr. Severin's, he is expecting us for tea."

*   *   *

"A very curious dream," said Severin, when I had finished my tale. He sat with his elbows on his knees, his chin resting in his delicately veined hands, lost in deep thought.

As I expected, he remained for a long while without moving, almost without breathing. I found nothing remarkable in his behavior, for over the last three years we had become very good friends and I was used to his eccentricities. He was undoubtedly an odd character, although he was not the dangerous madman that his neighbors and indeed the whole district of Kolome considered him to be. Not only did I find him interesting but I had a great liking

147

for him, and consequently I too was regarded by many people as a trifle mad. For a Galician gentleman and a landowner, especially considering his age (he was barely thirty), he was surprisingly lucid and serious almost to the point of pedantry. He followed a rigorous philosophical and practical system: each minute of his life obeyed the dictates of the thermometer, the barometer, the aerometer, the hydrometer, Hippocrates, Hufeland, Plato, Knigge and Lord Chesterfield. Occasionally, however, he was subject to attacks of such violence that he seemed about to burst through the very walls; at such times people would wisely avoid him.

While he sat there in silence one could hear the faint singing of the fire, the humming of the venerable samovar, the creak of the old rocking chair on which I sat smoking my cigar, and the chirrup of the cricket in the wall. I let my gaze wander over the curious collection of objects: skeletons of animals, stuffed birds, globes, plaster casts. Suddenly my eyes alighted on a picture that I had often seen before but which today in the red glow of the fire made a particularly strange impression on me.

It was a large oil painting done in the powerful colors of the Flemish School, and its subject was quite unusual. A beautiful woman, naked beneath her dark furs, was resting on an ottoman, supported on her left arm. A playful smile hovered on her lips and her thick hair was tied in a Grecian knot and dusted with snow-white powder. Her right hand played with a whip while her bare foot rested nonchalantly on a man who lay on the ground before her like a slave, like a dog. The pronounced but well-shaped features of the man showed quiet melancholy and helpless passion; he gazed up at her with the fanatical, burning eyes of a martyr. This man, this footstool for her feet, was Severin, beardless and ten years younger by the look of him.

"Venus in Furs!" I cried, pointing at the picture. "That is how I saw her in my dream."

"I, too," said Severin, "but I was dreaming with my eyes open."

"What do you mean?"

"Oh, it is a ridiculous story."

"It appears that my dream was prompted by your picture," I pursued. "Do tell me what is behind it, and how it came to play such an important part in your life. I cannot wait to hear."

"Then look at the picture facing it," said my friend, without answering my question.

It was a remarkably good copy of Titian's famous *Venus with the Mirror* which hangs in the Dresden art gallery.

"Yes, but what of it?"

Severin rose and pointed to the furs in which Titian had draped his goddess.

"She is also a Venus in furs," he said, smiling subtly. "I do not think the venerable Venetian had any ulterior motive; he simply painted the portrait of some distinguished Messalina coldly inspecting her majestic charms, and he was tactful enough to paint in Cupid holding the mirror, with some reluctance I may add. The picture is merely a piece of flattery. Later some connoisseur of the baroque dubbed the lady 'Venus,' and the despot's furs in which Titian's model wrapped herself (more out of fear of catching cold than from modesty) became the symbol of the tyranny and cruelty that are common to beautiful women. But what does it matter? As it stands, the painting is a biting satire on modern love: Venus must hide herself in a vast fur lest she catch cold in our abstract northern climate, in the icy realm of Christianity."

Severin laughed and lit another cigarette.

Just then the door opened and a pretty, plump blond with an amiable and intelligent air, wearing a black silk dress, trotted in with a tray of cold meat and eggs for our tea. Severin picked up an egg and opened it with his knife.

"Did I not tell you that I wanted them soft-boiled?" he shouted, with a violence that made the young woman quake with fear.

"But my dear Sewtschu," she began fearfully.

"What do you mean, 'Sewtschu'?" he shouted. "You are to obey, do you hear?"

Whereupon he tore down a knout that was hanging beside his weapons. The pretty woman fled from the room like a frightened doe.

"Let me catch you doing that again!" he shouted after her.

"But, Severin," I said, placing my hand on his arm, "how can you treat a lovely little woman like that?"

"Take a look at her," he said, with a sly wink. "If I had flattered her she would have tied a noose around my neck; but because I train her with a knout she worships me."

"What nonsense!"

"Nonsense yourself. That is the way to train women."

"You may live like a pasha in your harem if you choose, but do not foist your theories on me."

"Why not?" he exclaimed. "Goethe's words, 'Be the anvil or be the hammer' are never more true than when applied to the relations between man and woman. Incidentally, the Lady Venus informed you of this in your dream. Woman's power lies in the passion she can arouse in man and which she will exploit to her own advantage unless he remains always on his guard. Man has only one choice: to be a slave or to be a tyrant. If he surrenders to her the yoke will begin to weigh on his neck and soon he will feel the touch of the whip."

"What odd maxims!"

"Not maxims, but personal experience," he replied, with a nod. "I have been thoroughly whipped myself and it cured me. Would you like to read about it?"

He rose and took from his massive desk a small manuscript which he laid in front of me.

"You asked me what the picture was about and I have long owed you an explanation. Here you are — read this!"

Severin sat by the fire with his back toward me, lost in reverie. Everything became quiet: the fire singing in the hearth, the samovar and the cricket were heard once more.

I opened the manuscript and read: "Confessions of a Supersensualist."

The margin of the manuscript bore in the form of an epigraph an adaptation of the famous lines from *Faust*:

Thou sensual, supersensual libertine,
A little girl can lead thee by the nose.

I turned the page and read:

Since I believe that it is impossible to describe the past objectively, I have compiled the following from the personal diary I kept during the period in question. Thus my story will have a flavor of the present.

*　*　*

Gogol, the Russian Molière, once wrote, I cannot remember where: "The true muse of comedy is a woman with tearful eyes under a smiling mask." Remarkable!

A strange feeling comes over me as I write these words. The air seems laden with intoxicating smells that make my head spin and ache; the smoke of the fire rises in spirals that turn into figures: gray-bearded gnomes point at me mockingly, chubby cupids ride on the back of my chair and climb onto my knee. I smile in spite of myself; I even laugh aloud when I think of my adventures. And yet I am writing with no ordinary ink but with the red blood that drips from my heart; the wounds that were healed long ago have opened up again and throb with pain; now and then a tear falls onto the page.

\* \* \*

The days drift aimlessly by in the little Carpathian health resort. I see nobody and nobody sees me. It is so dull here that one might take to writing idylls. There would be time enough to fill a gallery with paintings, or write enough plays for a whole season, enough trios and duets for a dozen virtuosi, but when it comes to the point all that I manage to do is to stretch the canvas, smooth the bow and line the music paper. For the truth is (no false modesty, Severin, you can deceive others but alas, not yourself) I am nothing but a dilettante, an amateur in painting, poetry, and music and in all the arts that are supposed to be unprofitable but that can nevertheless earn one the income of a cabinet minister or even of a minor potentate. The truth is that I am an amateur in life.

Up to now I have lived exactly as I have painted and written poetry, that is, I have never progressed far beyond the first brushstroke, the outline of the plot, the first stanza. Some people begin everything and finish nothing: I am one of those.

But let us get to the point.

I lie on my window seat, gazing at the setting of my despair, savoring its poetry: before me, a breathtaking view of the blue mountains bathed in a mist of golden sunlight and veined with silver torrents. How clear the sky is, with its towering snowy domes! How green and fresh the wooded slopes and meadows where small herds are grazing, down to the tawny waves of corn where the reapers stoop and rise rhythmically.

The house where I am staying is in a sort of park, or forest, or wilderness, whatever it may be, and is very isolated. Its only other inhabitants are a widow from Lwow and the landlady, Madame Tartakowska, a little old woman who grows older and smaller each day, an aged dog with a lame leg and a kitten that plays endlessly with a ball of yarn — the ball, I believe, belongs to the lovely widow.

The widow is said to be very beautiful, still young — twenty-four at the most — and very rich too. She lives on the first floor; her green shutters are always drawn and her balcony is overgrown with green creepers. I occupy the ground floor, and the garden affords a pleasant leafy bower where I read, write, paint and sing like a bird on the tree. I can see what is happening on the balcony and sometimes I catch sight of a white gown gleaming through the thick tangle of foliage.

And yet the beautiful woman up there does not really interest me, for I am enamored of another. My love is quite without hope, and I am far more miserable than the Knight of Toggenburg or the Chevalier in Manon Lescaut: my beloved is made of stone.

In the garden, or rather the small neglected park, there is a charming meadow where a few does graze peacefully. In its center stands a statue of Venus, the original of which I believe is in Florence. This Venus is the most beautiful woman I have ever seen; of course this does not mean much, for I have seen few beautiful women, in fact few women at all. In love, too, I am an amateur who never gets beyond the first brushstrokes, the first act of the play. But why talk in superlatives, as though beauty could ever be surpassed? It is enough to say that she is beautiful and that I love her madly, passionately, with feverish intensity, as one can only love a woman who responds to one with a petrified smile, ever calm and unchanging. I adore her absolutely.

Often, when the dappled sunlight shimmers beneath the trees, I lie in the shelter of a young birch, reading. Often at night I pay a visit to my cold, cruel beloved; clasping her knees, I press my face against her cold pedestal and worship her.

The rising moon, which just now is waxing, creates an indescribable effect; it swims between the trees and floods the meadow with a silvery sheen. The goddess, as if transfigured, seems to bathe in the soft glow. One evening as I was returning from my place of worship along a wooded path I suddenly caught sight of a figure through the screen of trees, a woman's form, white as stone and shining in the moonlight. It was as though my dream had come true: the lovely creature had come down from her pedestal to follow me. I was seized with a nameless fear and my heart pounded as if it would burst.

I am an amateur, there is no doubt about it. As usual, I stopped short after the first stanza, or rather I did not stop, I fled as fast as my feet could carry me.

*   *   *

What a stroke of luck! A Jewish dealer in photographs has found me a replica of my ideal. It is a small reproduction entitled *Venus with the Mirror*. What a woman! I want to compose a poem but instead I write on the back of the photograph:

"*Venus in Furs*. You are cold and yet you fire the hearts of men. Wrap yourself in your despot's furs, for they become no one so well as you, cruel goddess of Beauty and Love!"

A while later I add a few verses from a poem by Goethe that I have found in the Paralipomena to *Faust*:

TO LOVE!
His wings belie his nature
And his arrows are but claws;
Beneath his crown are budding horns,
For without any doubt he is,

Like all the gods of Ancient Greece,
A devil in disguise.

Then I set the picture before me propped on a book and contemplate it.

I am enchanted but at the same time filled with horror by the
cold coquetry of the splendid woman enveloping her charms in
dark furs, and by the severity and harshness in her marble features.

I take up the pen again and write the following lines:

"To love and to be loved, what joy! And yet how this splendor pales in comparison with the blissful torment of worshiping a woman who treats one as a plaything, of being the slave
of a beautiful tyrant who mercilessly tramples one underfoot.
Even Samson, the hero, the giant, put himself into the hands
of Delilah who had already betrayed him once, only to be
betrayed yet again. And when he was captured and blinded by
the Philistines, he kept his brave and loving eyes fixed upon
the fair traitress until the very end."

\* \* \*

I breakfasted under the arbor, reading the book of Judith. I
could not help envying the heathen Holofernes who came to such
a bloody end, beheaded by a regal lady.

"The Lord hath smitten him by the hand of a woman."

This sentence made a deep impression on me. "How unchival-
rous these Jews are," I thought. As for their God, he might choose
his words better when speaking of the fair sex.

"The Lord hath smitten him by the hand of a woman." What
must I do for him to smite *me?*

Good heavens, here comes our landlady — she has become
smaller still overnight. And up there between the creepers I catch

sight of the white dress again: is it Venus or the widow?

This time it must be the widow, for Madame Tartakowska curt-
sies to me and asks me on the lady's behalf for something to read.
I rush to my room and quickly collect a few books.

I remember too late that the photograph of my Venus is in one
of them. The lady in white must now be deciphering my outpour-
ings; what will she make of them?

I hear her laugh – is she mocking me?

*   *   *

A full moon rises over the small fir trees that border the park.
A silvery mist drifts across the terrace and the copses and into
the landscape as far as the eye can see. The horizon is blurred like
trembling water.

I feel a strange and urgent call which I am powerless to resist.
I dress again and go out into the garden. I feel irresistibly drawn
toward the meadow, toward my goddess, my beloved.

The night is cool; I shiver. The air is laden with the heavy
smell of flowers and foliage. It is intoxicating. What splendor!
What music! A nightingale sighs. The stars quiver in the milky
glow of the sky. The meadow is smooth as a mirror, like a frozen lake, and there in the center stands the statue of Venus, shining and stately.

But what is this? The goddess is draped in fur: a dark sable
cloak flows from her marble shoulders down to her feet. I stand
bewildered, transfixed; again I am gripped by an indescribable
panic. I take flight. In my hurry I take the wrong path and just
as I am about to turn off into one of the leafy avenues, there
before me, seated on a bench – is Venus; not the marble beauty
of a moment ago, but the goddess of Love in person, with warm
blood and a beating heart! She has come to life for my benefit
like Pygmalion's statue. The miracle is not quite complete, for her

hair still seems made of marble and her white dress gleams like moonlight — or is it satin? The dark fur drapes her from shoulder to toe. But her lips are becoming redder, her cheeks are taking on color, suddenly her eyes shine with a wicked green glitter — she is laughing!

Her laughter is so strange, so — ah! Indescribable. It is breath-taking. I take to my heels and run, but each time I pause to catch my breath I hear the mocking laughter, it follows me down the alleys of scented foliage, over the shining lawns, into the moon-flecked shadow of the thickets. I wander utterly lost, cold beads of sweat on my forehead. At last I stop and say to myself sharply (with oneself one is either very polite or very rude): "You fool!"

The effect is immediate, like a magic formula; at once I recover my self-possession and become perfectly calm. Delighted with the discovery I go on repeating: "You fool!"

Now everything has become clear and distinct. There is the fountain, there the alley of boxwood and over there the house which I am slowly approaching.

Then all of a sudden, through the screen of foliage embroid-ered with silver moonlight, I catch sight of the white figure again, the beautiful woman whom I worship and from whom I flee in terror. In no time I am inside the house, panting. What game is this that I am playing, I wonder? Am I a mere amateur or a complete fool?

*     *     *

The morning is sultry, the air full of intoxicating smells. I am again seated under my arbor, reading the *Odyssey*; I have come upon the story of the delightful witch who changed her suitors into wild beasts — a spicy tale of love in ancient times!

Suddenly there is a rustling in the branches and in the grass, in the leaves of my elm tree, on the terrace: a woman's dress. It is she, Venus, but without her furs; the widow again, and yet it is Venus. Oh, what a woman!

She stands clothed in a vaporous white morning-gown, looking at me. What a graceful and poetic figure! She is not tall, but not short either; her face is not so much beautiful as charming and piquant as in the time of the French marquises. What sensitivity, what sweet impishness play about her features, her full lips, her not-too-small mouth! Her skin is so delicate that her blue veins show through even under the fine muslin that covers her arms and breasts. Her red hair — yes, she is a redhead, not blond or golden-haired — is gathered in thick curls that tumble with tantalizing charm onto the nape of her neck. Her eyes alight on me like a shaft of green lightning — yes, her eyes are green and indescribably soft and powerful, green like precious stones, like the unfathomable depths of mountain lakes. She notices my intense disquiet that has made me impolite (for I have remained seated and still have my cap on my head) and she smiles mischievously.

I finally rise and bow to her, and she comes toward me with a loud, almost childlike laugh. I stammer, as only an amateur or a fool can do on such an occasion.

Thus we made acquaintance.

The goddess asked my name and told me hers: she is called Wanda von Dunajew and she is none other than my Venus.

"Madam, what an idea! What made you think of it?"

"A little picture in one of your books."

"I do not recall...."

"Those strange lines on the back...."

"Why strange?"

She looked at me. "I have always wanted to meet a true romantic, someone really different, and I suspect you are even wilder than I thought."

"Really, madam, I...." Again the stupid despicable stammering; what is more, I began to blush, more like a boy of sixteen than a man ten years older.

"I frightened you last night."

"Yes, indeed, but...will you not take a seat?"

She sat down, delighted at my discomfiture, for I was even more afraid of her now in the broad daylight. A charming expression of contempt quivered on her upper lip.

"It would seem," she began, "that for you love and particularly women are hostile forces; you try to defend yourself against them. However, you are quite overcome by the pleasurable torments and exquisite pain which they afford you. A very modern view."

"You do not share it?"

"No, I do not," she said boldly and decisively, with a shake of her head that sent her red curls flying like flames. "I admire the serene sensuality of the Greeks – pleasure without pain; it is the ideal I strive to realize. I do not believe in the love preached by Christianity and our modern knights of the spirit. Take a look at me: I am worse than a heretic, I am a pagan.

'Thinkest thou that for long the goddess of Love did consider
When once in fair Ida's grove Anchises charmed her eye?'

"These lines from Goethe's *Roman Elegies* have always delighted me. The love we find in nature is the love of heroic times, 'When the gods and goddesses did love.' In those days, 'Desire would follow upon look, enjoyment on desire'; all else was an affectation, a lie. It was Christianity, whose cruel emblem, the cross, has always seemed to me somewhat horrific, that first brought an alien and hostile element into nature and its innocent instincts. The struggle of the spirit against the senses is the gospel of modern man. I do not wish to have any part in it."

"Yes, madam, you belong on Mount Olympus," I replied. "But

we moderns can no longer tolerate the carefree philosophy of the ancients, especially in matters of love. The idea of sharing a woman with others, even if she is an Aspasia, is revolting to us. Like our God we are jealous. We have made the name of the lovely Phryne into a term of abuse. We prefer a pale, thin virgin of Holbein, who belongs to us alone, to an antique Venus, no matter how divine her beauty, who today loves Anchises, tomorrow Paris and the day after Adonis. And if Nature gains the upper hand and we succumb in passionate ardor to such a woman, her serene happiness seems diabolical and cruel, and our bliss becomes a sin for which we have to atone."

"So you too are content with the women of today, these poor hysterical creatures who pursue like sleepwalkers the dream of an ideal man, while failing to appreciate the best of men. They are always lamenting their inability to uphold Christian morals; they deceive and are deceived, they search, choose and reject; they are never happy and cannot give happiness, and they complain about their fate instead of calmly admitting that they would rather live as Helen and Aspasia did. Nature admits of no stability in the relations between man and woman."

"Madam...."

"Allow me to finish. It is only man's egoism that seeks to bury woman like some treasure. Despite holy ceremonies, oaths and contracts, no permanence can ever be imposed on love; it is the most changeable element in our transient lives. Can you deny that our Christian world is falling into decay?"

"But...."

"But, you will say, the individual who revolts against the institutions of society is immediately rejected, ostracized, stoned. So be it; I am willing to take the risk. My principles are deliberately pagan; I wish to live as I please, and as for your hypocritical respect, I prefer happiness. Whoever invented Christian marriage was right to have invented morality at the same time. I do not for a moment believe that I am eternal; when I take my last breath, and life on earth is at an end for Wanda von Dunajew, what difference will it make to me whether my pure spirit joins the choirs of angels or whether the dust of my body produces new beings? Since the time will come when I shall no longer exist in my present form, what is the point of self-denial? Shall I belong to a husband I no longer love, under the pretext that I once loved him? No, I shall deny myself nothing, I shall love everyone who attracts me and give happiness to everyone I love. Is that such a dreadful thing? No, it is better by far than to rejoice at the torments that my charms produce, and virtuously turn away from the poor man who burns with passion for me. I am young, rich and beautiful, and I live for pleasure."

As she spoke her eyes sparkled with mischief. I had taken hold of her hand without knowing quite what I would do with it, and in true amateurish fashion I quickly let it drop again.

"Your frankness delights me," I said, "and not only that...." Again the confounded awkwardness paralyzed my throat.

"You were saying...."

"I was saying...I would like to say...Forgive me, madam, I interrupted you."

"Oh, really?"

A long silence. She must be thinking something which in my idiom would no doubt be summed up by the word "fool."

"If I may ask, madam," I ventured at last, "how did you arrive at these opinions?"

"It is quite simple. My father was a sensible man. From early childhood I was surrounded by replicas of classical sculptures. At the age of ten I read *Gil Blas*, at twelve, *The Maid of Orleans*. Where other children had Tom Thumb, Bluebeard or Cinderella as friends, mine were Venus, Apollo, Hercules and Laocoön. My

husband was of a happy disposition, and even the incurable illness that struck him shortly after our marriage did not more than
cast a brief shadow over his natural gaiety. The night before his
death he took me into his bed, and often, during the long months
when he lay dying in his wheelchair, he would say to me playfully: "Well now, have you taken a lover yet?" I used to blush with
shame. "Do not hide anything from me," he said. "Although the
thought pains me, I know that you must find yourself a congenial husband, or even several. You are a good wife, but you are still
a child and you need playthings." Needless to say that as long as
he lived I had no lovers, but it was he who helped me to find my
true self, the Grecian woman."

"The goddess," I interrupted.

She smiled. "Which goddess?"

"Venus."

She frowned and threatened me with her finger. "Perhaps even
Venus in Furs. Wait, I have a very large fur that would cover you
from head to foot — I shall catch you in it like a fish in a net."

"Do you believe," I said with feeling (for an idea had just
occurred to me, quite an inept and commonplace idea which at
the time seemed remarkably profound), "do you believe that your
theories could be put into practice in our present century? Do
you think Venus could display with impunity her joyous, naked
charms in the world of today?"

"Not naked, of course, but dressed in furs, yes," she laughed.
"Would you care to see her?"

"But what then?"

"How do you mean, what then?"

"Beautiful, carefree creatures such as the ancient Greeks can
only exist if there are slaves to carry out the prosaic tasks of life."

"True," she replied mischievously, "an Olympian goddess such
as I must have a whole army of slaves. Beware of me!"

"Why?"

I was frightened at the boldness of my "why," but she did not appear in the least perturbed. Her lips curled up slightly to reveal her small white teeth and she asked lightly, as though it were of no consequence:

"Do you want to be my slave?"

"In matters of love there is no equality," I answered solemnly. "If I were faced with the choice of dominating or being dominated, I would choose the latter. It would be far more satisfying to be the slave of a beautiful woman. But I should hate her to be a petty, nagging tyrant — where should I find a woman to dominate me in a serene and fully conscious manner?"

"Come now, that should not be so difficult?"

"You think not?"

"I, for example." She laughed and arched her back proudly. "I have a certain talent for playing despotic roles.... I also have the indispensable furs.... You were seriously afraid last night, were you not?"

"I was."

"And now?"

"Now I am beginning to be truly terrified of you."

\*     \*     \*

We now see a great deal of each other, I and...Venus: we breakfast under my arbor and take tea in her sitting room. I have the opportunity of revealing my pusillanimous talents: why become versed in science and the arts if not to impress a lovely little woman? But she is not really such a "little woman" — in fact she intimidates me dreadfully.

Today I made a portrait of her and became aware for the first time how inappropriate is modern clothing to her cameolike beauty. There is little of the Roman in her features but much of the Greek. At times I should like to paint her as Psyche, or again as Astarte, as her expression changes from gaiety to languor, ardor to voluptuous weariness; but she would like me to make a straightforward portrait.

Let us see: I shall put her in furs. How could I have hesitated; surely nothing could suit her better than regal fur!

*　　*　　*

I was sitting with her yesterday, reading aloud from the *Roman Elegies*. I laid the book aside and we conversed a little. She seemed enchanted and listened raptly to my every word, her bosom heaving. Or was I mistaken?

The rain beat mournfully on the windowpane and the fire crackled in the hearth as in midwinter. I felt so much at ease with her that for a moment I forget my fear at being in the presence of such a beautiful woman. I kissed her hand and she did not resist me.

Then I seated myself at her feet and read a short poem I had written for her:

### VENUS IN FURS
Rest your foot upon your slave,
Lady of fables, tender demon,
Your marble body reclining
Among the myrtles and the aloes.

And so on. This time I had indeed gone beyond the first verse, but in obedience to her wishes I gave her the poem, retaining no copy. Now that I would like to transcribe it into my diary, I am only able to remember this particular verse.

I am experiencing strange emotions. I do not think I am in love with Wanda, at least I did not feel when we first met an overwhelming surge of passion. I am aware, however, that her truly divine beauty is working a magical spell on me. It is not a sentimental inclination but a physical surrender that is coming over me gradually and inexorably.

Each day I suffer more, but she does nothing but smile.

\*    \*    \*

Today she said to me suddenly, without provocation: "You interest me. Most men are so common, so lacking in verve and poetry; but there is a depth in you, an enthusiasm and above all a serious-mindedness that warm my heart. I could become attached to you."

\*    \*    \*

After a brief and violent rainstorm we went to pay a visit to the statue of Venus. All around us the earth was steaming; clouds of mist rose like the smoke of sacrificial offerings and the fragments of a rainbow still hovered in the sky. The sparrows had reappeared in the dripping trees and were twittering and hopping from branch to branch in secret delight. The countryside was drenched with fresh odors. We could not cross the meadow, which was still under water, and we stood watching the reflection of the statue on its shimmering surface. A halo of gnats danced around the goddess' head.

Wanda was enchanted by the scene, and since we could not sit on the damp benches, she gently leant on my arm to rest. A sweet weariness had overcome her, her eyes were half closed and I felt the caress of her breath on my cheek.

How I managed to pluck up the courage I do not know, but I took her hand in mine and asked: "Could you love me?"

"Why not?" she replied, giving me a glance that was both serene and playful. I promptly knelt before her and buried my feverish face in the perfumed muslin of her gown.

"Severin, this is indecent," she protested.

But I took hold of her little foot and pressed my lips to it.

"You are taking more and more liberties," she exclaimed. She disengaged herself and fled toward the house, leaving her adorable slipper in my hands.

Is this an omen?

*   *   *

I dared not approach her for the rest of the day, but toward evening, as I was sitting under my arbor, her charming red head peeped through the green foliage of the balcony. "Why do you not come up?" she called impatiently.

I ran up the stairs, but on reaching the top I felt my courage leave me and gave a timid knock on the door. She did not tell me to come in but came to open the door herself and stood on the threshold.

"Where is my slipper?"

"It is...I have...I want to..." I stammered.

"Go and fetch it and we shall take tea together and chat."

When I returned she was busy making tea. I ceremoniously placed the slipper on the table and stood in a corner like a child waiting to be punished.

I noticed that she was frowning slightly and her mouth wore a severe and domineering expression that enchanted me. Suddenly she burst out laughing.

"So you are really in love with me?"

"Yes, and it is making me suffer more than you can imagine."

"You are suffering?" She laughed again.

I was ashamed and mortified, but apparently without reason, for she then said: "Why? I am good to you — I am very fond of you." She held out her hand and gave me the friendliest smile.

166

"Would you like to be my wife?"

Wanda looked at me — how can I describe that look? Slightly surprised and then a trifle mocking.

"How is it that you have suddenly become so bold?" she asked.

"Bold?"

"Yes, bold enough to ask someone to marry you, and me in particular." She pointed to the slipper. "Have you already made a friend? But joking aside, do you really want to marry me?"

"I do."

"Severin, this is a serious matter. I believe you are fond of me, and I of you; better still, we find each other interesting and there is no risk of our being bored together. However, as you know, I am a frivolous woman, which is why I take marriage very seriously; if I undertake something I want to be sure of carrying it out, and I am afraid. . . . No, this will wound you."

"I beg of you, be frank with me."

"Well then, frankly speaking, I do not think I could love a man longer than. . . ." She leaned her head gracefully to one side and mused.

"A year?"

"Good heavens, no! A month perhaps."

"Even me?"

"Yes, even you. Or perhaps in your case, two months."

"Two months!"

"Two months is too long."

"Madam, this is outdoing the ancient Greeks."

"You see, you cannot bear the truth."

Wanda rose and walked across the room; she leant her arm on the mantelpiece and looked at me thoughtfully.

"What shall I do with you?" she asked.

"Do what you will," I replied with resignation, "whatever you please."

"What inconsistency! First you want me to be your wife, then you offer yourself to me as a plaything."

"Wanda, I love you."

"We are back where we began. You love me and want me to be your wife, and I do not want to remarry because I have no belief in the permanence of either your feelings or mine."

"But if I am willing to take the risk of committing myself to you?"

"Your proposal demands that I, too, should commit myself," she replied calmly. "I can indeed imagine belonging to one man for life, but he would have to be a real man who commands my respect and enslaves me by his innate power. Do you understand? And I know from experience that as soon as a man falls in love he becomes weak, pliable and ridiculous; he surrenders to the woman and goes down on his knees to her. And I could only love a man before whom I myself should have to kneel. However, I have become so fond of you that I am willing to give you a trial."

I threw myself at her feet.

"My goodness, you are already on your knees! A promising beginning." When I had risen, she continued: "I shall give you a year to win my love, to convince me that we are suited to each other and that we might live together. If you succeed, I am your wife – a wife, Severin, who will perform her duties faithfully. During this year we shall live as man and wife."

The blood rushed to my head and her cheeks, too, were set ablaze.

"We shall live together in the daytime," she pursued, "and share all our habits so that we may find out whether we are really suited to each other. I shall grant you all the rights of a husband, a lover and a friend. Are you satisfied?"

"I have no choice."

"You are not forced to accept."

"So be it."

"Splendid! Now you are talking like a man. Here is my hand."

* * *

For ten days I have not left her side for a single hour, except at night. I am allowed to gaze into her eyes continuously, to accompany her everywhere. My love is like a bottomless abyss into which I seem to be sinking deeper and deeper and from which nothing can save me now.

This afternoon we were seated at the foot of the statue of Venus; I was picking flowers and tossing them into her lap, while she wove them into floral chains with which to adorn our goddess. Suddenly Wanda looked at me so strangely that my senses ran wild and passion enveloped me like a net of flames. I abandoned all restraint, threw my arms around her and kissed her lips, while she pressed me against her heaving breast.

"Are you angry?" I asked.

"I am never angry about things that are natural," she replied, "but I am afraid that you are suffering."

"Oh, I am suffering dreadfully."

"My poor friend!" She smoothed the tangled hair from my forehead. "I hope it is not my fault."

"No," I replied, "but my love for you has become a kind of madness. The thought that I could lose you, that I may well lose you one day, is a constant torture."

"But you do not even possess me," said Wanda, with the same vibrant look, both dewy-eyed and consuming, that had produced such a turmoil within me. She rose and with her small transparent hands placed a crown of blue anemones on the white stone curls of the statue. I could scarcely resist putting my arm around her waist.

"I can no longer live without you, O beautiful woman. Only believe me, these are not just fine words, this is no mere fancy; I feel in the depths of my soul that my life is bound up with yours; if you leave me, I shall be lost. I shall perish utterly."

"But that will not be necessary, since I love you." She took me by the chin: "You simpleton."

"But you will only be mine under conditions, while I belong to you unconditionally."

"Severin, this is all wrong," she said, in an almost frightened voice, "do you not know me yet, do you absolutely refuse to know me? I am kind when people behave reasonably, but if they are totally submissive to me then I become tyrannical."

"So be it! Be a tyrant, be a despot," I cried with exaltation, "but be mine, mine forever!" I prostrated myself before her and threw my arms around her knees.

"This will end badly, my friend," she said severely and without the least emotion.

"Oh, it must never end!" I cried, beside myself. "Only death shall part us. If you cannot be mine entirely and forever then I want to be your slave, I want to suffer anything to be able to stay by your side."

"Calm yourself," she said, bending down to kiss my forehead. "I am kind to you but you are not taking the right road to win me and keep me."

"I will do anything, anything you wish, only never leave me!"

"Get up!"

I obeyed.

"You are a peculiar man," said Wanda. "So you want to possess me at all costs?"

"Yes, at all costs."

"But what would be the value of possessing me if, for example..." she thought for a moment and eyed me in a disquieting manner, "if I did not love you anymore, if I belonged to another man?"

This was too much for me. I looked at her as she sat before me, confident and controlled; her eyes had an icy brilliance.

"You see," she went on, "the thought terrifies you." A gentle smile lit up her face.

"It is true, I am horrified to think that the woman I love, the woman who has accepted my love, could ever give herself to another without any thought for me. But would I still be free to choose? If I love this woman, if I love her to distraction, should I turn my back on her and perish for the sake of my pride – should I put a bullet through my head? There are two kinds of woman that I can love. If I cannot find a noble and spirited woman willing to share my destiny in complete faithfulness, then give me no half-measures, no lukewarm compromises. I prefer to be at the mercy of a woman without virtue, fidelity or pity, for she is also my ideal, in her magnificent selfishness. If I cannot enjoy to the full love's perfect bliss, then let me empty to the dregs its cup of bitterness and woe, let me be ill-treated by the woman I love, and the more cruelly the better. For this is also a form of pleasure."

"Are you aware of what you are saying?" exclaimed Wanda.

"I love you with all my soul," I continued, "with all my senses. You are necessary to my very existence, you and all that emanates from you. You must choose: make of me what you will, your husband or your slave."

"Very well," said Wanda tersely, knitting her arched eyebrows, "it will be most amusing to have complete power over a man who interests me and who loves me. At least I am sure to be entertained. You are rash enough to leave the choice to me, so I am choosing: I want you to be my slave; I shall treat you like a plaything."

"Oh, do!" I cried, with a mixture of fear and rapture. "Marriage can only be founded on equality and mutual understanding, but great passions are born from the meeting of opposites. It is because we are opposites – indeed almost enemies – that my love for you is part hatred, part fear. But in such relations one person must be the hammer, the other, the anvil. I choose to be the anvil: I cannot be happy if I must look down on the woman I love. I want to be able to worship a woman, and I can only do so if she is cruel to me."

"But, Severin," replied Wanda almost angrily, "do you believe me capable of maltreating a man who loves me as you do, and whom I love?"

"Why not, if I adore you all the more for it? I am only truly able to love a woman who dominates me, who overpowers me with her beauty, her temperament, her intelligence and her will-power, a woman who rules over me."

"Then you are attracted by what others find repulsive?"

"That is right. It is my peculiar nature."

"Come now, there is really nothing so peculiar nor remarkable about your passion. Who does not find beautiful furs irresistible? We all know, we all sense how closely related are sensual pleasure and cruelty."

"But in my case these things are taken to extremes."

"You mean that reason has little power over you and that you are weak and sensuous by nature?"

"Were the martyrs also weak and sensuous?"

"The martyrs?"

"Precisely, the martyrs were supersensual beings who found positive pleasure in pain and who sought horrible tortures, even death, as others seek enjoyment. I too am supersensual, madam, just as they were."

"Take care that you do not also become a martyr to love, the martyr of a woman."

\*   \*   \*

We were seated on Wanda's balcony; the night was warm and filled with the perfumes of summer; a twofold roof sheltered us, first the green ceiling of climbing plants, then the vault of heaven strewn with innumerable stars. The low, plaintive call of a love-sick cat floated in from the park, while I sat at the feet of my goddess, telling her about my childhood.

"Were these tendencies already marked in you in those days?" asked Wanda.

"Certainly. I cannot remember a period when I was not subject to them. Already in my cradle, as my mother later recounted, I was a supersensualist: I spurned the breast of my sturdy nurse and had to be fed on goat's milk. As a little boy I was inexplicably shy with women, which merely went to show that they affected me profoundly. I was oppressed by the high vaults and shadowy interior of churches, and was seized with anxiety before the glittering altars and the holy images. At times I would steal into my father's library, as if to enjoy a forbidden pleasure, and would gaze upon a plaster statue of Venus. I would kneel before her and recite the prayers I had been taught, the Lord's Prayer, the Hail Mary and the Creed.

"One night I left my bed to pay her a visit; the light from the crescent moon fell upon me and bathed the goddess in a cold blue light. I prostrated myself before her and kissed her feet in the way I had seen my fellow countrymen kiss the feet of the dead Savior. An insuperable desire took hold of me; I stood up, threw my arms around her beautiful body and kissed her ice-cold lips. A deep shudder went through me. Later in a dream the goddess appeared to me, standing by my bed and raising her arm in a threatening gesture.

"I was sent to school at an early age and soon graduated to the gymnasium. I greedily seized upon all that the world of antiquity could offer me, and I soon became more familiar with the

173

gods of Greece than with the religion of Jesus. With Paris I gave Venus the fateful apple, I saw Troy burn and I followed Ulysses on his adventures. The archetypes of all that is beautiful deeply penetrated my consciousness, and consequently at an age when other boys are rude and uncouth, I showed extreme disgust for everything base, common and ugly. When I first began to think about love, it seemed to my raw adolescent's eyes particularly crude and vulgar; I avoided all contact with the fair sex, while being supersensual in the extreme.

"When I was about fourteen my mother engaged a charming chambermaid, young and pretty, with a well-rounded figure. One day as I was studying Tacitus and going into raptures over the virtues of the Germanic tribes, she came to sweep my room. Suddenly she stopped, bent over me with her broom in her hand, and her delicious lips gently touched mine. The kiss of this amorous kitten sent a shiver down my spine, but I raised my *Germania* to shield me against the temptress and left the room in indignation."

Wanda broke into a peal of delighted laughter: "You really are an exceptional man. But do go on."

"There is another event from the same period which I shall never forget. A distant aunt of mine, Countess Sobol, came to stay with my parents. She was a beautiful, stately woman with a charming smile, but I hated her because of her reputation in the family of being a Messalina, and I was as rude, nasty and loutish with her as I could be. One day when my parents had gone to town, my aunt decided to take advantage of their absence to administer justice to me. Wearing her kazabaika, her fur-lined jacket, she burst into my room, followed by the cook, the kitchen-maid and the little kitten whom I had spurned. Without asking any questions, they seized me and in spite of my resistance, bound me hand and foot. Then with a wicked smile my aunt rolled up her sleeve and began to beat me with a long switch. She laid about me so hard that she drew blood, and although I tried to be heroic I screamed and wept and finally begged for mercy. She had me unbound but I then had to go down on my knees to her, thank her for the punishment and kiss her hand.

"What a supersensual lunatic I was! My taste for women was awakened by the blows of a beautiful and voluptuous creature in a fur jacket who looked like an angry queen. From that day on my aunt became the most desirable woman on God's earth.

"My Cato-like austerity and my shyness in the presence of women were nothing more than an excessively developed aestheticism. Sensuality became my own personal cult, and I swore never to squander its sacred treasures on any ordinary being, but to reserve them for the ideal woman, if possible for the goddess of Love herself.

"I was very young when I went to the university in the capital, which was where my aunt lived. In those days my room looked like that of Doctor Faustus: everything was thrown together in wild disorder, large closets stuffed with books which I bought secondhand from a Jew in Servanica, globes, atlases, phials, astronomical charts, animal skeletons, skulls and busts of famous men. At any moment Mephistopheles might have appeared behind my large green stove in the guise of a wandering scholar. I studied indiscriminately, without system or selection: chemistry, alchemy, history, astronomy, philosophy, jurisprudence, anatomy and literature. I read Homer, Virgil, Ossian, Schiller, Goethe, Shakespeare, Cervantes, Molière, the Koran, the Cosmos and the Memoirs of Casanova. As this chaos grew from day to day, so did my unbridled imagination and my supersensuality. I always carried the image of the ideal woman in my mind; sometimes she appeared on a bed of roses surrounded by Cupids, in a decor of skulls and leather-bound books; sometimes she loomed in Olympian garb, with the severe white face of the plaster Venus, and at other times I saw her with the thick tresses of brown hair, the laughing blue eyes and the kazabaika trimmed with ermine that were my pretty aunt's.

"One morning when her smiling beauty had once again emerged from the golden mists of my imagination, I set out to see Countess Sobol. My aunt received me in an agreeable and even cordial manner, giving me a kiss that threw my senses into a turmoil. She was approaching forty, but like most of the famous courtesans on whom time leaves no trace, she was still extremely desirable. She was wearing a kazabaika, but this time it was a green velvet one trimmed with mink. There was no longer any trace in her of the severity that had delighted me in the past. Far from treating me cruelly, she allowed me quite naturally to give her proof of my adoration.

"She found out all too soon what a supersensual, innocent fool I was, and it amused her to make me happy. Indeed I was as ecstatic as a young god. What delight to kneel before her and be allowed to kiss the hand that had once chastised me! What marvelous hands they were, so well shaped, so white and adorably plump! To tell the truth, I believe it was only those hands I was in love with. I played with them, hid them under the dark fur, held them in the light of the fire and could not have my fill of gazing at them."

I noticed Wanda involuntarily glancing at her own hands and could not help smiling.

"You may form an idea of the heights reached in those days by my supersensuality by the fact that I was in love solely with the fierce beating I had received from my aunt and, two years later, when I courted a young actress, with the roles she played onstage. I then fell in love with a most respectable woman who pretended to an inaccessible virtue, but who finally betrayed me with a rich Jew. You see, because I was sold and betrayed by a woman who affected the strictest principles and the most refined sensibility, I developed a hatred for poetic and sentimental virtue. Give me a woman honest enough to say: 'I am a La Pompadour, a Lucretia Borgia' – she is the woman I will worship."

Wanda rose and opened the window. "You have an extraordinary way of arousing one's imagination," she said. "My nerves are all on edge and my pulse is throbbing. If all you say is true, then you are giving vice a halo; your ideal is a brazen and inspired courtesan. Ah, you are the sort of man who will utterly corrupt a woman."

*   *   *

In the middle of the night I heard a tap on my window; I rose to open it and was struck with horror at the vision before me: it was Venus in Furs, as she had first appeared to me.

"Your stories have disturbed me so much that I have not been able to sleep a wink. Come and keep me company for a while."

"I shall be with you immediately."

When I entered her room, Wanda was huddled in front of the fireplace, where she had kindled a small fire.

"Autumn is drawing on," she began, "the nights are already chilly. I hope you will not mind, but I cannot take off my furs until the room is a little warmer."

"Not mind! Naughty lady, you know very well...."

I slipped my arm around her and kissed her.

"Of course, I know," she said, "but how did you acquire this fondness for furs?"

"I was born with it," I replied. "I already showed signs of it as a child. In any case it is a natural law that fur has a stimulating effect on highly strung people. It exerts a strong and mysterious physical attraction to which no one is immune. Science has recently established that there is a relation between electricity and heat and that their effect on the human body is similar. Torrid climates make for passionate natures and warm atmospheres produce exaltation; the same is true of electricity. This is why cats have always had such a beneficial and magical effect on spiritual and impressionable people: the movement of their long, graceful tails, their magnetism, their fur crackling with electricity.... No wonder they were the favorite pets of men such as Mahomet, Richelieu, Crébillon, Rousseau and Wieland."

"Then a woman in furs is nothing more than a large cat," exclaimed Wanda, "a sort of highly charged electric battery?"

"That is right," I replied, "and that is how I interpret the symbolic significance of furs as the attribute of power and beauty. In ancient times monarchs and noblemen claimed furs as their exclusive right, and great painters used them to adorn their queenly beauties. Raphael could find no more exquisite frame for the divine figure of La Fornarina, nor Titian for the roselike body of his beloved."

"Thank you for the learned discourse on eroticism," said Wanda. "But you have not told me everything. Does not fur have a special significance for you personally?"

"Certainly," I said, "I have often told you that pain holds a peculiar attraction for me, and that nothing kindles my passion quite so much as tyranny, cruelty and above all unfaithfulness in a beautiful woman. I cannot imagine this woman without furs; she is a strange ideal born of the aesthetics of ugliness, with the soul of Nero in the body of Phryne."

"I understand," said Wanda, "it gives a woman a haughty and imposing quality."

"That is not all," I continued. "As you know, I am a supersensualist; with me everything takes root in the imagination and finds its nourishment there. As a sensitive and mature youngster of about ten, I came across the *Lives of the Martyrs*. I read with a horror mingled with intense pleasure how they suffered the worst torments almost with a smile, how they languished in prison cells, were tortured on the rack, pierced by arrows, cast into boiling pitch, thrown to wild animals or nailed on the cross. To endure horrible tortures seemed from then on the highest form of delight, particularly if the torturer was a beautiful woman, for to my mind the poetic and the diabolical have always been united in woman. I turned this idea into a veritable religion. Sensuality took on a sacred quality, indeed it seemed the only sacred principle, and woman in her beauty became something divine, since she was called upon to perform the most important function in life, the continuation of the species. Woman seemed to be the personification of Nature, she was Isis, and man was her priest and slave; she treated him cruelly just as Nature casts aside whatever has served her purpose as soon as she has no more need of it. As for man, it seemed to me that to be abused by woman and even to die at her hand could only be pure bliss to him. I envied King Gunther who was fettered by the mighty Brunehilde on their wedding night; I envied the poor troubadour whose capricious mistress sewed him into a wolf's skin and hunted him like game; I envied the knight Ctivad trapped in the steppes of Prague by the fearless Amazon Scharka, who took him to her Divine Castle and after she had played with him for a while had him broken on the wheel."

"How abominable!" cried Wanda. "I would like you to fall into the hands of such a savage woman. When you were sewn in the wolf's skin, mauled by the hounds or stretched on the rack, poetry would quickly lose its charm."

"Do you think so? I doubt it."

"You are not in your right mind."

"That is quite possible; but let me continue.

"I went on avidly reading tales of the most fearful cruelty; I gazed with particular relish at paintings and engravings depicting such practices, and I noticed that in every scene furs were the attribute of the torturer. The most bloodthirsty tyrants that ever sat upon a throne, and murderous inquisitors who had heretics persecuted and burned, and all the women whom the great book of history has placed under the sign of beauty, lust and violence: Libussa, Lucretia Borgia, Agnes of Hungary, Queen Margot, Isabeau, the Sultana Roxelana and the Russian Tsarinas of the last century, all wore fur garments and ermine robes."

"So furs now arouse strange fantasies in you?" said Wanda coquettishly, twining the magnificent sable scarf about her so that the dark, shining fur played delightfully around her bust and arms. "Come now, how do you feel at this moment, half on the rack?"

Her piercing green eyes looked at me with a strange expression of mocking satisfaction. Overcome by passion I threw myself at her feet and put my arms around her.

"Yes, you have brought my dearest fantasies to life," I exclaimed. "They have lain dormant too long."

"And what are they?" She put her hand on the nape of my neck.

A sweet dizziness came over me on feeling the warmth of her little hand, and on meeting the tender, searching gaze that she let fall on me through half-closed eyes.

"To be the slave of a woman, a beautiful woman whom I love and worship."

"And who in return ill-treats you!" laughed Wanda.

"Yes, who fetters me, whips me and kicks me and who all the while belongs to another."

"And who has the impudence, after driving you mad with jealousy, to confront you with your happy rival, to hand you over to his brutality. Why not? Or does the final picture appeal to you less?"

I looked at Wanda in horror. "You exceed my wildest dreams."

"Ah, we women have fertile imaginations," she said. "Beware, if you do find your ideal you may well be treated more cruelly than you anticipated."

"I am afraid I have found my ideal," I cried, pressing my burning face against her knees.

"But not in me?" asked Wanda. She threw off her furs and began to dance around the room laughing; I could still hear her as I went downstairs, and as I emerged, thoughtful, into the courtyard below, her impish laughter floated down to me.

\*   \*   \*

"Am I to incarnate your ideal?" asked Wanda, with a mischievous air when we met in the park today.

At first I could find no answer. The most contradictory feelings battled within me. She sat down on one of the stone benches and began to play with a flower.

"Well then, shall I?"

I knelt before her and took her hands.

"I beg of you once more, be my wife, my faithful and honest wife, but if you cannot, then be my ideal, entirely and without reservations."

"You know that I will give you my hand in a year's time if you turn out to be the man for me," replied Wanda seriously, "but I do believe you would be grateful if I were to realize your fantasies. Come now, which would you prefer?"

"I believe that everything I have imagined is already present in your nature."

"You are under an illusion."

"I believe," I continued, "that you are quite delighted to have a man entirely in your power and that you would enjoy tormenting him."

"No, no!" she cried. "And yet...." She looked thoughtful. "I do not understand myself any longer, but I have a confession to make. You have so corrupted my imagination and inflamed my blood that I am beginning to find all this enjoyable. The enthusiasm with which you speak of such women as La Pompadour, Catherine II and all these selfish, cruel and frivolous creatures thrills me to the depths of my soul. I am prompted to become like these women who, in spite of their wicked ways, were slavishly worshiped all their lives and even after death. You are turning me into a miniature despot, a household Pompadour."

"Well, then," I said feverishly, "if it is in you, follow your natural bent. But no half-measures; if you cannot be a true and loyal wife, then be a demon!"

Excitement and lack of sleep and the proximity of such a beautiful woman had reduced me to a feverish state. I cannot remember what I said, but I know that I kissed her feet and lifted one of them to place it on my neck. She quickly withdrew it and rose almost angrily.

"If you love me, Severin," she said sternly, "never speak of this again, do you hear, never again, or I might really. . . ." She smiled and sat down again.

"I am perfectly serious," I replied. "I adore you to such a degree that I am prepared to put up with anything for the sake of spending my life by your side."

"Severin, again I am warning you."

"Your warnings are in vain. You may do as you will with me, only never send me away."

"Severin," said Wanda, "I am a young and frivolous woman. It is dangerous for you to surrender so totally to me, you will end up by becoming my plaything. Who will protect you then? I might take unfair advantage of your folly."

"You are too noble to dream of that."

"Power makes one presumptuous."

"Then be presumptuous!" I cried. "Trample on me!"

Wanda clasped her hands behind my neck and gazed into my eyes.

"I am afraid of not being capable of it, but for you I am willing to try, for I love you, Severin, as I have loved no other man."

\*     \*     \*

Today she suddenly put on her hat and shawl and ordered me to come shopping with her. She asked to see some whips, long ones with short handles such as are used on hounds.

"These should be suitable," said the shopkeeper.

"No, they are much too small," she said, giving me a sidelong glance. "I need a big one."

"For a bulldog, I suppose?" said the shopkeeper.

"Yes," she cried, "like those they use in Russia on disobedient slaves."

After some searching she finally chose a whip the very sight of which made me shiver.

"Now good-bye, Severin," she said, "there are a few other things that I want to buy alone."

I took leave of her and went for a walk. On my return I caught sight of Wanda coming out of a furriers. She beckoned to me.

"You ought to think again," she said gleefully. "I have never hidden the fact that I am fascinated by your combination of sensuality and earnestness. I am thrilled at the idea that the most serious-minded man in the world could be entirely devoted to my person, and actually lying at my feet in ecstasy. But will my excitement last? A woman can begin by loving a man, then she treats him like a slave and finally she kicks him away."

"Very well then, kick me away when you have had enough of me. I want to be your slave."

"I am aware of dangerous forces lurking within me," said Wanda, after we had gone a few steps. "You are awakening them, and it will do you no good. You paint such an attractive picture of pleasure-seeking, cruelty and arrogance — what would you say if I were to try my hand at them and make you my first victim? Remember the story of the tyrant Dionysius and the man who invented the torture of the bronze ox. To try out this new method of torture, Dionysius had the inventor shut up inside it and roasted alive to see whether his moans really imitated the lowing of an ox. Perhaps I am a female Dionysius?"

"Be one!" I cried. "All my dreams would be fulfilled. I belong to you for better or for worse, you must make the choice. I am driven by the destiny that has taken hold of me, a diabolical and all-powerful fate."

★   ★   ★

"My beloved,

I do not wish to see you today or tomorrow, only the evening of the day after, and then as my slave.

Your mistress,
WANDA"

"As my slave" was underlined. I read the note, which I had received early in the morning, a second time. I then saddled a little donkey and took to the mountains, to find relief from my yearning in the beauty of the Carpathian scenery.

I returned tired, hungry and above all in love. I quickly changed my clothes and knocked at her door.

"Come in."

I enter; she is standing in the middle of the room, wearing a gown of white satin that ripples over her body like liquid light, a red velvet kazabaika edged with rich ermine; a small diamond tiara rests on her powdered hair. She stands with her arms folded, a frown on her face.

184

"Wanda!" I run to put my arms around her and kiss her, but she retreats a step and eyes me from head to foot.

"Slave!"

"Mistress!" I kneel and kiss the hem of her gown.

"That is better."

"Oh, how beautiful you are!"

"Do I please you?" She postures in front of the mirror and looks at herself with proud satisfaction.

"You drive me to distraction!"

She gives a slight pout of contempt and looks at me with narrowed, mocking eyes.

"Give me the whip."

I look about the room.

"No," she cries, "stay on your knees." She goes over to the mantelpiece, takes the whip off the ledge and, watching me with a smile, makes it whistle through the air; then she slowly rolls up the sleeves of her fur jacket.

"Wonderful woman!" – the words escape from my mouth.

"Quiet, slave!" She scowls and suddenly strikes me with the whip. The next moment she bends over me with compassion and tenderly strokes the back of my neck.

"Did I hurt you?" she asks, torn between fear and shame.

"No," I reply, "and even if you had, the pain you cause is pure delight. Whip me if it gives you pleasure."

"But it does not give me pleasure."

Again the strange dizziness overcomes me.

"Whip me," I implore, "whip me without mercy!"

Wanda brandishes the whip and strikes twice.

"Have you had enough now?"

"No."

"Seriously not?"

"Whip me, I beg of you, it is a joy to me."

"Yes, because you know very well that I am not in earnest," she replies, "and that I have not the heart to do you harm. These barbaric games revolt me. If I were really the kind of woman who whips her slave you would be filled with horror."

"No, Wanda; I love you more than myself, I am utterly devoted to you. In all seriousness you may do whatever you wish with me, whatever your whims dictate."

"Severin!"

"Tread on me!" I cry, throwing myself before her.

"I dislike playacting," says Wanda impatiently.

"Then hurt me in earnest."

A disturbing silence.

"Severin, I am warning you one last time."

"If you love me, be cruel to me," I implore.

"If I love you?" repeats Wanda. "Very well!" She backs away and looks at me with a threatening smile. "Be my slave and know what it means to be at the mercy of a woman." Whereupon she gives me a kick.

"How do you like that?"

She brandishes the whip.

"Get up."

I begin to rise. "Not that way," she orders, "stay on your knees."

I obey and she proceeds to whip me.

The blows fall thick and fast on my back and arms. One of them cuts into my flesh and the burn lingers on, but the pain delights me, for it comes from her whom I adore and for whom at any moment I am ready to lay down my life.

She stops. "I am beginning to enjoy it," she says. "That is enough for today. But a diabolical curiosity has taken hold of me; I want to see how far your strength will go; I have a dreadful desire to see you tremble under my whip, to see you suffer, to hear at last your moans and screams, your cries for mercy, while I go on whipping you without pity, until you lose consciousness. Yes, you have awakened dangerous tendencies in me.... Now get up."

I seize her hand and press it to my lips.

"What impudence!" She shoves me away with her foot.

"Out of my sight, slave!"

\*   \*   \*

I wake after a feverish night troubled by nightmares. The dawn is just breaking.

Which of my confused memories are real? What have I experienced, what have I merely dreamed? I have been whipped, that much is certain; I can still feel each blow; I can count the burning weals on my body. And it was she who whipped me. Yes, now I know it all.

My dream has come true — what now? Has the realization of my fantasy liberated me? No, I am merely a little tired, and her cruelty fills me with rapture. Oh, how I love her, how I worship her! I cannot begin to express my feelings and the extent of my devotion to her. What bliss to be her slave!

\*   \*   \*

She calls me from her balcony. I race upstairs and find her standing on the doorstep holding out a friendly hand: "I am so ashamed," she says. I put my arms around her and she rests her head on my shoulder.

"Why?"

"Try to forget yesterday's horrible scene," she says, in a trembling voice. "For your sake I satisfied these mad wishes, now let us be reasonable. We shall be happy and love each other, and in a year's time I shall be your wife."

"My mistress," I cry, "and I your slave!"

"Not another word about slavery, cruelty or whips," interrupts

Wanda. "The only thing I shall still grant you is the fur jacket — come and help me into it."

\*     \*     \*

The little bronze clock surmounted by a Cupid informed us that it was midnight. I rose and prepared to leave. Wanda said nothing but embraced me, drew me back onto the ottoman and began to kiss me again. This silent language was so easy to understand and so persuasive.... It told me more than I dared interpret. A languid abandon came over her whole being. What voluptuous softness in her half-closed eyes, in her red hair shimmering under the white powder! The red and white satin rustled with each of her movements, and the ermine caressed her shoulders with a snakelike movement.

"I beg of you..." I stammered, "but you will be angry...."

"Do with me what you will," she whispered, "I belong to you."

"Then trample me underfoot, I implore you or I shall go mad."

"Have I not forbidden you...." said Wanda. "You are incorrigible."

"Alas, I am dreadfully in love." I fell on my knees and hid my burning face in her lap.

"I really believe," said Wanda thoughtfully, "that your madness is nothing but an unsatisfied, diabolical sensuality. Such afflictions are a product of our monstrous side — if you were less virtuous you would be perfectly sane."

"Then make me sane," I murmured. My hands ran wild over her hair and over the gleaming fur that rose and fell with her breast like a moonlit ocean, and threw my senses into confusion.

I kissed her; no, she kissed me — wildly, passionately, as though she wanted to devour me. I was almost delirious, and had long since lost my reason; panting, I tried to free myself from her arms.

"What is wrong?" asked Wanda.

"I am suffering horribly."

"You are suffering?" she broke into playful laughter.

"You may well laugh," I moaned. "Have you no notion...."

Suddenly she became serious again, took my head in her hands and pressed me to her breast.

"Wanda!" I stammered.

"You really do enjoy suffering," she said, and laughed again. "But wait, I shall bring you to your senses."

"I shall no longer ask you whether you want to belong to me forever or only for a brief instant," I cried. "I want to enjoy my happiness to the full. You are mine at this moment and I prefer to lose you than never to possess you."

"Now you are being unreasonable," she said, kissing me again with those fiendish lips. I tore off the ermine jacket and the lace and felt her naked bosom heaving against mine.

Then I lost consciousness.

The first thing I remember is when I saw blood dripping from my hand, and asked her in a flat voice: "Did you scratch me?"

"No, I believe I bit you."

* * *

It is strange how a love affair changes face as soon as a new character appears on the scene.

We spent many wonderful days together; we walked in the mountains and by the lakes, we read together, and all the while I completed my portrait of Wanda. How we loved one another! Her lovely face shone with happiness. Then one day a friend of hers arrives, a divorced woman, a little older, a little more experienced and less scrupulous than Wanda; she is already making her influence felt in many matters.

Wanda frowns often and shows a certain impatience with me. Does she no longer love me?

\*     \*     \*

This unbearable constraint has now lasted two weeks. The friend lives with Wanda and we can never be alone; furthermore, the two ladies are surrounded by an admiring circle of gentlemen. With my intensity and passion I cut a ridiculous figure as Wanda's lover – she treats me like a stranger.

Today while we were out walking she fell behind the others and waited for me to catch up with her; realizing that she had done this on purpose I was overjoyed. However, this is what she said:

"My friend does not understand how I can love you. She finds you neither handsome nor particularly attractive. She regales me from morning till night with tales of the brilliant and frivolous life to be led in the capital, the ambitions I might achieve, the advantages I would enjoy and the distinguished suitors I would attract. But what do I care for all that, since it is you I love?"

Her words took my breath away for a moment.

"In God's name, Wanda, do not let me stand in the way of your happiness. Do not be concerned about me." So saying, I raised my hat to her and let her walk ahead, which she did with a surprised look but without saying a word.

On the way back, when I found myself accidentally by her side, she squeezed my hand furtively and gave me a glance that was so warm and radiant that all the torments of the last few days were forgotten and all my wounds were healed. Now I know just how much I love her.

\*     \*     \*

"My friend has been complaining about you," said Wanda today. "She must have sensed that I despise her."

"But why do you despise her, you foolish man?" exclaimed Wanda, taking me by the ears.

"Because she is a hypocrite," I said. "I have time only for a woman who is truly virtuous, or who openly leads a life of pleasure."

"As I do," replied Wanda playfully. "But you see, my child, women can only live up to these ideals in special cases; they can be neither as purely sensual nor as spiritually free as men; their love is always a mixture of the sensual and the intellectual. Woman's heart desires to enchain man permanently while she herself is subject to change, with the result that discord, lying and deceitfulness invade her life, usually against her will, and her whole character is affected."

"That is certainly true," I said. "The transcendental quality that woman seeks to confer on love leads her into deception."

"But that is the way the world goes," Wanda interrupted. "Take this woman: she has a lover in Lwow and she has found a new admirer here; she deceives them both and yet she is worshiped by all and highly respected in society."

"That may well be so," I exclaimed, "but let her leave you out of it. She treats you like a vulgar object."

"Is there any harm in that?" asked Wanda. "Every woman has the instinct and the ability to make the most of her charms. It is an excellent thing to give oneself without love or pleasure: by keeping one's self-control one reaps all the advantages of the situation."

"Wanda, what are you saying?"

"Why not? Mark these words: never be sure of the woman you love, for there are more snares in her nature than you can ever imagine. Women are neither as good as their admirers maintain nor as bad as their detractors would have them be; their character is merely a lack of character. The best of women can momentarily flounder in the mud, just as the worst can unexpectedly rise to great heights of generosity, to the confusion of those who vilify her. Every woman, good or bad, is capable at any moment of the most diabolical thoughts, actions or emotions, as well as the most divine; the purest as well as the most sordid. In spite of all the advances of civilization, woman has remained as she was the day Nature's hands shaped her. She is like a wild animal, faithful or faithless, kindly or cruel, depending on the impulse that rules her. A profound and serious culture is needed to produce moral character. Man, even when he is selfish or wicked, lives by principles; woman only obeys her feelings. Never forget this, and never be sure of the woman you love."

\* \* \*

The friend has left; at last an evening alone with her. Wanda is so gracious, so tender, that one might think she had saved for this happy evening all the love she has denied me these last few days. What bliss to feel her lips so constantly close to mine, to swoon in her arms, and then, as she lies against my breast relaxed and totally mine, to melt into each other's pleasure-drunk eyes. I cannot yet understand that this woman is mine, totally mine.

"And yet she is right on one point," began Wanda, without moving nor even opening her eyes, as if she were asleep.

"Is she?"

She remained silent.

"Your friend?"

She nodded. "Yes, she is right, you are not a man, you are a romantic spirit, a charming suitor, and you would certainly make a priceless slave, but I cannot imagine you in the role of a husband."

I started.

"What is the matter? Are you trembling?"

"I tremble at the thought that I may lose you for no good reason."

"Come now, are you any the less happy at this moment?" she asked. "Does the knowledge that I have belonged to others before you and that others after you will possess me — does that rob you of your enjoyment? Would your pleasure be less great if another man were to share it?"

"Wanda!"

"Listen," she went on, "this could well be a solution. You want to keep me forever; as for me, I am fond of you, and you suit me so well that I would like to live with you permanently if I might, in addition to you...."

"What a thought!" I cried. "You horrify me."

"Do you love me any the less?"

"On the contrary."

Wanda raised herself on her left arm. "To hold a man permanently I believe one must above all not be faithful to him. What honest wife has ever been adored as much as a hetaera?"

"Yes, it is quite true that a woman's infidelity affords a painful but exquisite pleasure."

"And what if I were to grant you that pleasure?" taunted Wanda.

"I should suffer abominably but I should only adore you the more. You would have to be entirely honest with me, however, and have the diabolical grandeur to admit: I shall love no one but you, but I shall bestow my favors on anyone I please."

Wanda shook her head. "Lying is contrary to my nature, but what man is brave enough to take the truth? If I were to say to you: 'This joyful sensuality, this paganism is my ideal,' would you have the strength to bear it?"

"Certainly, I am ready to endure anything in order not to lose you. I am aware how tenuous is my link with you."

"But, Severin...."

"Yes, it is the truth," I said, "and that is why...."

"That is why you would like...." She smiled mischievously. "Have I guessed?"

"To be your slave," I cried, "your docile and will-less possession, without ever being a burden on you. While you drink from the cup of life, while you lie in the lap of luxury and enjoy every happiness, I would like to serve you, to put on your shoes on bended knee."

"You may well be right after all," replied Wanda, "for it is only as a slave that you could endure my loving others. What is more, the carefree pleasures of the ancient world are unthinkable without slavery. Ah, it must make one feel like a god to see a man kneel trembling before one! I want to have slaves, Severin, do you hear?"

"Am I not your slave?"

"Listen to me," said Wanda excitedly, grasping my hand. "I want to be yours for as long as I love you."

"For a month?"

"Maybe even two."

"And then?"

"And then you will be my slave."

"What about you?"

"What a question! I am a goddess; sometimes I steal down from my Olympian heights and secretly visit you. But what is all this?" She gazed into the distance, her chin in her hands. "A golden dream that will never come true." She was overcome by a strange melancholy, a wistfulness that I had never seen in her before.

"And why should it not be feasible?" I began.

"Because slavery does not exist any longer."

"Then let us go to a country where it does, to the Orient or Turkey," I said eagerly.

"Would you really like to?" said Wanda, her eyes shining.

"In all seriousness, I would. I want your power over me to become law; then my life will rest in your hands and I shall have no protection whatsoever against you. Ah, what delight to depend entirely on your whims, to be constantly at your beck and call! And then — what bliss! — when the goddess shows clemency, the slave will have permission to kiss the lips on which his life and death depend." I knelt and leaned my burning forehead on her knees.

"Severin, you are feverish," said Wanda compassionately. "Do you really love me so much?" She pressed me to her bosom and covered me with kisses. Her voice was trembling as she asked: "Is it really your wish?"

"I swear by God and my honor that I shall be your slave, wherever and whenever you wish, as soon as you command," I cried, beside myself with emotion.

"And what if I should take you at your word?"

"Do so!"

"What an attractive idea! That a man who worships me and whom I love with all my soul should be dependent on my every whim, that he should be my possession, my slave, while I...." She gave me a strange look. "It will be your fault if I become utterly frivolous. I think you are almost afraid of me now...but I have your oath."

"And I shall keep it."

"I shall see to that," she retorted. "The idea appeals to me so much that I cannot let it remain a fantasy any longer. You must become my slave, and as for me, I shall try to be Venus in Furs."

*　　*　　*

I thought I understood her at last but now I see that I must begin all over again. With what disgust she greeted my theories

a while ago, and with what eagerness she now prepares their exe-
cution! She has drawn up a contract by which I am to commit
myself on my honor to be her slave for as long as she wishes. Her
arm around my neck, she reads me this incredible document,
punctuating each sentence with a kiss.

"But this contract only mentions *my* duties," I said teasingly.

"Naturally," she replied, with great seriousness, "you are no
longer my lover, and therefore I am relieved of all duties and obligations toward you; you must regard my favors as pure benevolence. You can no longer lay claim to any rights, and there are no
limits to my power over you. Consider that you are little better
now than a dog or an object; you are my thing, the toy that I can
break if it gives me a moment of pleasure. You are nothing, I am
everything; do you understand?" She began to laugh and kissed
me again. A shudder ran through me.

"Will you allow me to make a few conditions?" I began.

"Conditions?" She frowned. "Ah, you are afraid already; perhaps you even regret your decision; but it is too late, I have your
oath and your word of honor. However, you may speak."

"First of all I would like the two following points to be included in our contract: that you should never separate yourself
from me completely, and that you should never abandon me to
the mercy of any of your admirers."

"But, Severin," exclaimed Wanda with tears in her eyes, "how
could you imagine...you, a man who loves me so and who puts
himself so totally in my power...that I could...."

"No, no!" I said, covering her hands with kisses. "I cannot believe that you would dishonor me. Forgive me this despicable moment."

Wanda smiled delightfully, put her cheek against mine and
seemed lost in thought.

"You have forgotten something," she whispered naughtily,

"the most important thing."

"A condition?"

"Yes, that I should always appear in my furs," she exclaimed. "But I promise you that I shall, if only because it makes me feel like a despot. I want to be very cruel with you, do you understand?"

"Shall I sign the contract?" I asked.

"Not yet," said Wanda, "I shall first add the conditions and then you can sign in all due form."

"In Constantinople?"

"No. I have thought things over. What is the point of having a slave in a country where slavery is common practice? I want to be the only one to own a slave. If we live in a cultivated, sensible, Philistine society, then you will belong to me, not by law, right or power, but purely on account of my beauty and of my whole being. The idea is most exciting. But let us go to a country where we are not known and where you can be my servant without embarrassment; Italy perhaps, Rome or Naples."

*　　*　　*

We were sitting on Wanda's ottoman. She wore her ermine-trimmed jacket and her hair was loose and wild as a lion's mane. She clung to my lips, drawing my soul from my body; my head was spinning, my heart beat violently against hers.

"I want to place myself entirely in your hands, Wanda," I exclaimed suddenly, in a storm of passion that deprived me of all reason, "without conditions, with no limitations on your power over me. I want to be at the mercy of your every whim." On saying these words I fell at her feet and gazed up at her, intoxicated.

"How handsome you are now," she exclaimed, "with your eyes half-closed in ecstasy; you enrapture me. How beautiful your gaze would be at the moment of expiring, after you had been beaten to death. You have the eyes of a martyr."

\*    \*    \*

I sometimes find it disturbing to be so totally at the mercy of a woman. With all the power in her hands, what if she were to take unfair advantage of my passion? I am now actually experiencing those things that have so preoccupied me from early childhood and have always filled me with such sweet fear. What senseless apprehension! She is playing a capricious game with me, no more. Of course she loves me; and she is so good, so noble — quite incapable of treachery. But everything rests in her hands; if she wants to betray me, she can. How exquisite is this agonizing doubt!

Now I understand Manon Lescaut and the unhappy Chevalier who even in the pillory still adored his faithless mistress. Love knows neither virtue nor merit; when we love, we forgive and forget everything, for we have no choice. It is not our judgment that leads us, it is not the qualities or faults that we discover in the loved one that inflame our passion or cause us to draw back in horror. We are driven by a gentle and mysterious power that deprives us of all will and reason, and we are swept along with no thought for the morrow.

\*    \*    \*

When we were in town today a Russian prince made his first appearance on the promenade. His athletic body, his well-shaped features and his splendid apparel aroused everyone's interest. The ladies in particular were all agape at the sight of this handsome wild animal, but the prince paid attention to no one and went his way with a somber air. He was accompanied by two servants, a Negro all dressed in red satin and a Tcherkesse in brilliant attire. Suddenly he noticed Wanda and fixed his cold, piercing eyes on her; he even turned around, and when she had passed he stood still and followed her with his gaze.

As for Wanda, she devoured him with her gleaming green eyes and seemed ready to give anything in the world to see him again. I felt a lump in my throat as I watched the refined coquetry of her walk, the studied gracefulness of her movements as she turned to look at him. When we were home I remarked on this. She frowned.

"What of it?" she said. "The prince is a man who could be attractive to me; in fact, if I may say so, he fascinates me. After all, I am free to do as I please."

"Do you no longer love me?" I asked in a trembling voice.

"I love no one but you," she replied, "but I shall let the prince pay court to me."

"Wanda!"

"Are you not my slave?" she asked calmly. "Am I not Venus, cruel Venus in the northern furs?"

I was silent; I felt crushed by her words; her cold stare pierced my heart like a dagger.

"I want you to find out immediately what the prince's name is, where he lives and everything you can learn about him, do you understand?"

"But...."

"No objections, obey!" she cried, with a sternness of which I would never have thought her capable. "Do not let me see you again until you have an answer to all my questions."

\* \* \*

It was not until afternoon that I could bring Wanda the desired information. She made me stand before her like a servant, while she reclined in an armchair, listening with a smile. She then nodded, apparently satisfied.

"Bring me my footstool," she ordered.

I obeyed, and after placing it before her and resting her feet on it, I remained on my knees.

"How will this end?" I asked despondently, after a brief silence.

Wanda chuckled: "It hasn't begun yet!"

"You are even more heartless than I thought," I replied, wounded.

"Severin," began Wanda earnestly, "I have done nothing yet, not the slightest thing, and you already call me heartless. What will happen when I fully satisfy your wishes and lead a carefree life surrounded by a circle of admirers, when I fulfill your ideal and kick and whip you?"

"You take my fantasies too seriously."

"Too seriously? When I undertake something, there can be no question of jesting. You know that I detest all playacting and melodrama. Was it my idea or yours? Did I lead you into this or is it you who aroused my imagination? At any rate we are now in earnest."

"Wanda," I replied tenderly, "be reasonable and listen to me. We have such enormous love for each other, we are so happy, would you sacrifice all our future to a whim?"

"This is no whim!"

"What is it then?" I asked fearfully.

"Something that was already in me," she said thoughtfully. "It might never have seen the light of day had you not aroused and cultivated these tendencies. Now that it has become a powerful impulse, now that I am enjoying the situation intensely, you want to turn back. Tell me, are you a man?"

"Dear sweet Wanda!" I began to caress and kiss her.

"Leave me alone. You are not a man."

"And what are you?" I asked, flushing with anger.

"I am selfish," she said, "you know that. I am not like you, strong in imagination and weak in action. When I make up my mind to do something, I carry it through, and the more resistance I meet with, the more determined I become. Leave me alone!"

She pushed me away and rose to her feet.

"Wanda!" I replied with emotion, tears filling my eyes. "You do not know how much I love you."

She pouted disdainfully.

"You are mistaken," I continued, "you are making yourself out to be more evil than you really are; you are far too good, far too noble by nature...."

"What do you know about my nature?" she interrupted violently. "You will get to know me as I really am."

"Wanda!"

"Make up your mind, will you submit unconditionally?"

"And what if I refuse?"

"Then——"

She came toward me, cold and ironic, and stood with her arms folded across her breast, that wicked smile on her lips; here indeed was the despotic woman of my dreams. Her features were harsh and I could read nothing in her eyes that promised kindness or mercy.

"Very well," she said at last.

"You are cruel," I said, "you are going to whip me."

"Oh, no. I shall let you go. You are free, I am not holding you."

"Wanda, I who love you so!"

"Yes, you sir, who worship me," she cried contemptuously, "you who are also a coward, a liar and a perjurer. Get out of my sight!"

"Wanda!"

"You wretch!"

The blood rose to my head. I threw myself at her feet and burst into tears.

"More tears!" She laughed — oh how dreadful that laugh was! "Away with you, I never want to see you again."

"Oh, my God!" I cried, beside myself. "I will do whatever you command, I will be your slave, your thing; you may treat me as you please, but do not reject me. I shall be lost, I cannot live without you." I embraced her knees and covered her hands with kisses.

"Yes, you must be a slave and taste the lash, for you are not a man," she said calmly. This is what hurt me most: she was neither angry nor even excited, but she spoke in an even voice.

"I know you now, I know your doglike nature; you worship whoever tramples you underfoot, and the more you are abused the more slavish your adoration. But you are only just about to discover me."

She stalked up and down while I remained on my knees, my head bowed and my face flooded with tears.

"Come and see me," ordered Wanda, settling on the ottoman. I obeyed and came to sit next to her. She gave me a somber look, then suddenly her eyes lit up with an inner glow and she drew me to her breast and dried my tears with kisses.

\*　\*　\*

The comic side of my situation is that I can escape but do not want to; I am ready to endure anything as soon as she threatens to set me free.

\*　\*　\*

If only she would take up the whip again! There is something uncanny in the way she treats me. I feel like a mouse held captive by a beautiful cat who plays with it daintily, and at any moment is ready to tear it to pieces; my mouse's heart beats so hard that it will break.

What are her plans? What does she intend to do with me?

\*　　\*　　\*

She seems to have forgotten completely about the contract and my status of slave. Or was it only ever a whim, and did she give up her plans as soon as I no longer offered her any resistance and yielded to her imperious will? How kind she is to me at present, how tender and loving! Blissful days float by.

\*　　\*　　\*

Today she asked me to read her the scene in *Faust* where Mephistopheles appears as a wandering scholar. She seemed strangely satisfied and could not take her eyes off me.

"I do not understand," she said when I had finished, "how a man can express such great and beautiful thoughts in such a clear way, so accurately and rationally, while being at the same time a romantic and a supersensualist."

"You enjoyed it?" I asked, kissing her hand.

She stroked my forehead affectionately.

"I love you, Severin," she murmured. "I believe I could never love anyone more than you. Let us be reasonable, shall we?"

Instead of replying, I folded her in my arms; my heart was filled with deep love and passionate longing, my eyes became moist and a tear fell on her hand.

"How can you cry?" she exclaimed. "What a child you are!"

\*　　\*　　\*

While we were out driving today we met the Russian prince. He looked disagreeably surprised to see me by Wanda's side, and looked as though he wanted to transpierce her with his magnetic green eyes. As for her – I could have knelt before her and kissed her feet – she did not appear to notice him, and let her gaze drift indifferently past him as though he were an object, a tree, for example; she then turned to me and smiled her adorable smile.

\*   \*   \*

Today, as I was saying good night to her, she seemed suddenly listless and distressed without reason. What could be preoccupying her?

"I am sorry to see you go," she began, as I stood on the threshold.

"It is entirely up to you to shorten my ordeal: cease tormenting me," I implored.

"Do you think this constraint is not also a torture for me?" she asked.

"Then bring it to an end," I said, embracing her. "Be my wife."

"Never, Severin," she said gently, but with great firmness.

"What do you mean?" I was stunned.

"You are not the husband for me."

I looked at her and slowly withdrawing my arm which was still around her waist, I left the room. She uttered not a word to call me back.

\*   \*   \*

A sleepless night, during which I took numerous decisions, only to discard them one after another. In the morning I wrote her a letter declaring our relations at an end. My hands trembled as I wrote and I burnt my fingers while sealing the letter.

As I went upstairs to give it to the chambermaid, my knees threatened to give way.

Suddenly the door opened and Wanda appeared with her hair in curlers.

"I have not yet arranged my hair," she said with a smile. "What have you there?"

"A letter."

"For me?"

I nodded.

"Aha, you want to break with me," she said ironically.

"Did you not tell me yesterday that I was not the husband for you?"

"I repeat it now."

"Then...." I was shaking from head to foot and my voice failed me. I handed her the letter.

"Keep it," she said, eyeing me coldly. "You forget that it is no longer relevant whether you satisfy me as a husband or not; as a slave you do well enough."

"Madam!" I gasped.

"Yes, that is how you are to address me in future," answered Wanda, throwing back her head in a gesture of unutterable contempt. "Have your belongings ready within twenty-four hours. I am leaving tomorrow for Italy and you will accompany me as my servant."

"Wanda!"

"I will not have any familiarity," she snapped. "What is more, you will have no right to visit me unless I call or ring for you, and you will not speak to me unless I address you first. From now on your name is no longer Severin, but Gregor."

I was trembling with rage but I cannot deny that I also felt a thrill of pleasure.

"But, madam," I said anxiously, "surely you know my situation — I am still financially dependent on my father and I am afraid that the large sum I shall require for such a journey...."

"That means that you have no money, Gregor," remarked Wanda delightedly. "So much the better; you will thus be completely dependent on me, and you will really be my slave."

"You do not think," I objected feebly, "that as a man of

honor I could possibly...."

"I think," she replied imperiously, "that as a man of honor you should, above all, keep your word to follow me everywhere as my slave and obey all my commands. Now off with you, Gregor."

I turned to go.

"Not yet, you may kiss my hand first."

She nonchalantly held out her hand to me, and I, pitiful amateur, fool, miserable slave, I pressed it with tenderness to my parched and burning lips. At last with a kindly nod she dismissed me.

*　　*　　*

Late that evening my lamp was still alight and the fire still burning in the large green stove, for I had letters and documents to put in order, and autumn had descended upon us suddenly, as it so often does in our country.

Suddenly she knocked on the windowpane with the handle of her whip. I opened the window and there she was, wearing her ermine-trimmed jacket and an ermine Cossack's toque, high and round, such as Catherine the Great liked to wear.

"Are you ready, Gregor?" she asked in a stern voice.

"Not yet, mistress."

"I like that word. You will always call me mistress, do you hear? We shall leave tomorrow at nine. Until we reach the main town you will be friend and partner, but from the moment we board the train, you will be my slave and my servant. Now close the window and open the door."

When I had carried out her orders and she had entered my room, she asked me with an ironic frown:

"Well, now, do you find me attractive?"

"Wanda, you are...."

"What impudence!" She dealt me a sharp blow with the whip.

"Mistress, you are marvelously beautiful."

Wanda smiled and seated herself in my armchair.

"Kneel down here, beside my chair."

I obeyed.

"Kiss my hand."

I grasped her cold little hand and kissed it.

"And my mouth."

In a frenzy of passion I flung my arms around my lovely cruel mistress and covered her face, her mouth, her breasts with burning kisses, which she returned with equal fervor, her eyes closed as in a dream. It was past midnight when she left.

\*    \*    \*

At nine o'clock sharp the next morning, as she had ordered, everything was ready for our departure. A comfortable carriage swept us away from the little Carpathian resort, the scene of the most interesting drama of my life whose denouement no one could have foretold.

All was still well. I was seated at Wanda's side and she chatted to me amiably and wittily about Italy, the latest novel of Pisemski and Wagner's operas. She wore a kind of Amazon's traveling dress in black linen, with a short jacket of the same stuff bordered with dark fur; it fitted closely and displayed her slender figure to its best advantage. On her Grecian chignon rested a little fur hat trimmed with a black veil. Wanda was in excellent humor, she fed me sweetmeats, combed my hair, undid my necktie and retied it more becomingly, spread her furs over my knee so that she could press my hand in secret, and when our Jewish coachman was looking ahead, she even gave me a kiss; her cold lips had the chilling fragrance of an autumnal rose blooming alone among bare trees and yellow leaves, as the first frosty mornings decorate its calyx with diamonds of ice.

207

\*   \*   \*

We arrive in the main town and alight at the railway station. Wanda throws off her furs, tosses them into my arms with a charming smile and goes to collect the tickets.

When she returns she is completely transformed.

"Here is your ticket, Gregor," she says, like an arrogant lady talking to her servant.

"A third-class ticket!" I exclaim in comic horror.

"Of course. Now make sure that you only get on the train once I am settled in my compartment and no longer need you. At each station you will hurry to my carriage to attend me. Do not forget. And now give me my furs."

After I have submissively helped her with these, she drags me off to find a first-class carriage. Supporting herself on my shoulder, she jumps on, and I wrap her feet in bearskins and place them on a hot-water bottle. She then dismisses me with a nod.

I struggle into a third-class carriage filled with a nauseating smell of tobacco – the court of Hades shrouded in the mists of the Acheron – and I have the leisure to meditate on the riddle of human existence, and on the greatest riddle of all, woman.

\*   \*   \*

Whenever the train stops I leap off, run to her carriage and await her orders, cap in hand. Now she wants coffee, now a glass of water; at one time she asks for a light supper, at another a bowl of warm water to wash her hands; and so it goes on. She flirts with a number of gentlemen who have got into her compartment. I am dying of jealousy and have to leap around like an antelope to serve her quickly and not miss the train. In this way the night passes, without my being able to eat a mouthful or sleep a wink. I share the foul air reeking of onions with Polish peasants, Jewish merchants and vulgar soldiers; when I climb up to her compartment I find her comfortably stretched out among cushions and pelts, like an Oriental princess, with the gentlemen sitting around her, bolt upright like Indian deities, hardly daring to breathe.

*   *   *

She stays in Vienna for a day to buy a few things, in particular a new series of luxurious outfits. She still treats me like a servant, and makes me follow her at the respectful distance of ten paces. She hands me her parcels without honoring me with so much as a friendly glance, and leaves me to pant along behind her, loaded like a donkey.

Before leaving she takes all my clothes and makes a gift of them to the hotel porter; she then orders me to wear her livery, which is a Crakovian costume in her colors, light blue with red facings, and a red toque decorated with a peacock feather. The overall effect is not unbecoming.

The silver buttons bear her coat of arms. I feel as though I have been sold or have pledged my soul to the devil.

*   *   *

My lovely devil leads me from Vienna to Florence. Instead of Mazurian peasants and greasy-haired Jews, my companions now consist of a flamboyant sergeant from the first Italian grenadiers and a poor German painter. The tobacco smoke no longer smells of onions but instead of sausages and cheese.

Night falls again, and I lie on a wooden bench that feels like a rack, and bruises my limbs cruelly. Yet my situation has a certain poetry about it: the sergeant has the face of the *Apollo Belvedere*, and the painter sings a lovely German ballad:

The evening shadows gather fast;
And one by one the stars appear;
The perfume of strange longings
Pours forth into the night.

Upon the sea of dreams
My lonely soul goes sailing,
Sailing without cease,
In thy soul to come to rest.

And I think of the divine creature peacefully sleeping a royal slumber in her soft furs.

Florence! The irritating bustle, the shouts, the porters, the coaches. Wanda hails a carriage and dismisses our porter.

"What do I have a servant for?" she says. "Gregor, here is the ticket, go and get the luggage."

She wraps herself in her furs and waits calmly in the carriage while I bring the heavy cases up one by one. Just as I am about to collapse under the weight of one of them an obliging *carabiniere* with a kind face comes to my rescue. She laughs:

"It must be heavy," she says, "all my furs are in it."

I climb up beside the coachman, mopping the sweat from my brow. A few minutes later we draw up in front of a brightly lit doorway.

"Have you any rooms?" she asks the footman.

"Yes, madam."

"Two for me and one for my servant, all with heating."

"Two elegant rooms for you, madam, both with fireplaces, and one without heat for your servant."

"Show me the rooms."

She gives them a cursory look.

"Good, I am satisfied, have the fires lit at once. The servant can sleep in the unheated room."

I give her a long hard stare, which she ignores.

"Bring up the cases, Gregor," she orders. "In the meantime I shall change and go to the dining room. You may also eat something later."

As she disappears into the adjoining room, I drag the cases upstairs and help the servant build a fire in her bedroom. He tries to question me in bad French about my "mistress." For a moment I gaze with mute envy at the crackling fire, the four-poster bed with its white fragrant sheets and the rugs that cover the floor. Tired and starving I make my way downstairs and ask for something to eat. A friendly waiter who was once a soldier in the Austrian army and makes a great effort to talk to me in German leads me to the dining room and waits on me. For the first time in thirty-six hours I have something fresh to drink and am just about to taste my first bite of warm food when she enters. I rise to my feet.

"What do you mean by serving me in the same dining room as my servant?" she says to the waiter, quivering with rage, and she turns around and walks out.

Meanwhile I thank heaven for being able at least to eat undisturbed. I then climb the four flights of stairs to my room: my small traveling case is already there, and a dirty oil lamp lights the room, which is tiny, has no fireplace and only a narrow vent for a window; if it were not so dreadfully cold, it would remind one of the Piombi of Venice. I burst out laughing in spite of myself, and the echo of my laugh startles me.

Suddenly the door is flung open and the servant exclaims with a theatrical gesture that could only be Italian: "Madam demands to see you." I pick up my toque, stumble down the steps that separate me from the first floor and knock excitedly at her door.

"Come in!"

★   ★   ★

I enter, close the door behind me, and stand to attention.

Wanda has settled in comfortably. Wearing a white muslin and lace negligee, she is seated on a red velvet sofa, her feet resting on a cushion of the same stuff. Around her shoulders is the fur cloak she wore when she first appeared to me as the goddess of Love.

The yellow light of the candelabras, their reflections in the great mirror and the red flames in the hearth cast a bewitching glow on the red velvet, the dark brown sable, the alabaster skin and the fiery red hair of the lovely creature; she turns toward me and lets her cool green eyes rest upon me.

"I am pleased with you, Gregor," she began.

I bowed.

"Come closer."

I obeyed.

"Closer still." She lowered her eyes and stroked the fur with her fingers. "Venus in Furs receives her slave. I can see that you are far more than an ordinary romantic; you do not fall short of your dreams, you become the man you imagine yourself to be, though it means nothing less than folly. I must admit that I am impressed by your behavior; it takes a certain strength, and one can only admire strength. I actually believe that in unusual circumstances and in a more exalted age than this, what appears to be your weakness would reveal itself as impressive power. Under the first emperors, you would have been a martyr, at the time of the Reformation an anabaptist; during the French Revolution you would have been one of those inspired Girondins who walked to the guillotine with the *Marseillaise* on their lips. But today you are my slave, my...."

She suddenly leapt up, her furs sliding to the ground, and threw her arms around my neck with tender abandon.

"My beloved slave, Severin! Oh, how I love you, how I adore you, how dashing you look in your Cracovian costume! But you are going to be cold tonight up there in your miserable room without a fire. Shall I give you one of my furs, dear heart, the large one there?"

She promptly picked it up, threw it over my shoulders and before I knew what had happened, I was completely wrapped up in it.

"Ah, how well fur becomes you, it brings out the true nobility of your features. When you are no longer my slave you must wear a velvet coat with sable, do you hear? Or I shall never wear my velvet jacket again."

She began to kiss and caress me, and drew me down beside her on the little sofa.

"You seem very pleased with yourself in furs," she said. "Quick, give them back to me or I shall lose all sense of dignity."

I placed the fur cloak about her shoulders and she slipped her right arm into the sleeve.

"This is the way they are worn in Titian's paintings. But enough joking. Do not look so miserable, you are making me sad. For the time being you are my servant in the eyes of the world only; you have not yet signed the contract, and you are still free to leave me at any time. You have played your part to perfection – I am quite satisfied. But are you not tired of it? Do you not find me abominable? Come now, speak, I order you."

"Must I confess it to you, Wanda?" I asked.

"Yes, you must."

"I am more in love with you than ever. Even if you abuse my devotion I shall only adore you the more fanatically. The more you hurt me as you have just done, the more you fire my heart and inflame my senses." I drew her to me and clung for a moment to her moist lips.

"Magnificent woman!" I exclaimed, and in my ardor I tore the fur from her shoulders and pressed my mouth against her neck.

"So you only love me when I am cruel?" said Wanda. "Go away! You bore me, do you hear?" And she slapped my face so hard that I saw stars and my ears hummed.

"Help me into my furs, slave."

I helped her as best I could.

"How clumsy!" she said, and slapped me again. I felt my cheeks grow pale.

"Did I hurt you?" she asked, gently resting her hand on me.

"No, no," I said.

"In any case, you have no reason to complain; you wished it to be this way. Come, give me another kiss."

I clasped her in my arms and her lips drank from mine. As she lay pressed against my breast in her large heavy furs, a strange and painful sensation came over me, as though I were in the clutches of a wild animal, a she-bear; I almost felt her claws gradually sinking into my flesh. But this time the bear was merciful and let me go.

My heart was full of joyful hopes as I climbed up to my servant's room and threw myself down on the hard bed.

"Life is very strange," I reflected. "A moment ago, the most beautiful of women, Venus herself, was resting against your breast. Then suddenly you find yourself tasting at first hand the hell of the Chinese — a hell where the damned are not thrown to the flames but chased out by devils into the icy plains. I should not be surprised if the founders of their religion slept in rooms without heating."

I awoke during the night with a cry of terror; I had been dreaming that I was stranded on a field of ice. An Eskimo appeared on a sled drawn by reindeer; he had the face of the servant who had shown me to my unheated room.

"What are you looking for here, sir?" he exclaimed. "This is the North Pole."

The next moment he had vanished and Wanda was skating on the frozen surface, her white satin skirt billowing and flapping behind her; the ermine on her jacket and her toque, and her face especially, shone whiter than the snow. She came toward me, folded me in her arms and kissed me. I felt a warm trickle of blood on my skin.

"What are you doing?" I asked in horror.

She laughed, and when I looked at her again it was not Wanda but a great white bear mauling my body with its claws. I cried out in desperation and awoke, but I could still hear her diabolical laughter; I looked about me, aghast.

\* \* \*

Early the next morning I stood in readiness before Wanda's door, and when the servant brought up the coffee, I took it from him and served it to my lovely mistress. She had just made her toilet and was fresh and resplendent. She gave me a friendly smile and even called me back as I prepared to withdraw respectfully.

"Hurry and take your breakfast, Gregor," she said. "We are leaving straight away to look for a house. It is dreadfully embarrassing here; when I chat with you at any length people are thinking: 'The Russian woman is having an affair with her servant. The race of Catherine the Great is obviously not extinct.' "

Half an hour later we were on our way, Wanda in her linen frock with her Russian toque, and I in my Cracovian costume. We made a sensation. I walked about ten steps behind her and wore a sinister expression, trying hard to repress my laughter.

There was not a single street where some attractive little house did not bear the sign: *Camere ammobiliate*. Wanda made me enter each of them, and only if the apartment seemed to suit her requirements did she come up herself. At noon I was as tired as a hound after the hunt.

We tried one house after another without finding a suitable place to stay; Wanda was beginning to lose her temper. Suddenly she said to me: "Severin, the seriousness with which you are playing your role is very endearing, and I find the constraint we are imposing on ourselves deeply exciting. I can no longer bear it, I am too fond of you, I must have a kiss; come into this house."

"But, madam," I objected.

"Gregor!" She slipped into the nearest entrance, climbed a few steps of the dark stairway, threw her arms about me and kissed me ardently.

"Ah, Severin, you are very clever; as a slave you are much more dangerous than I expected. I find you irresistible — I am afraid of falling in love with you again."

"Then you no longer love me now?" I asked, horror-stricken.

She nodded with a serious air, but kissed me again with her firm and fragrant lips.

We returned to the hotel where Wanda took luncheon and ordered me to eat something quickly.

I was naturally not served as promptly as she was, and just as I was carrying the second mouthful of beefsteak to my mouth, the waiter appeared and exclaimed in his theatrical way: "Madam wishes to see you immediately."

I painfully took leave of my luncheon, and tired and hungry that I was, hurried to join Wanda who was waiting in the street.

"I would never have thought you could be so cruel, mistress," I said reproachfully, "to prevent me from eating in peace after such a tiring morning!"

Wanda gave a hearty laugh.

"I thought you had finished," she said, "but what does it matter? Men are born to suffer, and you particularly so. Martyrs did not have beefsteak either."

I followed her resentfully, hunger gnawing at my stomach.

"I have given up the idea of living in town," she continued. "It is too difficult to find a whole floor to ourselves where we can live in privacy, and everything must be just so for such romantic and unusual relations as ours. I am going to rent a villa, and — wait, this will surprise you — I shall allow you to eat now and take a little walk around Florence. I shall not be home till this evening; if I need you I shall send for you."

*   *   *

I visited the cathedral, the Palazzo Vecchio, the Loggia dei Lanzi, and stood for a long while on the banks of the Arno. My gaze returned time and again to the ancient marvels of Florence; the domes and towers were delicately outlined against the cloudless sky, the yellow river churned under the wide arches of the splendid bridge, and around the town lay a circle of green hills dotted with slender cypresses, mansions, palaces and cloisters. It was another world, joyful, sensuous and laughing; even the countryside had none of the somber melancholy of our landscapes. The hills were bathed in sunlight and each little villa stood out in its whitewashed brilliance. The people here are less serious than we are; they think less, but they seem happier. They say it is easier to die in the south. I now know that there can be such a thing as a rose without a thorn, sensuality free from torment.

Wanda discovered a charming little house which she has rented for the summer. It is perched on a pleasant hill on the left bank of the Arno, opposite the Cascine, and has a beautiful garden with a bower, a lawn and a delightful alley bordered with camellias. It is built in the quadrangular Italian style and has two stories only. An open gallery runs along one side of the house, a sort of loggia with plaster casts of ancient statues; a few stone steps lead down into the garden. From the gallery one enters the bathroom, with a magnificent marble basin and a spiral staircase leading up to my mistress' bedroom.

Wanda is to occupy the first floor, and I have been assigned a room on the ground floor which is very pleasant and even has a fireplace.

I explored the garden and discovered a little temple built on a mound. It was locked, but on peering through a chink in the door I beheld the goddess of Love standing on a white pedestal. A shiver ran through me. She seemed to smile at me and say: "Is it you? I have been expecting you."

*  *  *

Toward evening a pretty little maid brought me orders to appear before my mistress. I climbed the wide marble stairs, passed through the antechamber which is a large, extravagantly furnished drawing room, and knocked on the bedroom door. I knocked softly, intimidated by the luxury displayed around me.

She did not hear me and I was left standing in front of the door. For a moment I imagined that I was waiting before the Great Catherine's bedroom, and that she was about to appear in a green morning-dress with fur trimmings, the red ribbon of her order across her naked breasts, and her neat curls whitely powdered.

I knocked again. Wanda flung the door open impatiently.

"Why so late?" she asked.

"I was standing in front of the door but you did not hear me knock," I replied timidly. She closed the door, slipped her arm into mine and led me to the red damask ottoman on which she had been reclining. The room was entirely furnished in red, the carpet, the curtains, the hangings and the canopy above the bed. A fine painting showing Samson and Delilah decorated the ceiling.

Wanda received me in captivating *déshabillé*: a white satin

morning dress that molded her slender body and fell in graceful folds, and over her bare shoulders, a green velvet jacket edged
with fur. Her red mane, casually retained by a string of black
pearls, tumbled down to her hips.

"Venus in Furs," I murmured, as she drew me to her breast
and smothered me with kisses. I was speechless and even beyond
thought, carried away in a storm of ecstasy.

Wanda gently disengaged herself from my embrace and gazed
at me, resting her head on her hand. I fell at her feet and she drew
me to her and played with my hair.

"Do you still love me?" she asked, her eyes misty with gentle
rapture.

"How can you ask such a question?"

"Do you remember your oath?" she continued, with a charming smile. "Now that all is ready and in order, I ask you once again:
are you in earnest, do you really wish to be my slave?"

"Am I not prepared for it?" I asked with surprise.

"You have not signed the papers yet."

"Papers? What papers?"

"Aha, you see, you have forgotten already," she said. "Then let
us drop the whole matter."

"But, Wanda," I said, "you know that nothing gives me greater
bliss than to serve you and be your slave; I will give anything
to be entirely at your mercy, to feel that my whole life lies in
your hands."

"How well enthusiasm becomes you," she murmured. "How
handsome you are when you speak with such passion! Ah, I am
more than ever in love with you, and yet I must be haughty, severe
and cruel toward you! I am afraid it will be impossible for me."

"Have no fears," I said with a smile. "Where are the papers?"

"Here." She pulled them out of her bodice, a little embarrassed, and handed them to me. "So that you will know what it

feels like to be entirely in my hands, I have drafted another statement according to which you undertake to put an end to your life. Thus I can even kill you if it pleases me to do so."

"Let me see."

While I looked at the documents, Wanda went to fetch pen and ink. She then sat next to me, put her arm around my neck and peered over my shoulder.

The first document read as follows:

"*Agreement between Mrs. Wanda von Dunajew and Mr. Severin von Kuziemski.*

"Mr. Severin von Kuziemski ceases from this date to be the fiancé of Mrs. Wanda von Dunajew and renounces all rights pertaining to this state; in return he undertakes, on his word as a man and a gentleman, to be the slave of this lady, until such time as she sets him at liberty.

"As the slave of Mrs. von Dunajew, he will take the name of Gregor, and will undertake to satisfy all the wishes of his mistress, to obey all her orders, to submit to her, and to regard the slightest kindness on her part as an extraordinary favor.

"Mrs. von Dunajew may not only chastise her slave for the slightest negligence or misdemeanor as and when she wishes, but she will also have the right to maltreat him according to her humor or even simply to amuse herself; she is also entitled to kill him if she so wishes; in short, he becomes her absolute property.

"Should Mrs. von Dunajew ever set her slave at liberty, Mr. von Kuziemski agrees to forget everything he has experienced or undergone in his capacity as slave, and will not entertain, under any pretext or in any manner, the thought of vengeance or reprisal.

"In return, Mrs. von Dunajew promises, in her capacity as his mistress, to appear as often as possible in furs, particularly when she is being cruel toward her slave."

The contract bore today's date.

The second document contained only a few words:

"Having been for many years weary of existence and the disappointments it brings, I have willfully ended my useless life."

A profound horror gripped me on reading these lines. It was still possible to turn back, but I was carried away by the madness of passion and the sight of the lovely creature nestling languidly against my breast.

"You must copy this one out, Severin," said Wanda, pointing to the second document. "It must be in your own hand. As for the contract, it will of course not be necessary."

I quickly copied out the note confirming my suicide and handed it to Wanda. She read it over and laid it on the table with a smile.

"Now are you brave enough to sign this one?" she asked, leaning her head to one side with a sweet smile.

I took up the pen.

"Let me sign first," said Wanda. "Your hand is shaking; are you so afraid of happiness?"

She snatched away the contract and the pen. In my hesitation I gazed up for a moment and only then did I realize the utter lack of historical character in the painting above me (as happens so often with painters of the Italian and Dutch schools); this gave it an uncanny quality. Delilah, an opulent creature with flaming red hair, reclines half-naked on a red ottoman, a sable cloak about her shoulders. She smiles and leans toward Samson, who has been bound and thrown at her feet by the Philistines. Her teasing, coquettish smile seems the very summit of cruelty; with half-closed eyes she gazes at Samson, while he regards her longingly, crazed with love. Already his enemy has laid a knee on his chest and is about to blind him with the white-hot sword.

"That's that," said Wanda. "But you look quite lost — what is the matter? Everything will be as it was, even after you have signed. Surely you know me, dear heart?"

She had placed her bold signature to the contract. I looked once more into those eyes that held me in their bewitching power, and then took up the pen.

"You are shaking," said Wanda calmly. "Shall I guide your hand?"

She gently took hold of my hand and my name appeared at the bottom of the contract. She read the two documents once more and placed them in the drawer of the table that stood by the ottoman.

"Good. Now give me your passport and your money."

I took out my pocketbook and handed it to her; she examined the contents, nodded and put it away with the rest. I then knelt down before her in sweet rapture and laid my head on her breast.

Suddenly she kicked me away, leapt up and pulled the bell-rope. Three slender young Negresses appeared, like ebony carvings, all dressed in red satin and each with a rope in her hand.

Realizing my situation I tried to rise, but Wanda turned her lovely cold face toward me, with its dark brows and mocking eyes, and confronted me in the stance of a domineering mistress. She signaled, and before I knew what was happening, the three Negresses had thrown me to the ground, tied my hands and feet and secured my arms behind me like a man about to be executed. I could hardly move an inch.

"Give me the whip, Haydée," ordered Wanda, with chilling composure. The Negress handed her mistress the whip on bended knee.

"Take off my fur, it hinders me."

The Negress obeyed.

"The jacket, over there!"

Haydée promptly brought the ermine-trimmed kazabaika from the bed and Wanda slipped it on with her inimitable grace.

"Tie him to the pillar here."

The blackamoors lifted me, wound a stout rope around my body and tied me upright to one of the massive pillars that held up the canopy of the big Italian bed.

Then they vanished suddenly as though the earth had swallowed them up.

Wanda stepped forward briskly. Her white satin dress flowed behind her in a long silver train, like moonlight; her hair flared like flames over the white fur of the jacket. Now she stood before me, her left hand on her hip, the whip in her right hand. She let out a peal of laughter.

"The game is over," she said coldly. "Now we are in deadly earnest, you senseless fellow! I despise the blind fool who puts himself at the mercy of a vain and capricious woman. You are no longer my lover, but my slave; your life and death are subject to my whims. You shall know me now! First of all, you shall taste the whip – seriously this time, and without having deserved it, so that you will know what awaits you if you are ever clumsy, disobedient or rebellious."

At these words she turned back her ermine cuffs with a gesture both graceful and savage, and lashed me across the back. I shuddered as the whip cut into my flesh like a knife.

"Well, how do you like that?" she exclaimed.

I was silent.

"You will see, I shall make you whimper like a dog beneath my lash," she said threateningly, and she began to whip me again.

The blows fell thick and fast with dreadful force on my back, arms and neck; I clenched my teeth not to cry out loud. Then she struck me full in the face. The warm blood began to run but she laughed and continued to whip me.

"I am only just beginning to understand you," she cried. "What a treat to have someone in one's power, especially a man who loves one – for you do love me, do you not? My pleasure grows with each blow; I shall tear you to shreds. Go on, writhe with pain, cry out, scream! You cannot arouse my pity."

Finally she seemed to grow tired. She dropped the whip, lay back on the ottoman and rang the bell.

The Negresses entered.

"Untie him."

When they loosened the ropes I fell to the ground like a log. The dusky creatures laughed, showing their white teeth.

"Undo the rope around his feet."

They did so and I was able to rise.

"Come and see me, Gregor."

I approached my cruel, mocking beauty who seemed more seductive than ever before.

"One step nearer!" ordered Wanda. "Kneel and kiss my foot."

She held out her foot beneath the white satin hem, and like the supersensitive madman that I was, I pressed my lips to it.

"You will not see me for a whole month, Gregor," she said solemnly. "I must become a stranger to you, so that our new relations may be easier for you to accept. You will work in the garden and await further orders. Away, slave."

\*   \*   \*

A month has gone by in the gray monotony of hard labor, in wistful longing and ardent desire to see her, she who is the source of all my sorrow. I have been put under the gardener's orders and must help him prune the trees and clip the hedges, transplant the flowers, weed the flower beds and rake the gravel paths; I share his frugal meals and his hard bed; I rise with the cockcrow and retire when the chickens do. Meanwhile I hear that our mistress is leading a gay life, surrounded by admirers. Once I even heard the sound of her playful laughter. I feel exceedingly stupid, and wonder whether this is due to the life I am leading or whether I have always been so. The day after tomorrow the month will end — what will she do with me? Perhaps she has forgotten me, and I shall spend the rest of my days clipping hedges and picking bouquets until a merciful end delivers me....

*　　*　　*

A written order arrives:
"The slave Gregor is hereby recalled to my personal service.
W.D."

*　　*　　*

The next morning, with beating heart, I drew back the damask curtains and entered my goddess' bedroom which still lay in half-darkness.

"Is that you, Gregor?" she asked, as I knelt before the hearth and prepared to the build the fire.

I started at the sound of my beloved's voice. I could not see her — she was lying behind the curtains of the four-poster bed.

"Yes, madam."

"What time is it?"

Past nine o'clock."

"My breakfast!"

I hurried to fetch it and knelt before her bed with the coffee tray.

"Here is your breakfast, mistress."

Wanda drew back the curtains and, curiously enough, as I saw her lying there among the pillows, her hair streaming over her shoulders, she seemed a perfect stranger; a beautiful woman, nothing more. These were not the beloved features, but a hard face with an expression of weariness and satiety that I found deeply disturbing. Or had I simply not noticed these traits before?

225

She stared at me with her green eyes that were curious rather than threatening or compassionate, and lazily pulled the dark fur in which she had been lying over her bare shoulders.

At that moment she was so charming, so bewitching, that I felt the blood rush to my head and the tray began to rattle in my hands. She noticed this and picked up the whip which lay on her bedside table.

"You are clumsy, slave," she said crossly.

I lowered my eyes and tried to hold the tray as steady as possible. She took her breakfast, yawned and stretched her voluptuous limbs in the magnificent fur.

\*　　\*　　\*

She has rung — I enter.

"Take this letter to Prince Corsini."

I hurry into town, hand the letter to the prince, a handsome young man with gleaming black eyes, and consumed with jealousy, bring the answer to my mistress.

"What is the matter?" she asks, giving me a sly look. "You are quite pale."

"Nothing, mistress, I merely ran rather fast."

\*　　\*　　\*

At lunch the prince is at her side and I am condemned to wait on them; they exchange jokes and ignore me totally.

As I am pouring out the Bordeaux, a dizzy spell comes over me; the wine spills over the tablecloth and onto my mistress's gown.

"How clumsy!" cries Wanda, and she slaps my face. The blood rushes to my head and they both laugh heartily.

\*　　\*　　\*

After luncheon she goes to the Cascine. She herself drives the little carriage drawn by elegant bay horses from England; I am seated behind her and watch her acknowledging each gentleman's greeting with a flirtatious glance.

As I help her down from her carriage, she leans lightly on my arm; her touch runs through me like an electric shock. Alas, she is truly a wonderful woman and I love her more than ever!

*     *     *

At six o'clock, a small circle of ladies and gentlemen are gathered for dinner. I am waiting at table and this time I do not spill wine on the tablecloth. A slap in the face is more effective than ten lectures, especially if it is delivered by the dimpled hand of a lady.

*     *     *

After dinner, she sets out for the Pergola Theater. As she descends the stairs in her black velvet gown with its wide ermine collar, a diadem of white roses in her hair, the effect is breathtaking. I open the carriage door and help her in. When we reach the theater, I leap down from my seat to assist her, and as she rests lightly on my arm I tremble under the sweet burden. I escort her to her box and take up my place in the corridor. The performance lasts four hours, during which time she receives continuous visits from her admirers, while I clench my teeth with rage.

*     *     *

It is long past midnight when my mistress rings for the last time.

"Light the fire," she orders briefly, and when the flames are crackling in the fireplace: "Some tea!"

When I return with the samovar, she has already undressed and with the aid of the Negress she slips into her white nightgown.

Haydée withdraws.

227

"Give me my furs," says Wanda, languidly stretching her beautiful limbs.

I take the furs off the armchair and hand them to her, and she slowly and lazily slips them on. Then she sinks into the cushions on the ottoman.

"Take off my shoes and put on my velvet slippers."

I kneel and try to pull off the dainty shoe without success.

"Quick!" cries Wanda. "You are hurting me. Wait a minute, I shall train you." And she deals me a blow with the whip. I finally succeed. "Now away with you!" Another kick and I am allowed to go to bed.

\*     \*     \*

Today I accompanied her to a soirée. In the hall she ordered me to help her off with her furs, and then sailed into the brilliantly lit room with a proud smile, confident of her success.

Hour after hour went by and I remained alone with my gloomy thoughts, occasionally catching a strain of music through the half-open doors. Some of the footmen tried to start a conversation with me, but since I know only a few words of Italian, they soon lost interest.

Finally I fell asleep and dreamed that in a fit of jealous rage I had killed Wanda, and was sentenced to death. I saw myself on the scaffold; I felt the blade fall, but I was still alive; then the executioner slapped me in the face.

But it was no executioner, it was Wanda who stood before me in a fury, demanding her furs. I immediately came to my senses and assisted her.

What a delicious sensation to help a magnificent creature into her furs, to feel the nape of her neck and her superb arms slip into the precious fleece, to lift her rippling curls and replace them on the collar!

And what delight when she throws off the fur and it retains the gentle warmth and faint perfume of her body — it makes one swoon!

\* \* \*

At last a day without guests, theater or other company. I breathe again. Wanda sits on the balcony reading and appears to have no orders to give me. As the silvery mist of evening retreats and twilight falls, she dines and I wait on her. Although she is eating alone, she has not a glance, not a word for me, not even a slap in the face!

Alas, how I pine for just one blow from her hand! The tears rise to my eyes, I feel that I have been humiliated so deeply that I am no longer even worth torturing.

Before retiring she rings for me.

"Tonight you will sleep in my room; I had horrible dreams last night and I am afraid of being alone. Take some cushions from the ottoman and come and lie on the bearskin at my feet."

With this, she puts out the lights, leaving only a small lamp burning, and climbs into bed.

"Do not move, so as not to wake me."

I do as she orders but cannot fall asleep for a long time. Like a goddess she lies wrapped in furs, her arms folded behind her neck, her hair scattered over the pillow. Her magnificent bosom heaves peacefully. When she makes the slightest stir I awake and listen in case she should need me.

But she has no need of me. My only function is to be there; I mean no more to her than the light of a nightlamp or a weapon kept by the side of the bed.

\* \* \*

Am I mad or is she? Has all this sprung from the vain fancy,

the inventive brain of a woman whose aim is to surpass my supersensual imagination? Or is she really a Nero, and does she take a
fiendish pleasure in trampling on a man who has thoughts, feelings and a will like hers, as though he were no more than a worm?

As I knelt before her bed with the coffee tray, Wanda suddenly laid her hand on my shoulder and gazed into the depths of
my eyes.

"What beautiful eyes you have!" she said gently. "Especially
now that you are suffering. Can you still love me?" And she drew
me to her with such violence that the crockery went flying and
the coffee ran over the carpet.

"Wanda, my Wanda!" I cried, embracing her ardently and covering her mouth, her face and her breasts with kisses. "This is
the sum of my misery: the worse you treat me, the more you
betray me, the more passionately I love you. Oh, I shall die of
pain and love and jealousy!"

"But I have not betrayed you yet, Severin," replied Wanda with
a smile.

"Have you not? Wanda, for the love of God, do not taunt
me so mercilessly," I cried. "Did I not deliver the letter to the
prince myself?"

"Certainly, it was an invitation to luncheon."

"Since we have been in Florence, you have...."

"I have remained entirely faithful to you," retorted Wanda. "I
swear by all that is holy to me. I have done all this merely to be
agreeable to you, to fulfill your dreams. But now I shall find
myself a lover, or I should only be doing things by halves and you
would eventually reproach me for not having been cruel enough.
My dear beautiful slave! However, today you shall be Severin again,
none other than my beloved. I have kept your clothes; you will
find them in that chest. Dress as you were in the Carpathian resort
where we loved each other so ardently. Forget everything that has

happened since then. Oh, you will soon forget in my arms; I shall kiss away all your sorrows."

She began to stroke me like a child, to kiss and caress me. Finally she said with a sweet smile:

"Go and get ready now. I shall dress also: shall I wear my fur jacket? Oh, yes, of course. Go quickly now."

When I returned she was standing in the middle of the room, wearing her white satin dress and her red kazabaika lined with ermine; her hair was powdered and she wore a small jeweled diadem. For a moment she reminded me in an uncanny way of Catherine II, but she gave me no time to think and drew me down beside her on the sofa. We spent two heavenly hours together. She was no longer a stern and capricious mistress but an elegant lady, a tender sweetheart. She showed me photographs and books that had just been published and she talked to me with such verve, lucidity and good taste that more than once I carried her hand to my lips, enraptured. She then had me read some poems of Lermontov, and at the height of my excitement she tenderly laid her little hand on mine and asked me, her eyes suffused with languor:

"Are you happy now?"

"Not yet."

She lay back on the cushions and slowly opened her kazabaika. But I promptly drew back the ermine over her half naked bosom.

"You are driving me insane!"

"Come to me."

I fell into her arms; her kisses were like a serpent's.

She whispered once again: "Are you happy?"

"Infinitely," I cried.

She burst out laughing, and her laughter had such an evil ring that it sent a cold shiver down my back.

"You dreamed of being the slave and the plaything of a beautiful woman, and now you imagine you are a free man; you think you are my lover, you insane fellow! I need only make one move and you become a slave again. Down on your knees!"

I fell at her feet, my hesitant eyes still fixed upon her.

"You cannot believe it." She looked at me with her arms folded across her breast. "I am bored and all you are good for is to amuse me awhile. Do not look at me in that way!"

She kicked me.

"You are whatever I want you to be, a man, a thing, an animal."

She rang. The black girls appeared.

"Tie his arms behind his back."

I remained on my knees and let them tie me up. They led me to the vineyard that lay along the south side of the garden. Maize had been planted between the vines and a few dry heads were still standing; a plough had been left there.

The blackamoors tied me to a stake and amused themselves by pricking me with golden hairpins. But this did not last long, for Wanda appeared with her ermine toque, her hands in the pockets of her jacket. She told them to untie me and fasten my hands behind my back. Then she had a yoke laid on my shoulders and I was harnessed to the plough.

The black demons pushed me on to the field; one drove the plough, the other led me on a leash, and the third goaded me with the whip, while Venus in Furs stood by, watching the scene.

*   *   *

The following day, as I was waiting on her at dinner, Wanda said to me:

"Lay another place, I want you to eat with me today." And as I was about to sit down opposite her, "No, next to me, close to my side."

She was in excellent humor. She gave me soup from her spoon, fed me with her fork, laid her head on the table like a playful kitten, and flirted with me. To my misfortune I paid a little more attention than I should have done to Haydée who was serving the meal in my place. For the first time I noticed her noble, almost European features, her statuesque bust that seemed chiseled in black marble. The lovely demon noticed that she was attractive to me and gave me a broad smile that revealed her dazzling teeth. No sooner had she left the room than Wanda flew into a rage.

"What! You dare look at another woman in my presence! She ought to suit you better than I — she is even more diabolical!"

I was terrified. I have never seen Wanda like this before; her face and even her lips grew as white as a sheet, and her whole body shook. Venus in Furs jealous of her slave! She tore the whip from its hook and lashed me full in the face, then she called the black servant girls and ordered me to be tied up and dragged to the cellar, where they flung me into a dark vault, a veritable prison cell.

The door closed behind me, the bolt was shot and the key ground in the lock. I was buried alive.

*　　*　　*

I do not know how long I have been lying on this pile of dank straw, like a calf waiting for the slaughter, without light, food or drink, and unable to sleep. She has everything she needs, but she is letting me die of hunger, if I do not freeze to death before then. I am shivering with cold — or is it fever? I believe I am beginning to hate her.

*　　*　　*

A blood-red streak of light falls across the floor — someone is opening the door.

Wanda appears on the threshold, wrapped in her furs, a lighted torch in her hand.

233

"Are you still alive?" she asks.

In a trice she is by my side; she kneels down and takes my head in her lap.

"Are you ill? Your eyes shine so! Do you love me? I want you to love me."

She draws a little dagger, and at the glint of its blade I am seized with terror, convinced that she is about to kill me. But she laughs and cuts the ropes that bind me.

\*     \*     \*

Every evening after dinner she sends for me. She demands that I read to her and then discuss various topics of interest. She seems completely transformed, as though she were ashamed of her savage behavior and of the severity with which she has treated me. A touching gentleness transfigures her whole being, and when she holds out her hand to bid me good-bye, her eyes shine with the saintly light of Goodness and Love that touches one to tears and wipes away all the miseries of existence and all the terror of death.

\*     \*     \*

I am reading her Manon Lescaut. She sees the association but does not refer to it, and merely smiles from time to time; finally she closes the little book.

"Do you not want me to read any further, madam?"

"Not today. I have decided to act the story of Manon in real life. I have a rendezvous at the Cascine and you, my dear chevalier, are to accompany me. You will, of course?"

"I obey all your commands."

"I am not commanding, but asking you," she said with irresistible charm. She rose, put her hand on my shoulder and looked at me. "Those eyes!" she exclaimed. "I love you, Severin, you have no idea how much I love you."

"Yes, I have," I replied bitterly. "You love me so much that you are going to a rendezvous with another man."

"I do this only to arouse your passion," she replied. "I am obliged to take admirers so as not to lose you. I do not ever want to lose you, do you hear? For I love you and you alone."

She clung passionately to my lips. "If only I could give you all my soul in this kiss! But come now."

She slipped into a simple black velvet coat and wrapped her head in a dark *baschlik*. She then walked rapidly down the gallery and entered the carriage.

"Gregor will drive," she called out to the coachman, who withdrew with a surprised look.

I climbed into the driver's seat and began to whip the horses furiously.

When we reached the Cascine, Wanda alighted at the point where the broad alley narrows to a corridor of lush foliage.

It was dark, and a sprinkling of stars shone through the overcast sky. On the banks of the Arno, a man stood watching the muddy waves; he wore a dark cloak that gave him the air of a brigand. Wanda quickly made her way through the shrubbery and tapped him on the shoulder. I can still see him turn toward her and take her hand; then they both disappeared behind the leafy wall.

A whole hour of torment! Finally I heard the rustle of leaves and they reappeared.

He accompanied her back to the carriage. The lantern revealed an incredibly young face that I had not seen before, with a gentle and melancholy expression. The bright light played upon his golden ringlets.

She held out her hand, which he kissed with deep respect; then she signaled to me and in a trice the carriage was speeding past the long line of trees that border the river like a green tapestry.

\* \* \*

The bell rings at the garden gate. It is a face I know — the man from the Cascine.

"Whom shall I announce?" I ask in French.

He shakes his head, embarrassed. "Do you understand a little German?"

"Of course, I was asking your name."

"Alas, I have none yet," he replied, ill at ease. "Tell your mistress that the German painter from the Cascine is here and that he would like to ask her.... But here she is."

Wanda appeared on the balcony and greeted the stranger.

"Gregor, show the gentleman to my apartment," she ordered.

I pointed the way.

"Please do not bother, I shall find it now.... Thank you, thank you very much." So saying he bounded upstairs.

I remained below, watching the poor German with a deep feeling of pity. Venus in Furs has trapped his soul in her red curls; he will paint her and lose his reason.

\*   \*   \*

A sunny winter's day: a golden haze trembles over the leaves of the trees and over the green carpet of the meadow. Below the balcony jewel-like camellias are bursting into flower.

Wanda is sitting in the loggia, drawing. The German stands opposite her, his hands clasped in adoration, looking, or rather gazing ecstatically at her face, utterly captivated by the vision before him.

But she ignores him; she has no eyes for me either as, spade in hand, I turn over the soil in the flower beds, so that I may see her and feel her presence that acts upon me like music, like poetry.

\*   \*   \*

The painter has left. It is extremely daring of me, but I take the plunge. I make my way up to the gallery, draw near to Wanda and ask:

"Do you love the painter, mistress?"

"I pity him," she answered, "but I do not love him. I love no one. I have loved you as ardently, as passionately, as deeply as I shall ever love, but it is no longer true at present. My heart is empty and dead, and it makes me very sad."

"Wanda!" I cried, in painful surprise.

"Soon you will not love me either," she went on. "Tell me when it has happened and I shall give you back your freedom."

"I shall remain your slave all my life, for I adore you and always shall," I cried, seized again by the frenzied passion that had repeatedly been so fatal to me.

Wanda looked at me with an oddly satisfied air.

"Consider this well," she said. "I have loved you infinitely and I have treated you tyrannically to gratify your desires. There are still some traces of the tender feelings that once found their echo in your heart, but when they too have disappeared, who knows whether I shall still want to free you? I could well become a monster of cruelty and have no other desire but to torment and torture you, to watch the man who adores me die of love, while I remain indifferent or even love another. Consider this well."

"I have thought about it for a long time," I answered, burning with fever. "I cannot exist without you; I shall die if you set me free. Let me be your slave, kill me, but do not turn me away!"

"Very well then, be my slave, only remember that I no longer love you and that consequently your love means no more to me than the attachment of a dog to its mistress. And dogs are meant to be kicked."

*    *    *

Today I went to see the *Venus de Medici*. It was early yet and the small octagonal chamber in the Tribuna was like a shadowy sanctuary. I stood in deep meditation, my hands clasped before the silent image of the goddess.

But I did not stay long in this position. There was no one in the gallery, not even an Englishman, and I knelt down before the statue. I gazed up at the maiden's sweet, lissom body, at her full breasts, her voluptuous face with its half-closed eyes, and the perfumed curls on either side of her head that seemed to conceal tiny horns.

\* \* \*

My mistress' bell. It was noon, but she was still in bed, with her arms folded behind her head.

"I am going to bathe," she said, "and you shall attend me. Lock the door."

I obeyed.

"Now go downstairs and make sure that everything is properly locked there as well."

As I descended the spiral staircase leading from her bedroom to the bath, my knees shook and I had to steady myself by clutching the banister.

After checking that the garden door was locked, I returned. Wanda was now seated on the bed, her hair undone, in her great velvet jacket edged with fur. A sudden movement revealed to me that she had nothing on but her jacket and I was inexplicably afraid. I felt like a condemned man who knows he must go to the scaffold and yet begins to tremble on seeing it.

"Come, Gregor, take me in your arms."

"What did you say, mistress?"

"You're to carry me, do you understand?"

I lifted her; she put her arms about my neck and I slowly

238

descended the stairs. Her hair brushed my cheek from time to time and her foot rested gently against my knee; I trembled under my lovely burden and thought I might fall at any moment.

The bathroom was a spacious rotunda, softly lit from a red glass dome in the ceiling. Two palm trees spread their broad leaves in a roof of green above the red velvet couch, and a few red carpeted steps led down to the wide marble bath in the center.

"There is a green ribbon on my bedside table," said Wanda, as I laid her on the couch. "Bring it to me, and also bring the whip."

I flew upstairs and down again and, kneeling before my sovereign lady, presented the two objects to her. She made me tie her heavy hair charged with electricity into a large chignon which I fastened with the velvet ribbon. I then had to prepare her bath and this I did very clumsily, for my hands and feet refused to obey me. From time to time I felt compelled to glance at my beauty, as though some magical force were driving me. At the sight of her lying on the red velvet cushions, her precious body peeping out between the folds of sable, I realized how powerfully sensuality and lust are aroused by flesh that is only partly revealed.

My feelings grew stronger still when the bath was filled and Wanda, in one sweep, threw off her fur wrap and appeared to me like the goddess of the Tribuna.

At that moment she seemed as saintly and chaste in her unveiled beauty as the statue of the goddess, and I fell on my knees before her and devoutly pressed my lips to her foot. My soul, that had been rocked a while ago by such a storm of emotion, was now suddenly pacified; there was not a trace of cruelty about her.

She slowly walked down the steps. I was able to contemplate her in peaceful joy, untouched by a single atom of suffering or desire. Her body gleamed through the crystal-clear water, and the waves she produced lapped lovingly around her. How right is the nihilist aesthete when he says that a real apple is more beauti-

239

ful than a painted apple, and a living body than a Venus of stone!

A silent rapture overcame my whole being when she rose from the bath, the drops of silvery water and the pink light streaming down her.

I wrapped the linen towel around her to dry her wonderful body, and the same peaceful bliss remained with me as she rested her foot upon me as on a footstool, and lay back on the cushions in her great velvet cloak. The supple furs greedily caressed her cold marble body. Her left arm, on which she supported herself, lay like a sleeping swan amid the dark sable, while her right hand toyed with the whip.

My eyes alighted by chance on the massive mirror that hung opposite and I let out a cry: our reflections in its golden frame were like a picture of extraordinary beauty. It was so strange and fantastic that I felt a deep pang of regret that its forms and colors would soon vanish like a cloud.

"What is it?" asked Wanda.

I pointed to the mirror.

"Ah, yes, it is beautiful," she said. "What a pity we cannot capture this moment."

"Why not?" I asked. "Would not the most famous painter be proud if you allowed him to immortalize you? I shudder to think that this extraordinary beauty, these mysterious green eyes and wild fiery hair, and all the splendor of this body should be lost forever. It fills me with the terror of death and nothingness. But the artist's hand must save you from this. You must not, like the rest of us, vanish irrevocably without leaving any trace of your existence. Your image must survive long after you have turned to dust; your beauty must triumph over death."

Wanda smiled.

"What a pity there is no Titian or Raphael in Italy today," she said. "However, love can be a substitute for genius. Who knows, perhaps our little German...." She mused.

"Yes, he must paint me.... And I shall ensure that love mixes the colors on his palette."

*   *   *

The young painter has set up a studio in the villa. She has captured him in her net.

He has just begun a Madonna, a Madonna with red hair and green eyes! Only the idealism of a German could make a virginal portrait of such a woman. The poor fellow is almost a bigger donkey than I, and our misfortune is that Titania has too soon discovered our ass' ears.

Now she is making fun of us, and how she laughs! I can hear the sounds of her mirth coming from the studio as I stand under her open window, waiting.

"Is it I? I cannot believe it, you must be mad to paint me as a Madonna!" She bursts out laughing again. "Wait a moment, I want to show you a portrait of me, one that I painted myself; you shall copy it."

Her head appears at the window, her hair fiery in the sunlight. "Gregor!"

I rush up the stairs, through the gallery and into the studio.

"Take him to the bathroom," orders Wanda, and she disappears.

We enter the rotunda and lock the door from the inside.

A few moments later Wanda arrives, dressed only in her furs, with the whip in her hand. She descends the stairs and stretches out on the velvet cushions as she had done before. I lie down in front of her and she places one of her feet on me while her right hand plays with the whip.

"Look at me," she says, "with your deep fanatical look. There, that is right."

The painter turns dreadfully pale; he devours the scene with his

241

beautiful melancholy eyes. His lips open, but he remains silent.

"Well, how do you like this picture?"

"Yes, that is how I shall paint you," says the German. But one could hardly say that he spoke, it was more like the moan of a soul sick unto death.

\* \* \*

The charcoal drawing is finished; the head and bust are sketched in. Already her diabolical face appears in a few bold lines, and life flickers in her green eyes.

Wanda stands before the canvas with folded arms. "This painting, like many of the Venetian school, is intended to be both a portrait and a story," declares the painter, still deathly pale.

"And you will call it?" she asks. "But what is the matter, are you ill?"

"I am afraid I..." he begins, darting a hungry glance at the lovely woman in furs. "But let us talk about the painting."

"Yes, let us talk about the painting."

"I imagine that the goddess of Love has come down from Olympus to visit a mortal. So as not to die of cold in this modern world of ours, she wraps her sublime body in great heavy furs and warms her feet on the prostrate body of her lover. I imagine the favorite of this beautiful despot, who is whipped when his mistress grows tired of kissing him, and whose love only grows more intense the more he is trampled underfoot. I shall call the picture *Venus in Furs*."

\* \* \*

The painter works slowly but his passion is fast increasing. I am afraid he will end up by killing himself. She teases him with riddles that he cannot solve and taunts him until he is driven to distraction.

During the sitting she sucks sweetmeats and rolls the wrappers into pellets which she flicks at him.

"I am glad you are in such high spirits, madam," says the painter, "but your face has completely lost the expression I need for my painting."

"The expression you need for your painting," she smiles. "Wait a moment."

She rises to her feet and deals me a blow with the whip. The painter gapes in childish wonder, half horrified and half admiring.

As she whips me, Wanda's face gradually recovers the cruel, ironic appearance that fills me with such rapture.

"Is this the right expression for your portrait?" she asks.

The painter is dumbfounded; he lowers his eyes to evade her piercing stare.

"That is the right expression," he stammers. "But I can no longer paint."

"What is the matter?" asks Wanda mockingly. "Can I be of any assistance?"

"Yes," cries the German, as though taken with madness. "Whip me, too!"

"With pleasure," she replies, shrugging her shoulders. "But if I am to whip you, I must do it properly."

"Whip me to death!" cries the painter.

"Will you let me tie you up?" she asks, with a smile.

"Yes," he sighs.

Wanda leaves the room for a moment and returns with a length of rope.

"Well, now, are you brave enough to put yourself at the mercy of Venus in Furs, the beautiful despot?" she taunts.

"Tie me up," replies the painter with the voice of a dying man.

Wanda ties his hands behind his back, winds a rope around his arms and another around his body, and attaches him to the bars of the window. She then throws off her furs, picks up the whip and stalks up to him.

The scene holds an awesome fascination: I feel my heart beat as she laughingly steps back to deal the first blow; the whip hisses through the air and he starts slightly as he feels its bite; then she begins to whip him without stopping, her mouth half-open, her teeth gleaming between her red lips, until the pitiful blue eyes beg for mercy. It is indescribable.

*  *  *

She now poses alone for him. He is working on her head. She has stationed me in the adjoining room, behind the heavy dividing curtain, where I can see everything without being seen. But what is she up to? Is she afraid of him? She has driven him mad enough. Or is this meant to be a new torture for me? My knees shake at the thought.

They are talking to one another: he is speaking in such a low voice that I cannot hear a thing, and she replies in the same tone. What does all this mean? Is there some secret understanding between them? I am suffering horribly and my heart threatens to leap from my breast.

Now he is kneeling before her. He embraces her and leans his head against hers, and she, the cruel woman, laughs and I hear her exclaim:

"Aha, you need the whip again!"

"Woman, goddess, is there no love in your heart?" cries the German. "Do you not know what it is to love, to be consumed with longing and passion? Can you not imagine what I suffer? Have you no pity for me?"

"No," she replies contemptuously, "but I have the whip."

She draws it deftly out of the pocket of her fur jacket and lashes him full in the face. He rises and staggers back.

"Can you paint now?" she asks indifferently.

He does not answer, but takes his place again before the easel.

\* \* \*

The picture is very successful; it is a good likeness, but it seems idealized because of the bright, supernatural, even diabolical colors. The painter has put into his work all his distress, his adoration and his wretchedness.

\* \* \*

Now he is painting me; we spend a few hours alone together each day. Today he turned to me suddenly and asked in a voice trembling with emotion:

"Do you love her?"

"Yes."

"I love her also." His eyes were filled with tears. He was silent for a moment, and turned back to the canvas.

"We have a mountain in Germany where she dwells," he murmured, as though to himself. "That woman is a demon."

\* \* \*

When the painting was finished, Wanda offered him a regal sum for his work.

"Oh, but you have paid me already," he said, with a pained smile.

Before leaving, he opened his portfolio with a mysterious air and allowed me to peep inside. It was a shock to see her face staring at me, as live as a reflection in a mirror.

"I am keeping that one," he said. "It is mine. She cannot take it away from me; I have earned it dearly enough."

"I really feel sorry for that poor painter," said Wanda today. "It is absurd to be as virtuous as I am, do you not think?"

I dared not reply.

"Oh, I forgot that I was speaking to a slave.... I must go out; I want to be distracted, to forget; quick, my carriage!"

*　*　*

Another fabulous outfit! Russian boots of mauve velvet lined with ermine, a dress of the same stuff gathered by narrow bands of fur, a short jacket matching the rest, tight-fitting and also lined with ermine. She wears a tall ermine toque in the style of Catherine the Great, with a plume fastened by a diamond clip, and her red hair lies loose over her back. Thus she climbs onto the driver's seat, and I take my place behind her. How she whips the horses! The team flies at breakneck speed.

Today she seems to want to attract attention at all costs, and fully succeeds. She is the lioness of the Cascine. People greet her from their carriages; they gather in groups to discuss her, but she ignores them all, and merely acknowledges the greetings of the older gentlemen with a nod.

Suddenly a young man appears on a prancing black horse. As soon as he sees Wanda he slows his mount to a walk and stops to let her go by. Their eyes meet: the lioness beholds the lion. As she passes before him, she is so drawn by the magnetic power of his eyes that she turns to look after him.

My heart stands still at the look of amazement and rapture that she casts over him like a net. He deserves it, however – what a beautiful man, by God! I have never seen his like in the flesh, only his marble replica in the *Belvedere*: he has the same slender, steely musculature, the delicate features, the wavy locks and the feature that makes him so distinctive: he has no beard. If his hips were less slender, he could be taken for a woman in disguise. But the strange expression of the mouth, the leonine muzzle and the bared teeth lend a fleeting cruelty to his magnificent face. Apollo flaying Marsyas!

He wears high black boots, closely fitting breeches of white leather and a black linen jacket in the style of Italian cavalry officers, trimmed with astrakhan and rich braid. On his dark curls, a red fez.

I cannot remain indifferent to his erotic power and my heart is filled with admiration for Socrates, who had the strength to resist the seductive Alcibiades.

I have never before seen my lioness so excited. Her cheeks burned as she jumped down from the carriage and hurried up the villa steps, ordering me to follow her.

Pacing up and down her room, she said with disturbing eagerness:

"You must find out immediately about the man we saw in the Cascine. . . . Oh, what a man! Did you see him? What do you think of him? Speak!"

"The man is handsome," I replied in a dull voice.

"He is so handsome," she paused and steadied herself on the back of the chair, "that he quite took my breath away."

"I can understand the impression he made on you," I answered. "I, too, was swept off my feet. In fact I formed the wild fantasy that. . . ."

"That this man was my lover and that he whipped you, to your great delight!" she said, bursting into laughter. "Off with you now, go!"

Before nightfall I had the required information. When I returned, Wanda was still wearing her magnificent attire, but she was lying on the ottoman, her face buried in her hands, her hair disheveled like a lion's mane.

"What is his name?" she asked in a strangely calm voice.

"Alexis Papadopolis."

"A Greek?"

I nodded.

"Is he very young?"

"Scarcely older than you. They say he was educated in Paris and that he is an atheist. He fought the Turks at Candia and is said to have distinguished himself no less by his race-hatred and cruelty than by his bravery."

"A man, in fact," she exclaimed, her eyes gleaming.

"He is living in Florence at present," I went on. "They say he is fabulously rich."

"I did not ask you about that," she interrupted. "This man is dangerous — are you not afraid of him? I am. Has he a wife?"

"No."

"A mistress?"

"Neither."

"What theater does he frequent?"

"Tonight he will be going to the Nicolini Theater, where the talented Virginia Marini is appearing with Salvini, the greatest living actor in Italy and perhaps in Europe."

"Do what you can to get a box, quickly!" she ordered.

"But, mistress...."

"Do you want a taste of the whip?"

\*     \*     \*

"You can wait in the stalls," she says, when I have laid the opera glasses and the program before her and arranged her footstool comfortably.

I support myself against the wall, hardly able to stand, my jealousy and anger are so great.... No, anger is not the right word; it is mortal anguish.

I can see her, in her blue moiré dress, her ermine cloak laid over her bare shoulders. Their boxes are face to face; I can see them devouring each other with their eyes. What do they care for Goldini's *Pamela*, Salvini, La Marini, the audience? For them the world has disappeared. As for me, what am I at this moment?

\* \* \*

Today she is attending the Greek ambassador's ball — does she know whom she will meet there?

At any rate she is dressed for the occasion: a heavy green silk dress molds her heavenly figure and reveals her arms and breasts. Her hair, which is tied in a large fiery knot, is adorned with a water lily and a spray of green rushes that sweeps down on to the nape of her neck. She no longer shows any trace of excitement. The fever and agitation have vanished, and she is calm, so calm that my blood freezes and I feel my heart grow cold under her gaze.

With slow stateliness she climbs the marble stairs, slips off her precious coat and carelessly drifts into the room filled with the silvery smoke of a thousand candles.

For a moment I follow her with my eyes, dumbfounded, and then I notice that I am holding her furs in my hands, still warm from the heat of her body. I deposit a kiss on them and my eyes fill with tears.

Here he is. In his black velvet jacket sumptuously lined with dark fur, he is a proud, handsome despot who plays with the lives and souls of men. He stands in the doorway, looking about him proudly. He catches sight of me and gives me a piercing stare.

Under his icy gaze I am again seized with a deadly terror, a premonition that this man will capture and enslave her, that he has the power to subjugate her entirely. Confronted with such fierce virility I feel ashamed and envious.

I am no more than a feeble, confused being. My weakest point is that I want to hate him but cannot. Why did he notice me among the army of servants?

With an aristocratic gesture he signals to me to come to him.

"Help me off with my coat," he orders calmly.

My whole body trembles with rebellion but I obey humbly, like a slave.

*   *   *

I wait all night long in the antechamber, in a state of feverish delirium. Strange visions pass before my eyes. I see their meeting, their first lingering exchange of glances; I see her whirling through the ballroom in his arms, giddy, resting with half-closed eyes against his breast; I see him in all the sanctity of love, not as a slave but as a lord, lying on the ottoman with her at his feet; I see myself kneeling before him, waiting on him, the tea tray trembling in my hands; I see him reach for the whip.

The footmen are talking about him now. Like a woman, he knows he is beautiful and behaves accordingly. Always elegant, he changes his costume four or even five times a day like a courtesan. He has been seen in Paris dressed as a woman and men showered him with love letters. An Italian singer famous for his talent and for his passionate temperament forced his way into his house and threatened to kill himself if our hero did not yield to him.

"I regret," the Greek replied with a smile, "I should have granted you my favors with pleasure, but alas, I can only sign your death warrant, for I am a man."

*   *   *

The ballroom is nearly empty, but she has apparently no thought of leaving.

Dawn is already peeping through the blinds.

Finally I hear the rustle of the heavy dress that flows behind her like a green wave. She is drawing slowly near, chatting to him. I hardly exist for her: she does not even bother to give me orders.

"Madam's coat," he commands. Naturally he does not think of assisting her himself.

While I help her with her furs, he stands by with folded arms. As I kneel to put on her fur boots, she leans lightly on his shoulder and asks:

"How does the story go, about the lioness?"

"When the lion she has chosen to live with is attacked by another," says the Greek, "the lioness lies down and watches the fight. If her companion is losing, she does not come to his rescue, but looks on indifferently while he is mauled to death by his opponent. Then she follows the victor, the stronger; that is woman's nature."

At that point my lioness gives me a strange look that makes me shudder, and the red light of dawn bathes all three of us in blood.

*   *   *

She did not go to bed, but took off her ball dress and untied her hair. Then she ordered me to light a fire, and she sat by the hearth staring into the flames.

"Do you still need me, mistress?" I asked in a faltering voice.

Wanda shook her head.

I left the room, walked through the gallery and sat down on the steps that led to the garden. A gentle north wind blew a cool dampness from the Arno, the green hills lay under a rosy mist, and golden vapors shrouded the town and billowed over the dome of the cathedral. A few stars glimmered in the pale sky.

I tore off my coat and pressed my burning forehead against the marble. Everything that had happened so far seemed like a child's game; now things were serious, horribly serious. I felt the approach of a catastrophe; I could see it before me and almost touch it with my hand, but I did not have the courage to go toward it and meet it. I was a broken man.

To be honest, it was not the suffering or the thought of being maltreated that frightened me. I was possessed by one fear only, that of losing the one I loved so passionately, and the fear was so violent and harrowing that I began to sob like a child.

\*   \*   \*

She remained in her room all day, waited on by the Negress. When the evening star rose in the sky I caught sight of her crossing the garden, and following her stealthily, I saw her enter the temple of Venus. I crept up behind her and watched through a crack in the door.

She stood before the majestic statue, her hands joined in prayer, and the light of the star of love cast a blue ray upon her.

\*   \*   \*

That night on my couch I was seized with the terror of losing her, and was so overwhelmed by feelings of doubt that I decided to play the part of a libertine hero. I lit the red oil lamp that hung in the passage under a pious image, and crept into her bedroom, shielding the light with my hand.

The vanquished lioness was the picture of exhaustion: she lay asleep on her back, sprawled over the cushions, her fists clenched, her breathing heavy. She seemed in the midst of an alarming dream. I slowly took my hand away from the light and let it fall on her magnificent face. But she did not awake.

I gently placed the lamp on the floor and fell on my knees by Wanda's bed, resting my head on her warm, soft arm. She stirred but did not wake.

I do not know how long I stayed in this prostrate position, in the dead of night, gripped by dreadful torment. At last a fit of violent trembling came over me and I was able to weep. I flooded her arm with my tears; she started several times, then finally awoke, rubbed her eyes and looked at me.

"Severin!" she cried, more frightened than angry.

I could not reply.

"Severin," she said again gently, "what is wrong? Are you sick?"

Her voice was so compassionate, so kind and tender, that it was like a red-hot iron piercing my breast and I began to sob aloud.

"Severin, my poor friend, my unhappy friend!" She gently stroked my hair. "I am very sorry for you, but I cannot help you; with the best will in the world, I can think of no remedy for you."

"Oh, Wanda, must it be so?" I moaned in my grief.

"What, Severin, what do you mean?"

"Do you no longer love me at all? Have you not a little pity left for me, or has the handsome stranger taken it all from you?"

"I cannot lie," she answered gently after a moment's silence. "He has made an impression on me that I cannot yet understand: I live in pain and fear. I have seen this feeling described in poetry and on the stage, but I had taken it for a figment of the imagination. Oh, he is a lion of a man, strong, handsome, proud, yet sensitive, not coarse like the men of our northern countries. I pity you, believe me, Severin, but I must possess him — what am I saying! — I must give myself to him, if he will have me."

"Think of your honor, Wanda. You have kept it unsullied till now," I exclaimed. "Even if I no longer mean anything to you...."

"I am considering it," she replied. "I want to be strong for as long as I can, but I want...." She hid her face shyly in the cushions: "I want to be his wife...if he will have me."

"Wanda!" I gasped, seized by the fatal anguish which made me lose all control. "You want to be his wife; you want to belong to him forever! Oh, do not send me away from you. He does not love you."

"Who told you that?" she cried.

"He does not love you," I went on passionately, "but I do; I love you, I adore you, I am your slave; I want you to tread me underfoot; I want to carry you in my arms all my life."

"Who told you that he does not love me?" she asked again, interrupting me violently.

"Oh, be mine!" I pleaded. "I cannot live, I cannot exist without you. Have pity, Wanda, have pity!"

She gazed at me with her cold, insensitive look, and smiled wickedly.

"You say he does not love me," she said. "Very well then, let that idea comfort you." And she turned her back on me with a disdainful air.

"Good God!" I sobbed. "Are you not a woman of flesh and blood, have you not a heart like mine?"

"You know what I am," she answered harshly. "I am a woman of stone, Venus in Furs, your ideal. Kneel down and worship me."

"Wanda," I pleaded, "have mercy!"

She laughed. I buried my face in the cushions and let the tears flow to relieve my pain.

For a long while all was silent, then Wanda slowly rose.

"You bore me," she said.

"Wanda!"

"I am weary, let me sleep."

"Have pity on me," I pleaded, "do not reject me; no man can love you as I do."

"Let me sleep."

She turned her back on me again. I leapt to my feet and seized the dagger that hung next to her bed; I drew it from the scabbard and pointed it at my breast.

"I shall kill myself before your eyes," I sobbed.

"Do as you please," replied Wanda, with perfect indifference, "but let me sleep." She yawned loudly: "I am tired."

For a moment I was stunned, then I began to laugh and cry at the same time. Finally I stuck the dagger in my belt and again fell on my knees before her.

"Wanda, listen to me one moment," I pleaded.

"I want to sleep, do you hear?" she cried, leaping angrily out of bed and giving me a kick. "Are you forgetting that I am your mistress?"

As I did not move an inch, she seized the whip and dealt me a blow. I rose. She struck me again, this time full in the face.

"Animal, slave!"

With my clenched fists raised to the sky, I resolutely left the room. She flung down the whip and burst into a loud peal of laughter. I imagine my theatrical attitude must have seemed the height of comedy.

*　　*　　*

I am resolved to cut myself off from the heartless woman who has treated me so cruelly and is now prepared to betray me in reward for my servile adoration and all that I have suffered. I tie the little I possess into a bundle and write her the following note:

"Madam,

I have loved you like a madman, I have given myself to you as no man has ever done, but you have abused my sacred emotions and have played a frivolous and shameless game with me. So long as you were only pitiless and cruel I was able still to love you, but you are now becoming vulgar. I am no longer the slave who let you trample and whip him; you yourself have given me back my freedom and I am leaving a woman that I can now only hate and despise.

SEVERIN KUZIEMSKI"

I entrust this note to the black servant girl and escape as fast as I can.

*　　*　　*

I arrive breathless at the railway station; suddenly a pain shoots through my heart and I begin to weep. Oh, how shameful this is! I want to run away but I cannot; I turn back — but whither? To her, the one I abominate and adore.

Again I change my mind: I cannot return; I have no right to return.

But how can I leave Florence? I realize that I have no money, not a penny. Then I shall travel on foot; it is better to be an honest beggar than to eat the bread of a courtesan.

But I cannot leave: she has my word of honor. I must return; perhaps she will free me from my pledge.

I take a few steps, then stop once more. She has my word, yes, I have sworn to be her slave for as long as she wishes, until she sets me free; however, I do have the right to kill myself.

I walk through the Cascine and down to the Arno, where the yellow waves lap monotonously around the trunks of a few lonely willows. I sit down and draw up an account of my existence; I review the whole of my life and find it a sorry affair: a few joys, an infinite amount of boredom and futility, and in the middle, a well of grief, anguish, disappointment and vain hopes.

I think of my mother whom I loved so dearly and whom I saw die of a dreadful illness, of my brother who perished in the flower of his youth, without ever tasting the pleasures of life; I think of my dead nurse, of my childhood playmates, of the friends who studied with me, of all those who are lying under the cold earth. I think of the turtledove who used to come cooing and bowing to me instead of going to his mate. All is dust and returns to dust.

I burst out laughing and slide into the river; but at the same time I save myself by clutching a willow branch overhanging the muddy waters. As in a vision, the woman who has made me so wretched appears before me; she hovers above the water, the sun shines through her transparent form and her head is surrounded by red flames. She turns toward me and smiles.

* * *

Here I am back again, soaked to the skin and burning with shame and fever. The servant girl has delivered my letter, I am condemned, lost, delivered into the hands of a heartless woman whom I have now insulted. She may even kill me; well, let her do so, for although I do not want to live any longer, I am unable to take my own life.

I walk to the back of the house and see her on the terrace, leaning over the railing with her head in full sunlight and her green eyes gleaming.

"Are you still alive?" she asks, without moving. I remain silent and hang my head.

"Give me back my dagger," she says. "It is of no use to you, since you have not even the courage to kill yourself."

"I have lost it," I reply, shivering with cold.

She eyes me scornfully.

"Did you lose it in the Arno?" she shrugged. "Ah, well. Why didn't you leave?"

I murmur something which neither she nor I can understand.

"Oh, you have no money," she exclaims. "Here!"

And she tosses me her purse with a contemptuous gesture.

I leave it on the ground. For a long time we are both silent.

"So you do not want to go?"

"I cannot."

* * *

Wanda goes to the Cascine and to the theater without me; when she entertains the Negresses wait on her. No one inquires about me. I roam anxiously in the garden like an animal that has lost its master.

As I was lying in the copse today, watching a few sparrows fight for a handful of seed, I suddenly heard the rustle of a woman's dress.

Wanda drew near, wearing a dark silk gown modestly fastened at the neck. The Greek was with her. An agitated exchange took place, but I could not catch a word. Then I saw him stamp his foot, sending the gravel flying, and lash the air with his riding crop. Wanda started – was she afraid he would strike her?

He left. She called him back, but he did not hear, or rather did not want to hear.

Wanda shook her head sadly and sat down on the nearest stone bench. For a long time she remained deep in thought. I watched her with wicked glee; finally I regained possession of myself and came toward her with an ironic look.

She stood up, her whole body trembling.

"I only come to wish you great happiness," I said, bowing to her. "I see, madam, that you have found your master."

"Yes, thank God," she cried. "Not another slave, I have had enough of them: a master. Women need to have a master to worship."

"So you worship him, Wanda?" I exclaimed. "You worship that barbarian?"

"I love him as I have never loved before."

"Wanda!"

I clenched my fists, but the tears were already rising to my eyes, and I was overcome by the delirium of passion.

"Very well then, choose him, take him for your husband, let him become your master, but I want to remain your slave for as long as I live."

"You want to be my slave even then? That would be amusing, but I am afraid he would not accept it."

"*He* would not?"

"He is already jealous of you!" she exclaimed. "Yes, he of you! He insists that I dismiss you on the spot, and when I told him who you were...."

"You told him?" I gasped.

"I told him everything. I related all our story to him, all our oddities, everything, and instead of laughing he grew angry and stamped his foot."

"And threatened to beat you?"

Wanda lowered her eyes and was silent.

"Yes, yes," I said with bitter irony, "you are afraid of him." I threw myself at her feet and in my exaltation embraced her knees. "I want nothing from you, nothing but the permission to be near you always, to be your slave!"

"Do you realize that you bore me?" said Wanda in a neutral voice.

I leapt to my feet; my blood was boiling.

"You are not cruel now, you are vulgar!" I said, giving the word its precise, wounding meaning.

"That is already in your letter," replied Wanda with a shrug. "A man of wit does not repeat himself."

"Then how would you describe your behavior toward me?" I asked furiously.

"I could make you see sense," she replied mockingly, "but I prefer this time to answer you by argument rather than with the whip. You have no right to blame me; I have always been honest with you. Have I not warned you more than once? Have I not loved you with all my heart, passionately, and have I in any way hidden from you the danger of lowering yourself before me? Have I not told you that I want to be dominated? But you wished to be my plaything, my slave! Your greatest delight was to be kicked and whipped by a proud and cruel woman. What do you want now? Dangerous tendencies were lurking in me, and you were

259

the one who awakened them; if I now take pleasure in hurting and tormenting you, it is entirely your fault. You have made me what I am, and you are so weak and unmanly that you are now blaming me."

"Yes, I am guilty," I replied, "but have I not suffered enough now? Cease this cruel game!"

"That is exactly my intention," she replied, with a strange look.

"Wanda," I cried, "do not drive me to desperation; you can see that I have become a man again."

"A flash in the pan," she replied, "it disappears as quickly as it flares up. You think you can intimidate me, but you are only making yourself ridiculous. If you had been the man I thought you were at first, a serious-minded and intelligent man, I should have loved you faithfully and become your wife. Women desire men they can look up to; a man such as you, who willfully places his neck under a woman's foot, is only an amusing toy that she throws away when she is bored."

"Try to throw me away," I said ironically. "Some toys are dangerous."

"Do not provoke me," cried Wanda. Her eyes began to sparkle, her cheeks to flame.

"If I cannot possess you," I said, in a voice strangled with anger, "then no other man shall."

"What play is that from?" she mocked. Then she seized me by the coat. "Do not provoke me," she repeated. "I am not a cruel woman, but who knows how far I might go, or whether there is any limit to what I might do to you?"

"What can you do that would be worse for me than to take him for your lover?" I said, hardly able to contain myself.

"I could make you his slave," she replied. "Are you not in my power? Do I not have the contract? But naturally it would merely be a pleasure for you if I were to have you bound and were to tell him: 'Now do with him as you please.' "

"Woman, are you mad?"

"I am perfectly rational. I am warning you for the last time. Do not offer me any resistance; I have gone so far now that it is easy for me to go still further. I now feel something akin to hatred for you; to see you whipped by him would be a veritable pleasure, but I am still restraining myself at present."

At my wit's end, I seized her by the wrist and forced her to kneel before me.

"Severin!" she cried, her features twisted in fear and rage.

"I shall kill you if you become his wife."

The voice that came out of my throat was toneless and hoarse. "You are mine and I shall not let you go. I love you too much." I clutched her tightly and unthinkingly grasped the dagger that was still in my belt.

Wanda looked up at me with her gentle unfathomable eyes.

"This is the way I like you," she said calmly. "Rightly now you are a man and I know that I still love you."

"Wanda!"

Tears of delight sprang to my eyes. I leaned down and covered her adorable face with kisses. But she suddenly broke into gay laughter and cried:

"Have you had enough of your ideal, now? Are you pleased with me?"

"What? Were you not serious?"

"I am serious," she replied in a playful tone, "when I say that I love you, and you alone. But you sweet madman, you simpleton, did you not even notice that it was all a game, a joke? Did you not see how hard it was for me to whip you, when all I wanted to do was to take your face in my hands and cover it with kisses? But that is enough now; I have played my cruel role better than you expected. Now I am sure you will be content with a nice little wife, clever and not too ugly. We shall live very sensibly, and...."

"You will be my wife!" I could not help exclaiming, overjoyed.

"Yes, your wife, my dear, darling husband," whispered Wanda, kissing my hand.

I threw my arms around her.

"Now you are no longer my slave, Gregor; you are my dear Severin again, my husband."

"And what about him? Do you not love him?"

"How could you think I could ever love that barbarian? You were blind. I was so afraid for you."

"I nearly took my life because of you."

"Truly?" she exclaimed. "Ah, I shudder to think that you were already in the Arno."

"But it was you who saved me," I said tenderly. "You were hovering above the waters, smiling, and your smile called me back to life."

\* \* \*

A new calmness has come over me now that I hold her in my arms. She rests peacefully against my breast, she lets me kiss her and smiles. It is as though I were emerging from a fever beset by fantastic visions, as though I were a shipwrecked sailor safely washed up onshore after a long and perilous battle against the waves.

\* \* \*

"I hate this town where you have been so unhappy," she said, as I wished her good night. "I want to leave immediately, tomorrow. Be so good as to write a few letters for me, and in the meantime I will pay my farewell calls. Does that suit you?"

"Of course, my dear, sweet, beautiful wife."

\* \* \*

Early next morning she knocked at my door and asked me tenderly how I had slept. I would never have thought that gentleness could become her so.

*　*　*

She has now been gone for over four hours. I have long since finished the letters and am sitting on the balcony, watching for her carriage to appear. I am a little worried about her although, goodness knows, there is not the slightest cause for doubt or alarm. But the feeling is there, weighing on my chest, and I cannot rid myself of it. No doubt my soul is still darkened by the sufferings of the past days.

*　*　*

She is back, radiating happiness and satisfaction.

"Well, did everything go as you wished?" I ask, kissing her hand tenderly.

"Yes, dear heart," she replies, "and we are leaving tonight. Help me pack my cases."

*　*　*

During the evening she asked me to go to the post office and mail her letters myself. I took the carriage and returned within an hour.

"The mistress wants to see you," said the black girl with a smile, as I climbed the wide marble stairs.

"Has someone called?"

"No one," she replied, crouching on the stairs like a black cat.

*　*　*

Slowly I passed through the hall and found myself before her bedroom door. Why was my heart beating so? I was perfectly happy. Slowly I opened the door and drew back the curtain.

Wanda was lying on the ottoman and did not seem to notice me. How lovely she looked in her silver-gray silk dress that molded her figure and revealed her arms and her incomparable breasts! Her hair was tied with a black velvet ribbon. A great fire crackled in the hearth, the lamp cast a red glow, and the whole room seemed bathed in blood.

"Wanda!" I cried at last.

"Oh, Severin," she said, leaping up and embracing me, "I have missed you so!" She sat down again among the sumptuous cushions and tried to draw me to her, but I fell on my knees and gently rested my head in her lap.

"Do you know, I am very much in love with you today?" she murmured, stroking a lock of hair from my forehead and kissing my eyes. "What beautiful eyes you have! They have always been the most attractive part of you, but today they quite enrapture me. I am overwhelmed." She stretched her marvelous limbs and gazed tenderly at me through her red eyelashes. "But you are so cold, you are holding me as though I were a block of wood. Wait a moment, I shall make you amorous." She pressed her lips languorously against mine. "I am no longer attractive to you; you still want me to treat you cruelly — no doubt I have been too kind today. Do you know what, you little fool? I think I shall whip you."

"But my child...."

"I want to."

"Wanda!"

"Come, let me tie you up," she went on, skipping gleefully across the room. "I want to see you very much in love, do you understand? Here are the ropes: I wonder if I shall still be able to do it?"

She began to tie my feet together, then she fastened my hands securely behind my back and finally she wound a rope around me like a prisoner.

"There," she said with playful eagerness. "Can you move?"

"No."

"Good."

She tied a loop in a stout rope, threw it over my head and let it fall to my hips, then drew it tight and secured me to the pillar.

A strange shudder went through me.

"I feel like a condemned man," I murmured.

"That is because you are to be thoroughly whipped today," she said.

"Then wear your fur jacket, I beg of you."

"I shall grant you that pleasure."

She fetched her kazabaika and put it on with a smile. Then she stood before me with her arms crossed, and looked at me with half-closed eyes.

"Do you know the story of the ox of Dionysius?" she asked.

"I remember it vaguely. Why?"

"A courtier invented a new instrument of torture for the tyrant of Syracuse. The victim was to be put inside a hollow bronze ox under which a fire was to be lit. It was intended that as the metal grew hot the prisoner would howl with pain and thus imitate the bellowing of an ox. Dionysius expressed interest in the invention and decided to try it out on the spot; so he had the inventor himself placed inside the ox. A very instructive story. It is you who have taught me selfishness, pride and cruelty, and you shall be my first victim. I am now feeling intense pleasure in having at my mercy someone who, like me, has thoughts, feelings and desires, a man who is my superior, both physically and intellectually, and above all a man who loves me — for you do still love me?"

"I love you madly!"

"Good! You will get all the more pleasure from what I am about to do to you."

"What has come over you? I do not understand you today. There is an unmistakable glint of cruelty in your eyes, and you are so strangely beautiful, quite the Venus in Furs."

Without answering, Wanda put her arm about my neck and kissed me. My passion flooded back in all its violence.

"Where is the whip?" I asked.

Wanda laughed and moved back a step or two.

"So you really want to be whipped?" she said, throwing back her head with a proud gesture.

"Yes."

Suddenly Wanda's face altered; it was transfigured by anger and seemed for a moment quite hideous.

"Then whip him!" she cried.

At that instant the dark, curly head of the Greek appeared behind the curtains of the four-poster bed. I was speechless and paralyzed. My situation was dreadfully comic and I should have laughed at it myself had it not also been so desperately humiliating.

It surpassed anything I had imagined. My rival stepped forth in his boots, his tight white breeches and his close-fitting jacket; the sight of his athletic build sent a shudder down my spine.

"You are indeed cruel," he said, turning to Wanda.

"Only thirsty for pleasure," she replied fiercely. "Pleasure alone makes life worthwhile; whoever suffers or lives in privation greets death as a friend, but whoever surrenders to pleasure does not easily part with life. The pleasure-seeker must take life joyfully, in the manner of the ancients. He should not be afraid of indulging himself at the expense of others; he must never feel pity. He must harness others to his carriage or his plough, like beasts. He should choose his slaves among men who live fully and would enjoy life as he does, and he must use them for his own

266

pleasure, without any trace of remorse. It is not for him to ask whether they are fulfilled or mortified. He must always bear this idea in mind: if they had me in their power, they would act as I do, and I should have to pay for their pleasure with my sweat, my blood and my soul. This is how the ancients lived: pleasure and cruelty, freedom and slavery, always went hand in hand. Men who wish to live as the gods of Olympus did must have slaves to throw into their fish ponds and gladiators ready to do battle for them at their feasts. Little do they care if they are spattered by the fighters' blood."

Wanda's words brought me back to my senses.

"Untie me!" I cried.

"Are you not my slave, my property?" said Wanda. "Must I show you the contract?"

"Untie me," I threatened, "or else...." I strained against the ropes.

"Can he free himself?" she asked. "He has threatened to kill me."

"Have no fear," said the Greek, inspecting my bonds.

"I shall call for help," I said.

"No one will hear you, and no one will prevent me from abusing your sacred emotions and playing this frivolous game with you," replied Wanda, parodying the phrase from my letter with fierce humor. "Now do you find me cruel and merciless, or am I merely becoming vulgar? What do you say? Do you love me still or do you hate and despise me?"

"Here is the whip." She handed it to the Greek who eagerly stepped forward.

"Do not touch me!" I said, trembling with rage. "I shall not take anything from you."

"You object because I am not wearing furs," teased the Greek, and he took his short sable jacket from the bed.

"How charming you look!" exclaimed Wanda, giving him a kiss and helping him on with his furs.

"May I really whip him?" he asked.

"Do with him as you please," replied Wanda.

"Beast!" I cried, utterly revolted.

The Greek eyed me fiercely, like a tiger; his muscles swelled as he drew back his arm and the whip whistled through the air. Like Marsyas I was bound hand and foot and condemned to be flayed by Apollo.

My eyes drifted about the room and came to rest on the ceiling where Samson lay at Delilah's feet, about to be blinded by the Philistines. The painting suddenly appeared as a symbol, the timeless image of the love, the passion and the lust of man for woman. "Each of us ends up like Samson," I thought. "We are always betrayed by the woman we love, whether she wears a sable cloak or a linen smock."

"Now watch me train him!" cried the Greek.

He bared his teeth and his face wore the bloodthirsty expression that so frightened me the first time I saw him. And he began to whip me so mercilessly and with such dreadful force that I started at each blow and began to shake all over with pain; the tears streamed down my cheeks. Meanwhile Wanda lay on the ottoman, her head in her hand, watching the scene with fiendish curiosity and amusement.

The sensation of being whipped before the eyes of a woman one adores by a successful rival is quite indescribable; I was dying of shame and despair.

What was most humiliating was that I felt a wild and supersensual pleasure in my pitiful situation, lashed by Apollo's whip and mocked by the cruel laughter of my Venus.

But Apollo whipped all poetry from me, as one blow followed the next, until finally, clenching my teeth in impotent rage, I

cursed myself, my voluptuous imagination, and above all woman
and love. I suddenly saw with alarming clarity how blind passion
and lust have always led men, from the time of Holofernes and
Agamemnon, into the net of woman's treachery, into poverty,
slavery and death. It was as though I were awakening from a
long dream.

My blood was flowing under the whip; I curled up like a worm
being crushed, but still he continued to whip me without mercy
and she to laugh, and all the while to fasten her cases and slip
into her traveling furs. She was still laughing as they went downstairs arm in arm and got into the carriage.

A moment's silence. I held my breath.

The doors slammed, the horses moved off and the noise of the
carriage could be heard for a while; then all was quiet.

\*   \*   \*

For a moment I thought of revenge; I thought of killing him,
but I was bound by the wretched contract: I could do nothing
but keep my word and grit my teeth.

\*   \*   \*

The first thing I felt after this, the most cruel disaster of my
life, was the desire to live rough and experience danger and privation. I wanted to become a soldier and go to Asia or Algeria,
but my father was old and sick and wanted me to stay near him.
So I simply returned home and for two years shared his worries,
administered our estate, and also learned something which was
quite new to me and which now refreshed me like a draft of clear
water: to work and to fulfill my duties.

Then my father died and quite naturally and without altering
my way of life I became the master of the house. I donned my
father's boots of Spanish leather and continued to lead a well-

ordered life, as though he were still standing behind me, watching over my shoulder with his great wise eyes.

One day I received a box accompanied by a letter. I recognized Wanda's writing.

Strangely moved, I opened it and read.

"Sir,

Now that three years have elapsed since that night in Florence, I can admit that I loved you deeply. But it was you who stifled my feelings with your romantic devotion and insane passion. From the moment that you became my slave, I felt that it would be impossible for you ever to be my husband; but I found it exciting to realize your ideal and while I amused myself pleasantly, perhaps to cure you.

I found the strong man I needed and was as happy with him as it is possible to be on this funny ball of clay. But my happiness, like all things of this world, was short-lived: about a year ago he was killed in a duel, and since then I have been living in Paris like an Aspasia.

What about you? Your life will surely not lack sunshine if your imagination has ceased to govern you and those other qualities that first attracted me to you have gained the upper hand, I mean your clarity of thought, kindness of heart and above all virtuous austerity.

I hope that my whip has cured you, that the treatment, cruel though it was, has proved effective.

In memory of that time and of a woman who loved you passionately, I am sending you the portrait by the poor German painter.                    VENUS IN FURS"

\*　\*　\*

I could not help smiling and, as I sank into a daydream, I suddenly saw before me the lovely creature clad in her ermine jacket, with the whip in her hand. I smiled to think of the woman I had loved so much, of the jacket that had so delighted me in the past; I smiled at the thought of the whip; and finally I smiled to think of my own suffering, and said to myself: "The treatment was cruel but radical, and the main thing is that I am cured."

*     *     *

"And what is the moral of the tale?" I asked, replacing the manuscript on the table.

"That I was a fool!" he exclaimed, without turning around, as though embarrassed. "If only I had whipped her instead!"

"A curious method," I replied. "Perhaps with your peasant girls...."

"Oh, they are used to it. But think of the effect it would produce on our refined ladies with their nerves and hysterics!"

"But what about the moral?"

"The moral is that woman, as Nature created her and as man up to now has found her attractive, is man's enemy; she can be his slave or his mistress but never his companion. This she can only be when she has the same rights as he and is his equal in education and work. For the time being there is only one alternative: to be the hammer or the anvil. I was fool enough to let a woman make a slave of me, do you understand? Hence the moral of the tale: whoever allows himself to be whipped deserves to be whipped. But as you see, I have taken the blows well; the rosy mist of supersensuality has lifted, and no one will ever make me believe that the sacred wenches of Benares or Plato's rooster* are the images of God."

* Term used by Schopenhauer to designate women (footnote in 2nd edition). Diogenes threw a plucked rooster into Plato's school and exclaimed: "Here is Plato's man" (footnote in 1st edition).

# A Childhood Memory and Reflections

# on the Novel

Whether she is a princess or a peasant girl, whether she is clad in ermine or sheepskin, she is always the same woman: she wears furs, she wields a whip, she treats men as slaves and she is both my creation and the true Sarmatian woman.

I believe that every artistic creation develops in the same way that this Sarmatian woman took shape in my imagination. First there is the innate tendency common to all of us to capture a subject that has eluded most other artists; then the author's own experience intervenes and provides him with the living being whose prototype already exists in his imagination. This figure preoccupies him, seduces him, captivates him, because it corresponds to his innate tendencies and mirrors his particular nature; he then transforms it and gives it body and soul. Finally, in the reality which he has transformed into a work of art, he encounters the problem that is the source of all subsequent images. The inverse path that leads from the problem back to the configuration is not an artistic one.

When I was still a child I showed a predilection for the "cruel" in fiction; reading this type of story would send shivers through me and produce lustful feelings. And yet I was a compassionate soul who would not have hurt a fly. I would sit in a dark secluded corner of my great-aunt's house, devouring the legends of the Saints; I was plunged into a state of feverish excitement on reading about the torments suffered by the martyrs.

At the age of ten I already had an ideal woman. I yearned for a distant relative of my father's — let us call her Countess Zenobia — the most beautiful and also the most promiscuous woman in the country.

It happened on a Sunday afternoon; I shall never forget it. I had come to play with the children of my aunt-in-law — as we called her — and we were left alone with the maid. Suddenly the countess, proud and resplendent in her great sable cloak, entered the room, greeted us, kissed me (which always sent me into raptures) and then exclaimed: "Come, Leopold, I want you to help me off with my furs." She did not have to ask me twice. I followed her into the bedroom, took off the heavy furs that I could barely lift, and helped her into the magnificent green velvet jacket trimmed with squirrel that she wore about the house. I then knelt to put on her gold-embroidered slippers. On feeling her tiny feet in my hands I forgot myself and kissed them passionately. At first my aunt stared at me in surprise, then she burst out laughing and gave me a little kick.

While she was preparing our tea we played hide-and-seek; I do not know what devil prompted me to hide in my aunt's bedroom. As I stood concealed behind a clothes rack, I heard the doorbell and a few moments later my aunt entered the bedroom followed by a handsome young man. She closed the door without locking it and drew her lover into her arms.

I did not understand what they were saying, still less what they were doing, but my heart began to pound, for I was acutely aware of my situation: if they discovered me I would be taken for a spy. Overcome with dread, I closed my eyes and blocked my ears. I was about to betray my presence by sneezing, when suddenly the door was flung open and my aunt's husband rushed into the room accompanied by two friends. His face was crimson and his eyes flashed with anger. But as he hesitated for a moment, wondering no doubt which of the two lovers to strike first, Zenobia anticipated him.

Without a word, she rose, strode up to her husband and gave him an energetic punch on the nose. He staggered; blood was pouring from his nose and mouth. But my aunt was still not satisfied; she picked up a whip and, brandishing it, showed my uncle and his friends the door. The gentlemen were only too glad to slip away, and not last among them, the young admirer. At that moment the wretched clothes rack fell to the ground and all the fury of Madam Zenobia was poured out on me: "So you were hiding, were you? I shall teach you to play at spying."

I tried in vain to explain my presence, but in a trice she had seized me by the hair and thrown me on the carpet; she then placed her knee on my shoulder and began to whip me vigorously. I clenched my teeth but could not prevent the tears from springing to my eyes. And yet I must admit that while I writhed under my aunt's cruel blows, I experienced acute pleasure. No doubt her husband had more than once enjoyed a similar sensation, for soon he returned to her room, not as an avenger but as a humble slave; it was he who fell down at the feet of the treacherous woman and begged her pardon, while she pushed him away with her foot. Then they locked the door. This time I was not ashamed, and did not block my ears, but listened attentively at the door – either from spite or childish jealousy – and again I heard the crack of the whip that I had tasted only a moment before.

This event became engraved on my soul as with a red-hot iron; I did not understand at the time how this woman in voluptuous furs could betray her husband and maltreat him afterward, but I both hated and loved the creature who seemed destined, by virtue

275

of her strength and diabolical beauty, to place her foot insolently on the neck of humanity.

Subsequently other strange scenes, other figures, in regal ermine, in bourgeois rabbit fur or in rustic lamb's fleece, produced new impressions on me; until one day this particular type of woman became crystallized in my mind, and took definite shape for the first time in the heroine of *The Emissary*.

Much later I isolated the problem that inspired the novel *Venus in Furs*. I became aware first of the mysterious affinity between cruelty and lust, and then of the natural enmity and hatred between the sexes which is temporarily overcome by love, only to reappear subsequently with elemental force, turning one of the partners into a hammer and the other into an anvil.

SACHER-MASOCH, "Choses Vécues"
*Revue Bleue*, 1888

# Two Contracts of von Sacher-Masoch

## Contract between Mrs. Fanny von Pistor and Leopold von Sacher-Masoch

On his word of honor, Mr. Leopold von Sacher-Masoch undertakes to be the slave of Mrs. von Pistor, and to carry out all her wishes for a period of six months.

On her behalf, Mrs. von Pistor shall not demand anything of him that would dishonor him in any way (as a man or as a citizen). Moreover, she shall allow him six hours a day for his personal work, and shall never look at his letters and writings. On the occurrence of any misdemeanor or negligence or act of lèse-majesté, the mistress (Fanny von Pistor) may punish her slave (Leopold von Sacher-Masoch) in whatever manner she pleases. In short, the subject shall obey his sovereign with complete servility and shall greet any benevolence on her part as a precious gift; he shall not lay claim to her love nor to any right to be her lover. On her behalf, Fanny von Pistor undertakes to wear furs as often as possible, especially when she is behaving cruelly.

[Later deleted] At the end of the six months, this period of enslavement shall be considered by both parties as not having occurred, and they shall make no serious allusion to it. Everything that happened is to be forgotten, and the previous loving relations restored.

These six months need not run consecutively: they may be subject to interruptions beginning and ending according to the whims of the sovereign lady.

We, the undersigned, hereby confirm this contract,

FANNY PISTOR BAGANOW

LEOPOLD, KNIGHT OF SACHER-MASOCH

Came into operation 8th December 1869.


### Contract between Wanda and Sacher-Masoch

My Slave,

The conditions under which I accept you as my slave and tolerate you at my side are as follows:

You shall renounce your identity completely.

You shall submit totally to my will.

In my hands you are a blind instrument that carries out all my orders without discussion. If ever you should forget that you are my slave and do not obey me implicitly in all matters, I shall have the right to punish and correct you as I please, without your daring to complain.

Anything pleasant and enjoyable that I shall grant you will be a favor on my part which you must acknowledge with gratitude. I shall always behave faultlessly toward you but shall have no obligations to do so.

You shall be neither a son nor a brother nor a friend; you shall be no more than my slave groveling in the dust.

Your body and your soul too shall belong to me, and even if this causes you great suffering, you shall submit your feelings and sentiments to my authority.

I shall be allowed to exercise the greatest cruelty, and if I should mutilate you, you shall bear it without complaint. You shall work for me like a slave and although I may wallow in luxury whilst leaving you in privation and treading you underfoot, you shall kiss the foot that tramples you without a murmur. I shall have the right to dismiss you at any time, but you shall not be allowed to leave me against my will, and if you should escape, you hereby recognize that I have the power and the right to torture you to death by the most horrible methods imaginable.

You have nothing save me; for you I am everything, your life, your future, your happiness, your unhappiness, your torment and your joy.

You shall carry out everything I ask of you, whether it is good or evil, and if I should demand that you commit a crime, you shall turn criminal to obey my will.

Your honor belongs to me, as does your blood, your mind and your ability to work.

Should you ever find my domination unendurable and should your chains ever become too heavy, you will be obliged to kill yourself, for I will never set you free.

"I undertake, on my word of honor, to be the slave of Mrs. Wanda von Dunajew, in the exact way that she demands, and to submit myself without resistance to everything she will impose on me."

DR. LEOPOLD, KNIGHT OF SACHER-MASOCH
(Quoted by Schlichtegroll, *Sacher-Masoch und der Masochismus*
and by Krafft-Ebing, *Psychopathia Sexualis*).

# The Adventure with Ludwig II

(Told by Wanda)

At the beginning of November 1877 my husband received the following letter:

> "What remains within you of the New Plato? What can your heart offer? Love for love? Think! If all your desires have not been a lie, you have found what you seek.
> I am because I *must* be,
>
> Your ANATOLE"

The letter was posted in Ischl, but gave a *post restante* address in another town — Salzburg, I believe. Leopold was thrown into a state of intense excitement and curiosity. The letter alluded to one of the stories in *The Heritage of Cain*, "The Love of Plato." The writing was that of a person of distinction. Who could it be? A man? It was impossible to tell. At any rate it seemed to promise an interesting adventure, and was not to be dismissed lightly. Trembling with emotion, Leopold answered:

> "Your words roused my soul as the storm rouses the ocean, as the wind lifts the waves to the stars, but needlessly, for a star has descended to me from the skies. . . .

"Friendship for friendship and love for love! How can I hesitate when you tell me that I have found the object of my sacred desire, the desire that dwells in me both in broad daylight and in the mysterious darkness of night, when Anatole has appeared in my dreams to deprive me of all rest, all sleep. If you are Anatole, I am yours, take me!

With all my soul,

LEOPOLD"

My husband awaited the reply with indescribable tension. At last it arrived, as follows:

"Have you never wept within yourself? Here I am, dry-eyed, and I feel the tears flowing one by one in my heart. I tremble with fear and my soul seems to struggle violently to free itself from its prison of flesh. You pervade all my being! I have just received your letter and since reading it I know only one thing, that I love you infinitely, as only you can be loved, as only Anatole can love! Anatole! Oh, it is I!...

"All that is good, noble and ideal in me will be yours; I want to kindle within me the divine spark that is in every man, until it grows into a flame dedicated to you — and if this pure, spiritual and sacred love does not make me your Anatole, then I am not he....

"I am Anatole, your Anatole. What a child I was to doubt it, to sin against the mysterious miracle working within us! Now it has come to me with terrifying clarity: we belong to each other for all eternity, ceaselessly, endlessly — or do you think that such a love can die with us? This is the aim of my life, the reason for my existence on this earth: to be the object of your longing, to link you to me irrevocably, proud, pure spirit! This is indeed great, this is divine!..."

282

It was eccentric but there was something to be said for it; it could add some spice to literature. It was exactly what Leopold needed. Besides, is a fine work of art any the less fine if it is made up of abnormality and falsehood? Thus I was determined to lend a hand in this venture, as far, naturally, as I should be allowed.

It was most interesting to observe Leopold. When he replied to the letters he was convinced that he really was the ideal man that others took him for, and yet he found himself very pathetic. But once he had sent off the letters his enthusiasm was somewhat dampened and he began to see the whole matter in a more practical light. Whereas the exaltation of his correspondent seemed quite genuine, my husband knew that his own was not, and that although he did not admit it to himself, he was entirely fabricating it. Besides, "The Love of Plato" was not his style at all, and the man who wrote under the name of Anatole must have known very little about Sacher-Masoch to have imagined otherwise.

Leopold believed and sincerely hoped that it was a woman, but because he was afraid of creating a conflict between us, he pretended to believe and to desire quite the opposite. In either case the spiritual relationship in question was nothing but a lie. However, it was the kind of lie to which he used to cling with all his might and which he never would have recognized as such, even if it had been exposed to the full light of the truth, because it was the foundation of his faith in himself and in his moral worth; without this faith he could not have survived.

This exalted Anatole, as blind as a child, this woman in love surrendering her soul, made me sorry, for I could see the day of disillusionment dawning: our correspondent seemed to know nothing of Sacher-Masoch's personal life. How could he be ignorant, for example, of the fact that he was *married*? Plato married! Anatole had certainly never dreamt of that.

The correspondence continued. As the letters were never

posted from the same place, and the address to which one had to reply was always different, the letters took a long time to arrive. They came from Salzburg, Vienna, Paris, Brussels or London. Clearly Anatole wanted at all costs to establish a personal relationship, even if the identity of his correspondent was to remain secret.

This irritated Anatole: what was the use of a personal relationship when their love was spiritual? He tried to avoid the issue, but he was not reckoning with Leopold's eloquence and persistence. Finally, after prolonged hesitation and, so to speak, in a gesture of despair, Anatole consented to an interview, under the express condition that Leopold follow point by point the instructions he would lay down for him. Obviously the man had much to lose from an indiscretion and was indeed afraid that one might occur.

Leopold naturally accepted the conditions. It was arranged that the interview should take place in Bruck. The choice of a place where we had lived for so long and had only recently left, where Sacher-Masoch was well known and where a chance occurrence could, without him being in any way responsible, reveal to him the identity of his friend, only confirmed my impression that Anatole knew nothing of the circumstances of our life.

It was a dreadfully cold December day when my husband set out. He had been told which train to take, and he was to stay at the Bernauer Hotel where he was to wait, blindfolded, in a completely dark room with tightly drawn curtains, until midnight, when he would hear three knocks at the door; at the third knock only he was to say: "Come in," and not make any movement.

Such precautions could only make sense if they were planned by a woman; coming from a man they would have seemed ridiculous. My husband therefore took leave of me tenderly, in the firm belief that he was about to spend the night with a beautiful woman.

That night I could not have slept more peacefully. I did not consider that I had the right to let any petty considerations interfere with an affair that could be so interesting and valuable to my husband. Once I had made up my mind on this point, I had the strength not to think of it further. Besides, Leopold, except where the sex of his new acquaintance was concerned, had shown complete loyalty to me, and I certainly considered this an attenuating circumstance to what was happening at that moment in Bruck.

He returned the next day as full of trepidation and doubt about Anatole as when he left. Here is what he told me. On arrival in Bruck he went directly to the Bernauer Hotel, took supper there and was given a room where he waited. After a short while, a letter from Anatole was delivered to him: three pages of close writing that expressed all his anguish at the thought of what he was about to do, his intense joy at the prospect of the interview and his dread of its consequences.

If Leopold had still harbored the slightest doubt about the sex of the person he was waiting for, this letter should have dispelled it. Only a woman, and a woman of high social position whom the slightest indiscretion could endanger gravely, could possibly write such a letter. It was so pleading, so desperate, it implied such great perils that Leopold was seized with pity and also with fear at the idea of the responsibility he was taking on. He thought for a moment of withdrawing, and regretted not being able to communicate this intention to Anatole, whose name he was not allowed to pronounce. He had no choice but to follow the course of events.

Besides, these feelings disappeared over the long waiting period: the desire awakened by the mysterious and beautiful woman soon had the better of his pity. When the hour of midnight approached, and he drew the curtains, blindfolded himself and waited, every nerve in his body taut, for the last few minutes to elapse, he was firmly resolved to grasp and never to lose hold of the happiness that fate was bringing within his reach.

On the last stroke of midnight, Leopold heard heavy steps ascending the stairs and drawing near to his room. He was convinced that it was a hotel servant bringing him another letter which would shatter his hopes, and was about to take the kerchief off his eyes, when he heard the three light, cautious knocks that were the agreed signal.

He cried "Come in!" and heard the door open, and then the same heavy steps ring out in the room.

So it was a man! As my husband tried to master his disappointment, a fine musical voice filled with emotion said, "Leopold, where are you? Guide me, I cannot see a thing."

My husband took the hand that was held out to him and led the unknown visitor toward the sofa where they both sat down.

"You must admit that you were expecting a woman," said the voice.

Leopold's agitation at the unexpected appearance of a man had soon died down. Since it was not a woman whom he could cast in the role of Venus in Furs, then he would make the man into "the Greek," which would be better still. So his voice was quite composed when he replied:

"After your last letter I was afraid it might be so; you surround yourself with such mystery."

"Afraid? Then you are not disappointed?"

The ice was soon broken and the two men began to converse. Anatole talked endlessly of love, but of a spiritual and immaterial love, and he finally confessed to Sacher-Masoch that although he was young and virile, he had never laid hands on a woman, but was "pure in both body and soul."

The man who said these words was no longer an adolescent; he was still young, it is true, but he was a man, taller and stronger than Leopold, and he had never touched a woman. What could this mean?

My husband possessed a dangerous eloquence that was gripping, if not convincing, and whoever found themselves exposed to it without warning never failed to succumb to its influence. This is what happened to Anatole, who was moreover in a very emotional state during the whole time the interview lasted. Leopold easily captured his mind and maneuvered him into the position he had planned. He told him that he was married, that he had a charming wife and a child as beautiful as an angel, and that it was delightful still to be in love with his wife after five years of marriage. Anatole, touched, said almost humbly:

"Oh, I am grateful to you. You have relieved me of a great fear."

"Are you handsome?" asked Sacher-Masoch, who was still blindfolded.

"I do not know."

"Are you considered handsome?"

"I am a man; who would ever tell me if I were?"

"You yourself. You are handsome, I can feel it; with such a voice you must be."

"But perhaps you would not find me attractive after all?"

"You! You are my master and my king! But if you are so afraid, show yourself first to my wife Wanda; she knows me; if she tells me that I may see you, then I shall believe her."

Thus one of them was being pressed by the other, and was retreating.

It was time to take leave; they exchanged adieus; my husband felt a burning kiss on his hand, and they parted. Leopold took the next train to Graz.

The correspondence started again. I was now involved personally. Leopold sent him photographs of us both, and asked him for his, but he always put off sending it. A correspondence subject to so many *détours* becomes tedious. Besides, excursions into the infinite realm of fantasy are the privilege of the idle rich; the practical problems and painful realities of life soon bring one down to earth. Even my husband's interest in the affair began to fade. He was sensitive to the wounding aspect of these continual protestations of love coupled with such mistrust. The mistrust was of course understandable, although Sacher-Masoch would have shown complete discretion in all respects. But it could not go on indefinitely; we were caught within an endless circle, and my head was beginning to spin; I therefore wrote Anatole an unequivocal letter. It had the desired result: we received a letter of farewell, covering many sad and painful pages.

"Leopold,

I have given up peace of mind, the gentle bliss of friendship, the joys of life and all the pleasure in the world in the exquisite hope of finding a resting-place in your heart. And what have I gained? An ardor, a torment that consume me, and the agony of my own desire increased a thousandfold by your senseless reproaches.

After a long struggle with myself I have finally embarked on the most difficult, the only action of my life. I am seized by dread when I think how you will interpret these words.

I have read Wanda's letter, and each sentence deeply touched my heart. "If you wish me to believe that your love is sincere, then act, act like a man." For two long days I have had to struggle with my selfish feelings – I have emerged victorious.

I am speaking to you for the last time, and I am calling you Leopold, my beloved, my greatest, most sacred gift, for Anatole bids you farewell. I have severed all relations with the mail and I shall receive no more letters after you read this one — you will write in vain. And now let me tell you how I reached this decision. Your desire to have me near you cannot be realized.... In this material world there is no spiritual love: even you cannot sustain it, and neither, perhaps, can I...."

Some months later we received the following letter:

"Leopold,

Come what may, I know that I do not want to leave you, that I cannot leave you. A blockhead of a bookseller has just sent me one of your books; it reached me in the middle of my struggle between renunciation, love and despair. Come what may, I am yours, you are mine, and you will have me by your side, but not just yet. Be patient for a few months and I shall be with you forever. I am willing to give up anything, to suffer anything for you. Do you still love me? Do you still believe in your Anatole?

A thousand kisses to Wanda"

And the old game started up again, with the same hesitation and the same doubts. A deceitful game, moreover: distrust on the one hand, dishonesty on the other. My husband, who still clung to the image of the Greek, was in a permanent state of tension and excitement. Now that I knew where the affair was bound to lead us, I regretted having taken any part in it; I was pleased when it was broken off and deplored that it had been resumed, for I was afraid it might come to an ugly end. In May, the day before an exceptional performance at the Thalia Theater — I cannot recall on what occasion — we received a note from Anatole, saying that he would be at the theater and would like to see us there.

We did not even know that he was in Graz. Leopold was very

excited. Sacha was coming with us, and Anatole would see our beautiful child. The open boxes of the Thalia Theater allowed their occupants to be seen clearly; Anatole, whom we did not know, had the advantage of being able to recognize us from our portrait, while we had no hope of distinguishing in a packed house a person we had never set eyes on. Anatole had mentioned in a letter that he looked like the young Lord Byron, and Leopold thought he had seen a man of this description hidden behind a pillar in the entrance hall, but he did not want to stare at him indiscreetly, and allowed himself to be carried along by the crowd.

What a strange sensation it is to sit for hours on end in the knowledge that somewhere two eyes are riveted on one, scrutinizing with feverish ardor every feature of one's face! This act of spying showed a lack of generosity on the part of our friend Anatole; but men who live in the clouds are no doubt more sensitive to divine than to human magnanimity. What a relief when the play was over and our self-exposure came to an end!

The next day another letter came from Anatole asking us this time to go to the Elephant Hotel. We were to wait in the dining room until he sent us word, for this time he wanted to speak with us. We obeyed his instructions, and after we had been sitting in the dining room for a little while, a servant asked Leopold to follow him to the gentleman who was expecting him. Leopold returned shortly afterward and told me that Anatole wished me to go to his room, and that a servant was waiting to take me there.

I went, determined to put an end to all this nonsense. The servant, who was no mere porter and had a certain style about him, led me up a staircase and along several corridors to an elegant and brilliantly lit drawing room, and then on into a room that was in complete darkness. I was left standing there, unable to see a thing.

"Oh, Wanda, please come here."

"Is it you, Anatole?"

"Yes."

"You will have to guide me, I cannot see."

A moment's silence, then a slow, hesitant step in my direction. A hand groped for mine and led me to the sofa.

The person who had drawn near to me and who was now sitting by my side was certainly not the Anatole that Leopold had spoken with in Bruck. He was small, and it was obvious even in the dark that he was deformed. His voice had the almost childlike tone of a hunchback's; it was not rich and deep like that of the Anatole who had so fascinated my husband. Who could he be? I spoke to him but the poor man was so frightened that he could hardly reply. I left quickly, out of pity for him.

When I told Leopold about *my* Anatole, he was as perplexed as I was. The person he had spoken to was the same as the one in Bruck, the same tall, well-built man with the beautiful deep voice.

Full of resentment, I wrote to Anatole as soon as we reached home. I allowed him to think that we had not noticed the difference, and I said that I now knew the true reason behind his refusal to let us see him, namely his appearance, and that I was saddened to think that he did not realize how such mistrust would wound us.... This is briefly the gist of what I wrote to him, and I posted the letter that very evening.

The next day, as we were all sitting in the dining room after luncheon, the doorbell rang. The maid handed me a letter, and said that the gentleman who wrote it was awaiting a reply. The note was from Anatole, or rather from the unfortunate man with whom I had spoken at the Elephant Hotel; he was asking me to see him alone.... As I entered my bedroom, which served as a sitting room, a short, deformed young man with reddish-blond hair and a pale, gentle and sad face such as many invalids have, entered through the other door. An indescribable and painful emotion caused him to tremble; his serious, soulful eyes looked at me, so pleading and so timid that I was seized with pity and I rushed up to him, took both his hands in mine and spoke to him affectionately. He fell on his knees before me and hid his face in my lap; stifled sobs wracked his poor deformed body. I laid my hands on his head to calm him down; I no longer remember what I said to him, but my words certainly came from the depth of my heart, for his boundless grief moved me to deep pity. When he raised his tear-stained face to me, his smile was full of happiness and gratitude.

"I am leaving tonight by the eleven o'clock train. Would you do me the kindness of coming to the National Theater with Leopold, so that I may see you until the last moment and breathe the same air as you? When the performance is over, I shall wait for you in my carriage, by the cathedral, in the hope that you will not refuse me the favor of a last handshake, a farewell kiss."

That evening we went to the theater and after the performance we walked across to the carriage which was standing in the shadow of the cathedral. As we drew close, a face wearing a mask appeared at the window of the carriage, and two arms reached out to Leopold and drew him close in a long embrace. In turn my hands were grasped and I felt his burning kiss upon them. The masked man slumped back into his seat, the window was shut and the carriage drew away. Not a word had been exchanged during the whole scene; we stood there speechless, our eyes following the flight of the mystery as it disappeared into the dark night.

Who was it? Anatole or the cripple? We had no idea.

We received another farewell letter which ended with a reproach: we had not been capable of spiritual love, and thus we had broken the spell, etc.... The letter was entirely confused and incomprehensible — perhaps intentionally so, although the writer claimed that he was expressing himself clearly and frankly. We did not reply.

A few years later, a chance occurrence convinced us almost with certainty of Anatole's identity. In 1881 we spent part of the summer in Heubach, near Passau, and we made the acquaintance of Dr. Grandauer. He was a physician, but did not practice, and held the position of director of the Munich Hoftheater. He was both a scientist and a great connoisseur of the arts, and we spent many pleasant hours in his witty and congenial company.

One day as we were talking about art and the treasures of the Bavarian royal castles, he mentioned the artistic tastes of Ludwig II, and spoke of the king's eccentricity, his relationship with Richard Wagner, their strange correspondence, the aversion the king had for the company of men, his distant attitude to women, his solitary nature, and his passionate and unsatisfied yearning for an ideal life.

Our interest was aroused by what Dr. Grandauer was saying: it had such a familiar ring about it.... We looked at each other with the same name on our lips: Anatole. When the doctor had finished speaking, I asked him point-blank: "What about the little deformed man who is said to be the king's friend?"

"Ah, you must be thinking of Prince Alexander of Orange, the eldest son of the King of Holland. A poor devil."

WANDA VON SACHER-MASOCH
*Confessions of My Life*

This edition designed by Bruce Mau
Type composed by Archetype